First published in Great Britain in 2001

ISBN: 0-954052-0-2

Published by Taunton Deane Borough Council
The Deane House
Belvedere Road
TAUNTON
SOMERSET
TA1 1HE
Tel: 01823 356493
Fax: 01823 356563
Email: heritage.landscape@tauntondeane.gov.uk
www.tauntondeane.gov.uk

Cover picture 'Taunton from Cotlake Hill, 1889' by Harry Frier.
The Quantock Hills in the background are composed of resistant Devonian slates and sandstone. Permo-Triassic red marls, alluvial silts and gravels underlie the lowland. His life and work are recorded by M. H. Jones' Harry Frier: Somerset's unknown painter (Jones, 1985).

Geology and Landscape
of Taunton Deane

A geological exploration of southwest Somerset

To Eric Robinson and Hugh Torrens
for their help and encouragement over many years.

HUGH PRUDDEN

Supported by: English Nature, Environment Agency, Quantock Hills AONB JAC,
Wessex Water, University of Plymouth, Quantock Geological Services,
Somerset Wildlife Trust, Hanson Environment Fund, Wyvern Waste.
Harvey Ham Hill Stone, Geologists' Association Curry Fund.
British Geological Survey, Royal Society for Nature Conservation

Taunton Deane Borough Council

Contents

Chapter 1 Introduction

This book is intended as an introduction to the geological features of the Taunton area and especially as a guide to places worth visiting. It has been prepared for both local people and visitors. It is not designed to serve as a systematic text book or to present a detailed account of the geology of the area. It does, however, provide a bridge to the technical literature. The Taunton area has a rich and varied geological inheritance awaiting your discovery.

Using the book

The Ordnance Survey's 1:50,000 Landranger Series (especially Sheet 193 Taunton and Lyme Regis) or better still the 1:25,000 Explorer Series (especially Sheet 128 Taunton and Blackdown Hills) are essential companions. Likewise the British Geological Survey's 1:50,000 Series geological maps (especially Sheet 295 Taunton) not only show the general pattern of rock outcrops but help identify what lies below the soil at specific places. The Appendices provide further information for reference. An extensive glossary is provided in order to reduce repetition; see items marked *. Copies of a number of the technical papers have been deposited in the Somerset Studies Library which holds a collection of geological maps and other literature.

The first part provides an introduction to topics such as basic geology, building stones, radon, soils, water supplies and conservation.

The Regional Studies highlight the many attractive localities which lie within some 15 miles of Taunton. Most of these are suitable for family outings and include a rich variety of landscapes and places of wildlife, architectural and historical interest. The Taunton Rock Trail offers a descriptive account of the principal building stones seen in the centre of Taunton; a visit to see the stones at first-hand is the best possible introduction to the geology of the area.

Access and safety

We have felt it wise to omit mention of a number of interesting localities where the consent of the landowner would be required. However, this need not deter keen geologists who discover or hear about these localities. Rarely will a polite request to visit an old quarry be refused. Every effort has been made to direct readers to places where there is open access. This does not include Gamlins Quarry (Figure 7.2) or the cave at Holwell (Figure 27.3). The localities mentioned in the text should be sufficient to satisfy most people. We do urge that visitors keep to footpaths and respect the rights of landowners.

Please remember that health and safety regulations, together with the possibility of a landowner incurring a claim for injury, mean that access is more difficult than in the past. Group leaders should certainly have indemnity against claims. Steep, slippery slopes, loose rock, deep pools, uneven footpaths, narrow busy roads all present hazards. Take care!

Scientific study

Description of the rocks is the first step to understanding their origin which is why we recommend the Taunton Rock Trail as the best starting point, bearing in mind the following advice in *The Geological Observer* by Sir Henry De la Beche in 1853.

> It has been well remarked by Humboldt that to behold is not necessarily to observe, that is, to compare and combine. The history of Geology, like that of all sciences depending for their effective advance on experiment or correct observation, amply proves the truth of this statement.

(Courtesy: Department of Geology National Museum of Wales).

FIG.1.1 Sir Henry De la Beche, FRS (1796-1855).

Henry De la Beche (1796-1855) was a key figure in the development of geology in the first half of the 19th century and he became the first Director of the Geological Survey of Great Britain. His geological surveys of Southwest England included west Somerset and are described in his *Report on the geology of Cornwall, Devon and west Somerset (1839).* We include a number of quotations from De la Beche and other pioneer geologists as it is both instructive and interesting to see the local geology through the eyes of earlier pioneers.

Another worthy was William Ussher, of the Geological Survey of Great Britain, who remapped much of the area and published many papers between 1875 and 1914. His sheet memoirs are still useful sources of information. His name is remembered in the title of the Ussher Society (Appendix H).

Geological delights

It might be thought that geological research today is the sole province of the university academic or the professional consultant but this is not so. An amateur can record a hole dug in the ground and relate it to the geological map. The local enthusiast is on the spot to observe, with permission and precautions, a trench dug across the fields. There will be an academic somewhere who would welcome the information. The specialist and beginner are both explorers. Exploring is exciting.

The Reverend Henry Winwood was one such Somerset amateur; he led field excursions and contributed to local journals in the late-19th and early-20th centuries. Winwood recommended the delights of geological study in a talk to the Bath Natural History Field Club in 1877.

> It is given generally to but few members of a mixed Field Club to feel the same intense interest in the rocks, as their brothers of the hammer do. But each intelligent mind has its own peculiar hobby........As one then of those who take an interest in the mighty forces, the long-continued but gentle influences, which have formed the rocks and sculptured the physical features of hill and dale around us, I unhesitatingly assert that the pursuit of geology will yield unbounded gratification to every one who tries to unravel its secrets; and that as a science it stands second to none in the healthy recreation it affords to both body and mind, giving strength to the one, and elevating thoughts to the other.
>
> (Winwood 1877)

Our only quibble with these sentiments is the use of the phrase 'gentle influences'. Many of the rocks of the Taunton area suggest forces that were far from gentle!

Time and change

The geologist and historian share an awareness of time and change albeit it on different scales. The landscape historian, W.G. Hoskins, has pointed out the association between rocks, landscape and buildings in the dimension of time.

> There is hardly a single aspect of local history, whether we are looking at documents or the landscape itself, that is not illuminated to some degree, sometimes completely explained, by a knowledge of the underlying rocks. At times like these the arid jargon of the geologist, which we have laboured to understand, is transmuted into a kind of poetry. The carving of a Norman doorway in a country church, still bold and clear because the Normans knew so well how to select the best stone from the quarry, gives us all the more pleasure if we recognise also the stone they chose and if we know its outcrop, so that we can go on down the very lane up which they brought it when Henry II reigned at Westminster, and push through the tangled undergrowth to the deserted pit itself.
>
> W. G. Hoskins,
> *Devon: a New Survey of England (1954).*

The study of rocks takes us back into prehistory and beyond, almost to the very beginning. The oldest rocks in Taunton Deane date back some 380 million years; this is well-before man or the dinosaur. There is evidence in the local rocks for all to read that tells of colliding continents, volcanic eruptions, tropical seas, semi-arid deserts and tundra conditions.

Church guides show a curious neglect of the types and sources of the stones used in churches However, medieval churches are one of the best places to start a study of the local geology since stone was usually drawn from the nearest suitable source. The stones are memorials to a thousand years or more of history and are an integral part of the landscape.

AISHOLT CHURCH

Have you seen it where
it squats on the edge
of its vast green nest,
musing hymns, compulsively,
through the brooding years?
Sometimes the close air
stills within the pallisade
of lusty trees on the steep
where we climb to the cool
white shadows waiting there
behind the church door
with its sliding latch
and wrinkled face
And there the God-place sits
while the seasons circle
within the circling years.
There is birth and death
but all are gathered to the
smiling hills
to be mothered and breasted
in the warm red earth

From *Aisholt and its Church*
by the Late Reverend Arthur Moss

Chapter 2
Rocks and Landforms

Geological thinking and investigation

The illustration of an old quarry (Figure 2.1), 12km SSE of Taunton, provides a useful example of how we can delve into the geological past. It is no longer visible but similar features may be studied on Kilve beach east of Watchet (ST 143445).

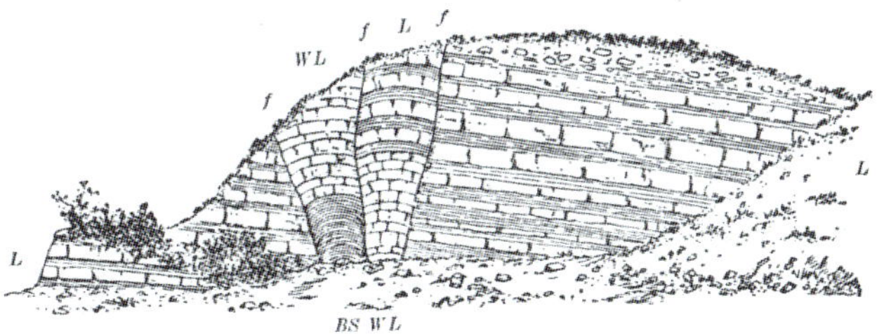

L Lower Lias limestone and clay = Blue Lias.
WL White Lias limestones.
BS Black Shales.
f Faults. (Ussher, 1906).

FIG.2.1 An old quarry near Bishopswood.

Observe that the beds are in regular layers but vary in thickness. Limestones alternate with dark shales. The beds show a tilt of 5° and are dislocated by faults*. The limestones have vertical cracks (joints). Note the rock debris at the top of the section.

One of the first tasks would be to become familiar with the section by collecting samples of the rocks and fossils, noting carefully which beds they come from. These are the raw material, so to speak, on which to work.

Do these beds contain marine creatures? Do the rocks contain clues as to the conditions on the sea floor which were favourable for the formation of limestones and shales? How did, what were presumably pale soft limy oozes and dark organic-rich muds, change into the limestones and shales? Can we observe changes in the succession of beds e.g. in their fossil or mineralogical content? Do these beds contain a succession of different ammonites bottom to top which can be used to match-up the beds in different locations as, for example, at Kilve beach?

At what stage were these strata dislocated by the faults? Today's land surface cuts across the various beds as a result of the erosion which has carved the valley at Bishopswood, thus exposing 200 million year old sediments at the surface. The land surface does not show vertical faces along the faults and so we conclude that the rocks were dislocated before the present-day land surface was formed. What was the stress regime that dislocated the rocks? The narrow faulted slices at Bishopswood are rather curious.

More questions arise: does each limestone bed have its own unique set of characteristics e.g. thickness, top surface, bottom surface, fauna, percentage of calcium carbonate, degree of bioturbation? Was the accumulation of sediments a slow gradual process or spasmodic? Can the same individual beds be detected at Lyme Regis?

What circumstances might have led to the preservation of fossils? Most animals are recycled when they die. Is the changing fossil fauna in the beds the result of migration or evolution?

We have not finished! Palaeontologists might wish to search for microscopic plant and animal remains. Were the black shales deposited in stagnant conditions lacking oxygen? Do they contain radioactive elements? Do the faults and limestones provide pathways for radon to reach the surface? Are metals present such as molybdenum, lead, zinc or copper which might contaminate the soil and vegetation? The presence of molybdenum can lead to copper deficiency in cattle.

Thus the geologist interrogates the rocks, cogitates and reconstructs the geological history of part of Somerset However, it is as well to remember that reading the rocks in order to discover the geological past is similar to reading an Ordnance Survey map: rocks and maps can indicate the elements of the scene, past or present, but they cannot paint the full, living, colourful picture.

We could also consult the geological map of the area published by the British Geological Survey (see Appendix E for details), or visit the public library to seek scientific papers and geological memoirs for the locality.

One of the wonders of scientific investigation is that as one question is answered, another arises. Geology is intellectually stimulating.

Geological sections

The sketch of the quarry face in Figure 2.1 shows a section in the rocks of some 20m width. However, it is also useful to study sections at smaller scales as in Figure 2.2 below. Remember that the geology is much simplified and generalised at this scale.

The section shows that the southern Quantocks are underlain by the Morte Slates rock formation of Devonian age. Slates, siltstones and sandstones can be seen locally in the buildings, road cuttings and old quarries. Ripple-marked silty-sandstones can be seen in the paving of the Edwardian Garden at Hestercombe. The Morte Slates are cut by the Hestercombe igneous* intrusion. Hot magma* was injected into cracks in the earth's crust and baked the adjacent sediments.

The red beds of the Mercia Mudstone Group overlie the Morte Slates. These beds are readily eroded, a fact which explains the reason for the low ground of the Vale of Taunton Deane. Notice that these beds rest on the eroded up-turned edges of the Morte Slates.

White and Blue Lias limestones cap Pickeridge Hill to the south. They form a line of hills which trend northeast towards Langport. These limestones are overlain by the Lower Lias clays on the lower slopes of the Blackdown Hills escarpment. They are the same clays that are seen in the cliffs at Charmouth in Dorset.

Finally, the Upper Greensand caps the Blackdown Hills which form an extensive plateau in East Devon.

The Cothelstone Fault dislocates the strata; the rocks are let down to the south. The fault is part of a complex of faults which are aligned NNW-SSE along the northwest side of the Quantocks. Comparison of rocks on either side of the fault suggests that there has been vertical and

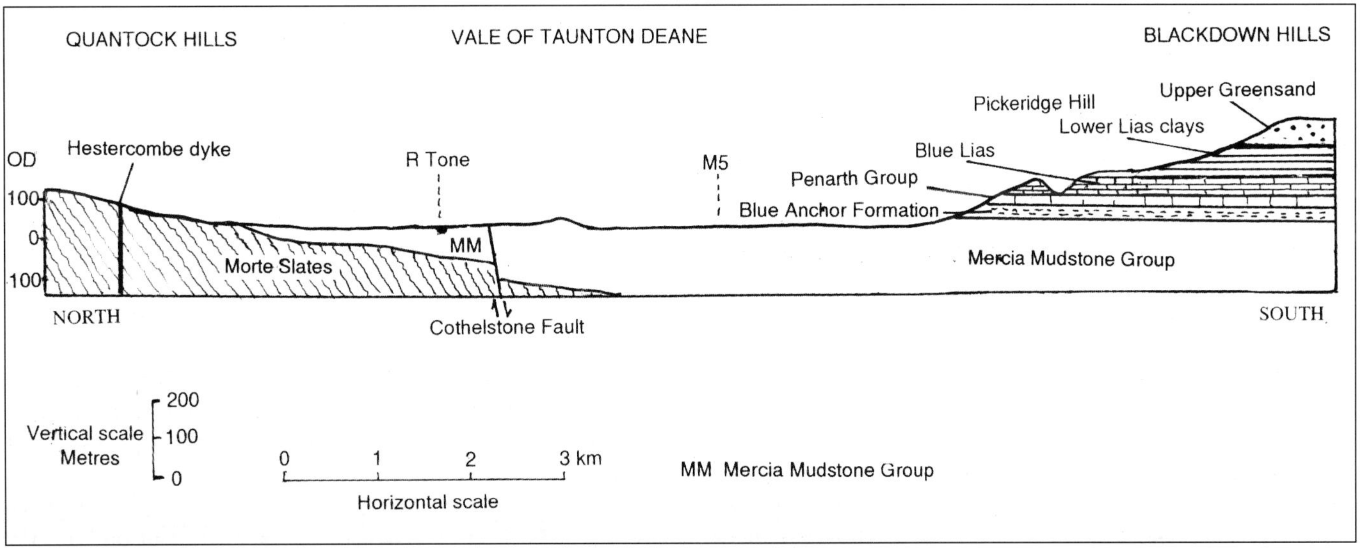

FIG. 2.2 Simplified geological section from the Quantocks to the Blackdown Hills.

horizontal movement at various times in the geological past. The Cothelstone Fault is rather similar to the San Andreas Fault in California except that the former is not in active mode (we hope).

It is worth noting the wide difference in the ages of the Morte Slates (367 Ma) and the Mercia Mudstone (223 Ma). During this long time-interval the Morte Slates were deeply buried, crumpled by earth movements, elevated into mountains and subsequently eroded. Proof is provided by the many fragments of the Morte Slates which can be found in the red beds of Taunton Deane.

Geological maps

Maps are essential in order to understand the geology of an area. Basically, they show the arrangement of rock formations at the surface. Figure 2.3 is a simplified geological map in which many different rock formations are lumped together. It shows the broad pattern.

Taunton sits on the red beds of Permo-Triassic age. To the west are the older beds of Devonian and Carboniferous age which are found on Exmoor, the Brendon Hills and the Quantocks. Jurassic formations to the east include the Lower Lias limestones and clays. To the south of Taunton is the Upper Greensand. The Key indicates the geological time 'Periods' to which the rocks belong.

Much of Britain is now covered by more detailed maps produced by the British Geological Survey at the 1:50,000 scale. Sheet 295 Taunton is a modern map and an invaluable companion. The rock formations are shown in order of their age in a 'Generalised vertical section' (bottom right of the sheet) with the oldest at the bottom i.e. the beds are in order of deposition. For example, the Otter Sandstone is represented by orange shading. Below it are the older Budleigh Salterton Pebble Beds and above is the younger Mercia Mudstone Group of rocks. 'Permian' and 'Triassic' indicates the geological time period to which these formations belong. These beds are often referred to as 'Permo-Triassic' for convenience.

The map itself shows where the Otter Sandstone comes to the surface, e.g. in grid square ST 2828 just east of the M5 where an arrow shows that the beds dip* at 5° to the south. Note the symbols shown to the right of the map. The term drift refers to superficial deposits such as river-deposited

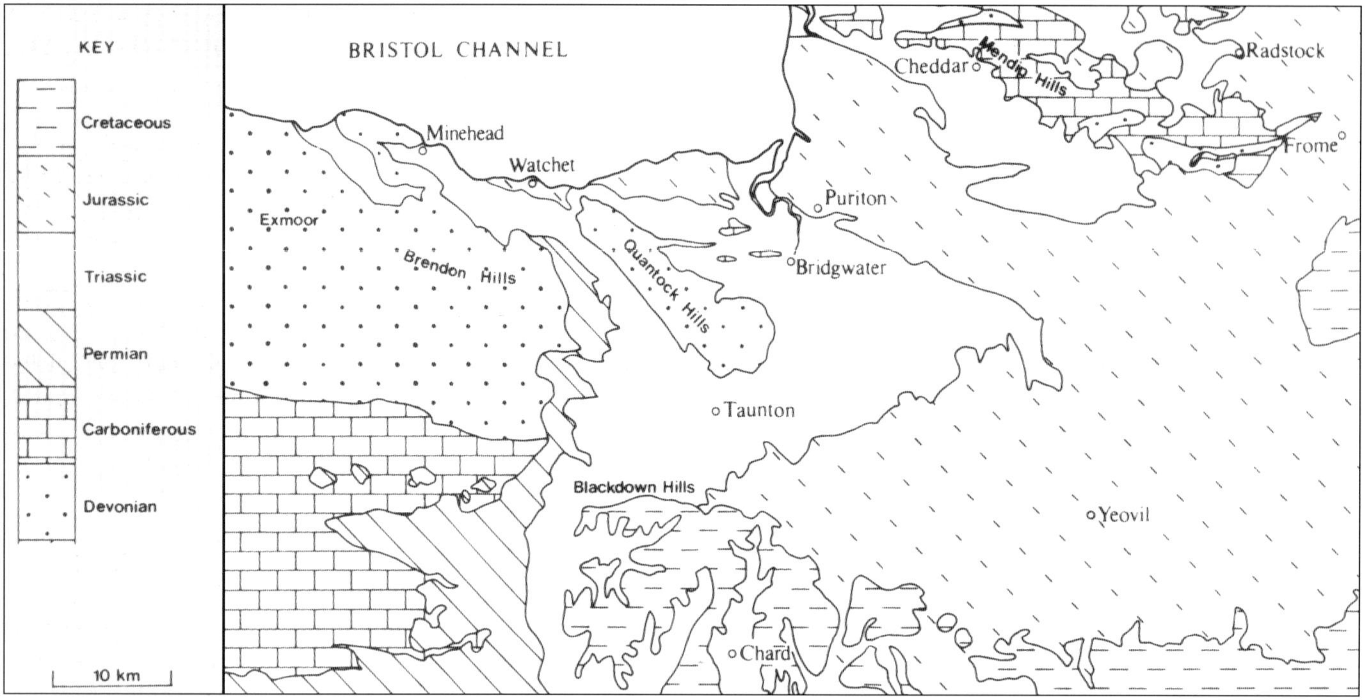

FIG. 2.3 Simplified geological map of Somerset

(Courtesy: H. Breeze and Somerset Wildlife Trust).

alluvium*. Examples can be found on the eastern side of the map. The two cross-sections below the map help one to visualise the geological structure. The sheet map gives a summary of each rock formation at the foot of the page.

The Taunton 1:50,000 geological map covers much of Taunton Deane and was surveyed in the 1980s. An explanatory memoir is available. The Wellington sheet and memoir mainly date from the late 19th century and the latter is out of print. Whilst the geology may not change, it is true to say that modern mapping is much more detailed. The maps can be ordered from bookshops or from the British Geological Survey (BGS) the address of which is given in Appendix E.

The colours of the rocks

Alec Clifton-Taylor has reminded us that colourful building stones are an important factor in producing regional character and diversity:

> ...but one really enters 'the red country' soon after leaving Taunton, and the effect upon the eyes as one approaches Exeter is unforgettable: the whole countryside seems to be bathed in a warm red glow. In west Somerset the hills (the Quantocks, Brendons, Exmoor) all belong to the Devonian formations, but down in the valleys between them, where the villages cluster, the soil is red marl over New Red Sandstone. Especially delightful are some of the church towers under the lee of the Quantocks... but at Bishop's Lydeard the tower is almost a wine red, a very rich shade which adds not a little to its attraction. (Clifton-Taylor, 1984)

The majority, but not all, of the Permo-Triassic sediments are reddened with a coating of iron oxide (haematite) and are thought to have been deposited in semi-arid climatic conditions. Yet present-day deserts tend to be yellow rather than red. The redness probably developed after the sand grains of the sediments were buried as a result of the decomposition of unstable minerals containing iron (eg mica) to provide iron-oxide coatings on the sediments. Anaerobic (without oxygen) bacteria may have been involved in the liberation of oxygen which would have combined with the iron. It is a complicated story.

Greenish-grey spots and patches in the Permo-Triassic sediments may be the result of the inclusion of organic matter which would have used up the oxygen during diagenesis*. Pale, cream-coloured patches seen in some of red Permo-Triassic sandstones may be the result of hydrocarbon gases passing through the pore spaces of the rock. Look out for this feature in some of the churches built of these sandstones.

These rocks are traditionally interpreted as deposited in arid conditions. They feature beds of salt, gypsum and calcretes* which are the result of the evaporation of lakes and ground water. The visitor to Coryton's Cove, Dawlish in Devon, can see fossil sand dunes. Perhaps the climate in the Permo-Triassic Periods was wetter than is sometimes imagined and more like today's savannas which have seasonal rainfall. The Permo-Triassic breccias, pebble beds, sandstones and silty beds around Taunton all imply water-assisted processes.

White Lias, Bath Stone, Portland Stone and Beer Stone are whitish in colour. They are mainly composed of calcium carbonate (CaCO3) in the form of shelly debris and lime-rich muds; iron compounds are generally subordinate. They were deposited in seas with a low input of terrestrial sediments from the land.

Whitish, opaque vein-quartz, which occurs widely in the Brendon Hills and Quantocks, is composed of silica. The golden-brown Ham Hill Stone and Guiting Stone are typical of limestones in which iron occurs in the hydrated form of ferric oxide (limonite).

The green beds in the Upper Greensand owe their colour to the mineral glauconite (hydrated silicate of iron and potassium). However, weathering has oxidised the glauconite in much of the Upper Greensand, as at the top of Golden Cap east of Lyme Regis, to yellow-brown limonite. The green colour of the Cockercombe Tuff is the result of the presence of the mineral chlorite (hydrated silicate of aluminium, iron and magnesium).

The Devonian Morte Slates may show as silvery grey, greenish grey and brown; the pale colours reflect the low content of organic matter. They are often stained red as a result of reddening from the overlying Permo-Triassic rocks.

Organic matter and finely-disseminated pyrite give rise to the blue-grey colours in the Blue Lias limestones and mudstones. Oxidation along cracks near the surface results in the conversion of iron to the yellow-brown ferric state in the hydrated form. Lighter-coloured beds in the Blue Lias have a higher calcium carbonate content.

Stratigraphical charts

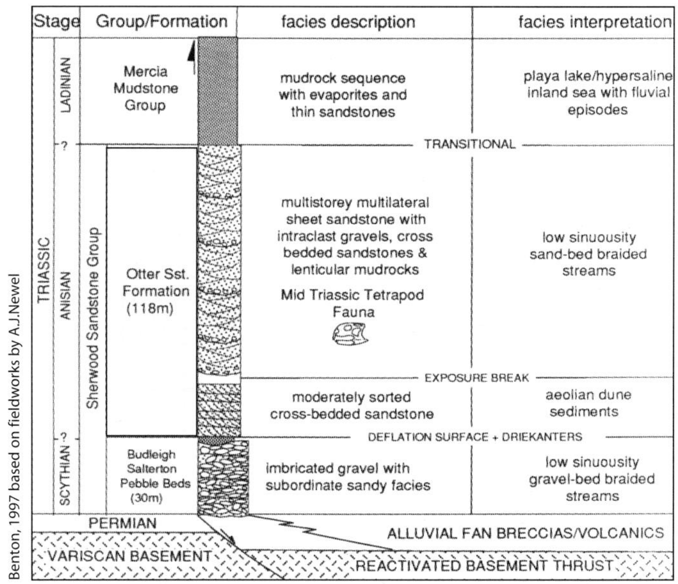

FIG. 2.4 Sedimentology and interpreted depositional environments of the Otter Sandstone Formation and adjacent units.

Most people pass their lives quite happily without ever consulting a stratigraphical chart. These charts and tables can be forbidding. However, they do have their uses. Geologists use them in order to summarise detailed observations and to show how rocks are related to one another. Here we present one such chart recently published in the *Proceedings of the Ussher Society* which concerns the Otter Sandstone (Figure 2.4). It is worth taking a little time in order to become familiar with the concepts. The information is based on a study of the superb cliff sections along the east Devon coastline.

The left-hand column provides the stratigraphic time framework e.g. the Anisian Stage refers to rocks laid down during one part of the Triassic Period. Historians and archaeologists use similar time labels e.g 'Victorian'.

The next column shows the names of rock units which can be mapped across country e.g. groups and/or formations. It is important to understand that these are independent of the time units. What is recognised as 'Otter Sandstone' in one place may be different in age at another. A delta growing out into the sea will vary in age.

There follows a graphic log which gives a visual impression of the sediments. The term 'facies' can be understood by comparing the last two columns with the definition given in the Glossary below. The sandstones occur in cycles on the coast, often with conglomeratic bases, and fine upwards through cross-bedded sandstones to ripple-marked sandstones (Benton, 1997).

The lower part of the diagram indicates that the basement rocks have had renewed movement which has affected the beds of Permian age.

Many lanes west and north of Taunton show good exposures of Otter Sandstone where traffic over the years has lowered the road level. Good road exposures in the Otter Sandstone are mentioned in the Milverton, Nynehead and Thurloxton chapter below. At North Newton (ST 294310) by Churchill Farm the sandstone has a lumpy appearance as a result of being cemented by calcium carbonate in an irregular manner to form calcretes. This is thought to be the result of ground water evaporating in semi-arid conditions with the result that calcium carbonate was precipitated in the sands.

The refinement of geological knowledge has resulted in a changing terminology which does make difficulties for readers. The term 'White Lias' is now used informally; Langport Member is now the adopted scientific label. The 'Keuper Marl' is now part of the Mercia Mudstone Group. The Otter Sandstone Formation and Budleigh Salterton Pebble Beds are combined in a higher order as the Sherwood Sandstone Group. Appendix C is an attempt to sort out the changing nomenclature.

Readers will meet the term 'New Red Sandstone' which has been used since the early days of geology to describe the dominantly red-bed continental rocks laid down in Britain during the Permian and Triassic periods. The survival of the term reflects the difficulty of subdividing these rocks. It is useful as a term to distinguish these red beds from rather similar, but older, red beds known as the Old Red Sandstone. Here we use the term 'Permo-Triassic'.

The Devonian Morte Slates Formation is mostly slate but does include quite a lot of sandstone. The term 'formation' refers to the basic formal unit used in mapping.

Landforms - the effects of structure and process

Following the deposition of the Upper Greensand and Chalk, parts of western Britain became a land surface with a semi-tropical climate. The East Devon plateau, that adjoins the Blackdown Hills to the south of Taunton, shows reddish Clay-with-Flints, silcretes* and ferricretes* which are interpreted as evidence for tropical weathering with a seasonal rainfall regime as explained in the Staple Fitzpaine chapter below. The hilltops appear to combine to form a level plateau surface. This is no optical illusion; the long-continued tropical weathering and erosion combined to produce a surface of low relief.

This 'surface', and its overlying deposits, has been warped and dislocated by faulting. One effect of the earth movements was to elevate much of western Britain including the East Devon plateau, Exmoor and the Quantocks. At the same time, faulting and downwarping caused other areas to subside and thus determined the broad shape of the British Isles including the Bristol Channel (Straw, 1995).

Subsequently, erosion of the weaker rocks has lowered the land surface. Especially vulnerable were most of the Permo-Triassic rocks in the vale of Taunton Deane, and the Liassic clays in the vale to the east of Taunton. A view across Taunton Deane along the line of the section in Figure 2.2 provides some idea of the amount of rock that has been eroded and transported to the Bristol Channel.

The older Palaeozoic rocks of the Quantocks, Brendon Hills and Exmoor were more resistant to erosion and is one reason why they form high ground. The resistant Upper Greensand (and Chalk in some places), that cap the Blackdown Hills escarpment and adjacent East Devon Plateau, preserved the former land surface on the ridge tops. Note that the more resistant rocks tend to have narrow valleys as in the Quantocks.

Much of the surface of Southwest England is hidden under a blanket of rock debris termed 'head'. This is the product of much colder winters and cooler summers than those of the present day. Freeze-thaw cycles disintegrated the surface rocks whilst the spring thaw would have released copious amounts of water which would have increased the mobility of the sodden mass; the result was widespread downslope movement of rock waste and hillslope recession especially on outcrops of clay and shale. Similar effects are seen on the 'active' cliff faces at Charmouth during wet winters. The downslope overturning of slates seen at Hestercombe and in the lanes at Thurloxton provide graphic evidence of these processes.

Figure 31.3 illustrates the general features of one of the most common landform combinations in south and west Somerset, namely the escarpment and dip slope, which result from erosion acting upon a combination of weak and strong rock layers which are tilted at an angle from the horizontal. The strong rock acts as a capping to the escarpment and protects the weaker beds below. The Budleigh Salterton Pebble Beds at Milverton, the Blue Lias at Curry Rivel and the Upper Greensand at Castle Neroche all form prominent escarpments. Outcrops of weaker rocks, such as the Lias Clay, form broad vales. Horizontal strata form a plateau instead of a dip slope e.g. the East Devon Plateau.

River channels and valleys

River channels and valleys can be classified broadly into three types:

(a) Goyles:
These are deep, steep-sided incisions to be seen in the headwaters of many streams in the Brendons, Quantocks and Blackdown Hills. The rock strewn channels have steep gradients, waterfalls and often reveal bedrock. They tend to be developed in weak beds such as those in the Upper Greensand and in the thick deposits of head

found in the Quantocks. There are frequent rockfalls and slumps where fast-flowing water undercuts steep slopes. Many are in wooded areas.

(b) Active streams with riffles and pools:
Goyles often widen out downstream where the gradient lessens. Channels are heavily charged with rocky debris; deep pools alternate with gravel bars as the flowing water swings from side to side in the channel. The point to remember is that these channel forms are the product of active erosion and deposition at bankfull stage when one can observe upwellings and whirlpools in the flood waters. Scouring of river banks eats into the adjacent farmland and one can often see material that has been dumped in efforts to control the erosion.

An example of riffles and pools at Hoccombe is described below in the The Brendon Hills (Elworthy to Oakhampton) chapter. The rivers draining south in the Blackdown Hills (e.g. the Yarty) are very active as is the River Axe in Devon owing to the relatively steep gradients and heavy bedloads of chert and flint. These rivers provide a variety of valuable habitats for wildlife; conservation policy now favours non-clearance.

(c) Broad floodplains:
The lower reaches with gentler gradients tend to have single, stabilised channels cut into alluvial silts and clays. Many are now embanked to contain floodwater. In their natural state, overbank floods would spill onto adjacent flood plains and be temporarily stored thus reducing the risk of flooding in the lowest reaches. Traditional geography textbooks told a story of the gradual build-up of floodplains as a result of flood events: suspended matter was gradually deposited in the still water adjacent to the turbulent flow in the main channel. However, archaeological research suggests that there may have been widespread soil erosion consequent upon forest clearance by prehistoric people and that the bulk of floodplain sediments may have resulted from their activities.

Many floodplains have beds of gravel underneath the alluvium. These gravels accumulated at an earlier date during cold phases in the Ice Age as a result of mass-wasting (solifluction) moving weathered debris downslope into the valley bottoms. Finer particles were removed in suspension whilst coarser debris choked the floodplains. The upward transition from coarse gravel to silty alluvium represents, in part, the climatic changes at the end of the last cold phase of the Ice Age. River gravels are frequently found some 10 to 30 m above adjacent present-day floodplains. These are remnants of floodplains surviving from times when rivers flowed at higher levels i.e. is before valleys were eroded to their present levels, as described in the Norton Fitzwarren chapter.

Drainage patterns

Figure 2.6 shows that the Rivers Isle, Parrett and Yeo flow north to the Bristol Channel whilst the Axe, Char, Brit and Frome flow a much shorter distance southwards to the English Channel. There appears to be a radial pattern. Is there any reason for this curious pattern?

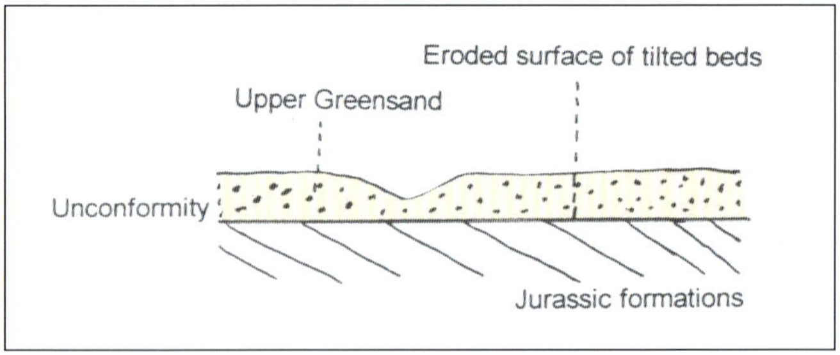

Fig. 2.5 Sketch section to show the planed-off surface below the Greensand.

The Upper Greensand rests unconformably upon the planed-off tops of a variety of tilted Jurassic rock formations as shown in Figure 2.5. Figure 2.6 shows the variations in height of this planed-off surface. Note the dome-like feature and its relationship to the radial pattern of the streams. Also note how streams run southwards from the Blackdowns. There does seem to be a remarkable correlation between the dome as shown by the base of the Greensand, and the modern drainage pattern. This feature was pointed out in 1958 in the Bridport and Yeovil sheet memoir (Wilson et al., 1958, p 204).

It is not unreasonable to assume that the undulations of the unconformity shown in Figure 2.6 are mainly the result of earth movements subsequent to the deposition of the Upper Greensand and that these earth movements may also have warped a plain of low relief and thus initiated a new drainage pattern Is there evidence for such a plain of low relief?

The view of the Blackdown Plateau from Golden Cap in Dorset near Lyme Regis (ST 407922), the contours on the topographic map and the experience of travelling along the Blackdown ridgetops all confirm that there are the remains of such a plain now raised some 200 m above sea level. The hilltops on the eastern side of the Blackdowns are covered with what are thought to be shallow-water marine gravels composed of rocks derived from the Palaeozoic rock formations (Waters, 1960); such a sea could have trimmed the surface. Before that there is evidence for a period of prolonged tropical or semi-tropical weathering following the retreat of the sea in which the Chalk was deposited; ideal conditions for the production of a plain of low-relief. These and allied features are discussed in the Otterford and Blackdown Plateau chapter.

The Blackdowns are unique in having the combination of warped unconformity (Figure 2.6), erosion surface and stream pattern which help explain the drainage pattern. The drainage patterns in other areas of Britain may well be a response to similar earth movements. For example the River Exe flows southwards from high ground close to the Bristol Channel and this is very suggestive of north-south tilting. The parallel rivers in the eastern Mendips, those on the Chalk dip slope between Dorchester and Blandford, and even the parallel streams in South Wales may well be the result of similar tilting of Tertiary land surfaces.

The streams initiated at this time would have been superimposed upon the underlying geological structures and this would explain examples of where river valleys cross discordant outcrops of relatively resistant rocks e.g. the Parrett at Langport (Blue Lias), the Yeo at Yeovil (Yeovil Sands) and the Bristol Avon in the Clifton Gorge (Carboniferous Limestone).

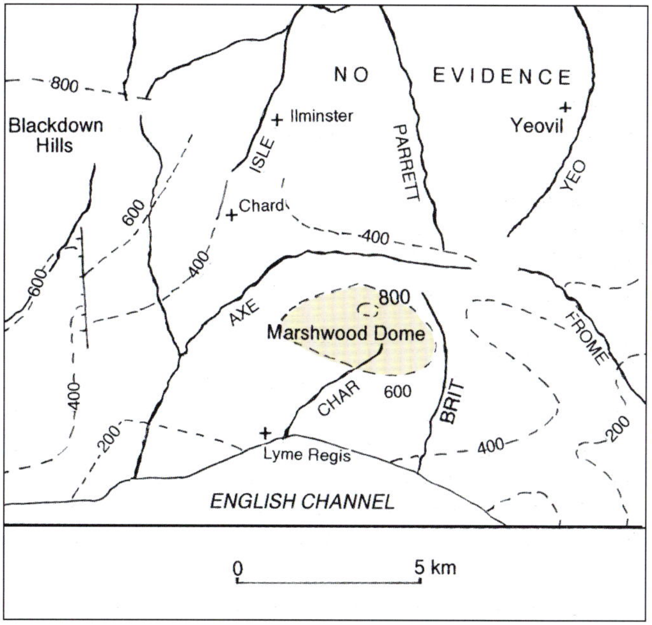

FIG. 2.6 Sketch map showing the relationship between the base of the Upper Greensand and the drainage pattern in West Dorset. Heights are in feet above above sea level.

Summary of the main geological events

Here we summarise the more important events in the geological history of the area The latest events, i.e. the youngest, are at the top:

- Continued denudation of rocks to produce present-day hills and valleys
- Ice age with periglacial and interglacial phases
- Faulting, including NNW-SSE wrench faults, and tilting of strata (Alpine Orogeny)
- Formation of silcretes and ferricretes under semi-tropical climate on what is now the East Devon Plateau
- Deposition of Upper Greensand and Chalk
- Deposition of Jurassic clays, sandstones and limestones
- Deposition of Permo-Triassic sediments
- Extensive E-W faulting producing basins and tilted blocks
- Intrusion of the Hestercombe magma
- Folding, faulting and thrusting of Devonian and Carboniferous sediments (Variscan Orogeny)
- Deposition of Devonian and Carboniferous sediments

Earth history can be simplified into a few major types of events:

(a) Crustal extension accompanied by deposition of sediments in subsiding basins

(b) Crustal compression accompanied by folding, thrusting, uplift and denudation

(c) Volcanic events which may happen in either of the above.

PERIODS	ROCK FORMATIONS
QUATERNARY	Peat Alluvium Valley Gravel Head
24 Ma	
TERTIARY	Plateau Deposits
65 Ma	
CRETACEOUS	Chalk Upper Greensand
145.6 Ma	
JURASSIC	Lower Lias Clay Blue Lias
208 Ma	
TRIASSIC AND PERMIAN	Penarth Group Blue Anchor Formation Mercia Mudstone Group North Curry Sandstone Otter Sandstone Budleigh Salterton Pebble Beds Littleham Mudstone Vexford Breccia Wiveliscombe Sandstone Hestercombe dyke
290 Ma	
CARBONIFEROUS	Carboniferous Limestone Upper Westleigh Limestone
362 Ma	
DEVONIAN	Pilton Shales Pickwell Down Sandstones Morte Slates Leighland Slates

The principal rock formations in the Taunton area and the geological periods to which they belong.

Ma - Age in million year

Chapter 3
Earthquakes

Reports of earthquakes

Among many fascinating folders in the Somerset Studies Library is one on local earthquakes.

On July 12, 1747 people who were sitting talking or supping in Taunton felt their seats move under them, and those who were in bed were awakened.

In 1863 on October 6 a loud report was first heard, which could easily have been imagined to be a terrific explosion at a distance, and many people believed that Taunton Prison had been blown up by Fenians until their own eyes convinced them otherwise, This was followed by a shaking of houses, bedroom furniture, windows etc. and many people, imagining that their houses were being ransacked by burglars, hastily slipped on garments and searched for the intruders. The shocks were also felt at Curry Rivel and in the Parrett Valley between Stoke-sub-Hamdon and Langport. In Bridgwater the ships lying in the river fairly rocked to and fro, and some portion of a large body of ice in the river near the bridge was broken up. This was a large earthquake with an epicentre in Herefordshire, felt over most of England and Wales. Incidentally, when was ice last seen on the river in early October?

> On January 4, 1680 of this year, about seven o'clock in the morning, there was an earthquake at Bridgwater, Chedzoy and for some miles around. It shook the houses pretty much, and was attended with a noise resembling a sudden gust of wind, or as others imagined, the shock and noise was not unlike that of some great thing thrown upon the ground.
>
> In the same year (15 May 1201) there was a great earthquake in the town, which is called Montacute, and for seven miles round, lasting for nearly two hours, so that the seats in the Monks choir were seen to shake, and the monks themselves trembled and were stupefied (Annnales Wintoni).

Mathew of Paris recorded the effects of the Wells' earthquake on December 21, 1248:

> ...an earthquake occurred in England, by which (as told to the writer of this work by the Bishop of Bath in whose diocese it occurred) the walls of the buildings were burst asunder, the stones were torn from their places, and gaps appeared in the ruined walls. The vaulted roof which has been placed on the top of the church of Wells by the great efforts of the builder, a mass of great size and weight, was hurled so as to strike great terror into all who heard it.....

The Somerset and Dorset Notes and Queries for 1895 gives details about a number of shocks in the Priddy, Wells, Shepton Mallet and Glastonbury area on December 30, 1893. At Wookey it seemed as if the earth was assuming an undulating motion, such as is observed on the waves of the sea. The first of the shocks, for there were several, was preceded by what seemed to be 'a terrific explosion' (Anon, 1895). In fact many accounts of earthquakes mention what sounded like large explosions.

Davison (1896) gives an account of the Exmoor Earthquake of the following year-January 23, 1894. Figure 3.1 shows where the effects were observed. Davison suggested that the earthquake was associated with movement on east-west faults.

Clearly there have been a significant number of earthquakes during historical time in Somerset yet the record cannot compare with the number and intensity of earthquakes in places such as Turkey or Alaska. However, we still need to know what are the chances of an earthquake compromising the safety of the reactors at Hinkley Point Nuclear Power Station. The Environmental Statement produced for the public enquiry into plans for a third reactor concluded that risks were minimal (CEGB, 1987). British Geological Survey (BGS) seismologists at Edinburgh have been investigating historical records of earthquakes in order to assess the degree and intensity of earthquake activity in Britain. There is an authoritative discussion of the 1248, 1747, 1894 and other earthquakes in the region in Musson, (1994).

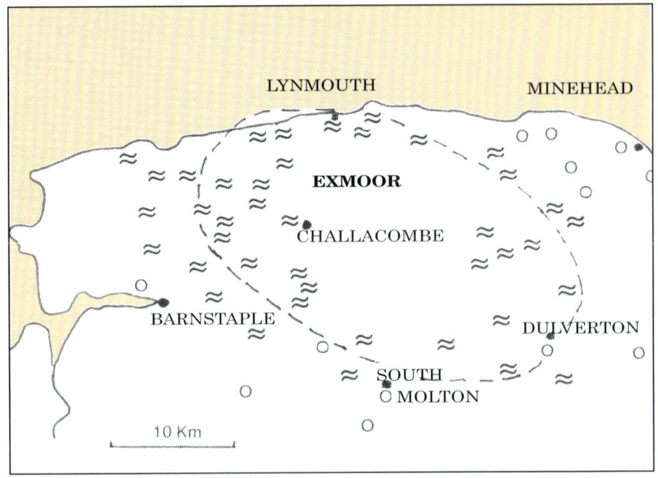

(based on Davison, 1896).

FIG 3.1 The effects of the 1894 Exmoor earthquake. The wavy symbol indicates places that reported feeling the effects; a circles marks a place where the effects were not observed. The pecked line encloses places with a 'Davison' intensity scale of 4 or over.

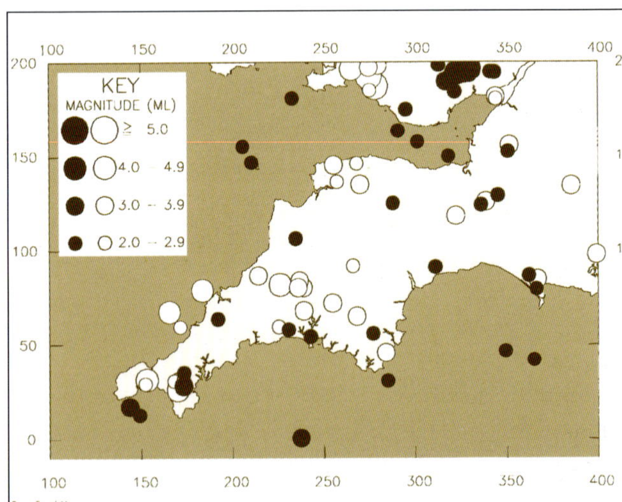

FIG 3.2 Distribution of recorded earthquakes in Southwestern England; open circles represent pre-1970 events whilst black circles are based upon instrumental monitoring.

Regional stresses and the pattern of faults

The distribution map of earthquake foci in Figure 3.2 has been specially prepared by the BGS Global Seismology Research Group. It is important to note that the open circles are pre-1970 events and the black circles represent post 1970 earthquakes whose location is based on BGS instrumental monitoring. We may note that the latter have averaged one per year including two near Taunton. Clearly there are stresses in the geological foundations of S W England.

Earthquakes are shock waves resulting from the release of stresses by sudden movement along faults. Faults in Somerset are the product of a long history of compression and tension. The most dramatic, the N-S compression which took place during the Variscan Orogeny, included thrusting, folding and considerable NNW-SSE strike-slip (sideways) movement along faults including the Cothelstone Fault. There followed N-S crustal extension which involved E-W faulting and the deposition of Permo-Triassic, Jurassic and Cretaceous sediments in subsiding basins. NW-SE compression during the succeeding Tertiary Period resulted in folding, thrusting and reactivation of Variscan faults.

The more recent episodes of compression have produced arrays of N-S/NNW-SSE vertical cracks (joints) in the rocks which can be seen in almost every Exmoor quarry, the Liassic cliffs and foreshore at Kilve and the quarry workings at Ham Hill near Yeovil among many other sites.

Is it possible to associate the recorded earthquakes with known faults and the present-day stress-field? Dollar (1963) has speculated on this subject but Dr Roger Musson, of the British Geological Survey Global Seismology Research Group in Edinburgh, makes the following comments (pers. comm.):

The issue of present stresses and active faults is highly contentious. One can say that the direction of principal compressive stress is roughly NW-SE from the opening of the Atlantic, and assuming that faults are more likely to be reactivated in a strike-slip sense, this would mean that faults trending N-S or E-W are more likely to be reactivated. But it only takes a small fault to make a British earthquake, and there are plenty of them. Given the three-dimensional uncertainty in any hypothetical location, it is very hard, if not impossible to pin blame for any particular quake on an individual fault, and my colleagues are always very doubtful of any attempts to do so. I would go so far as to question whether the concept of 'active fault' (inherited from California) is even useful in a British setting.

Evidence for earthquake activity in the rocks

It is reasonable to assume that earthquakes must have occurred in geological time as there is plenty of evidence that faulting took place which must surely have disturbed sediments on the seafloor. Yet very few possible examples are reported; this may be because geologists do not recognise the effects of earthquakes when they see them! However on the west side of St Audries Bay, some 3km east of Watchet (ST 103 431), one bed stands out from the evenly-bedded strata; it shows that the sediment has been plastically deformed into mini-buckles and highly contorted slump-folds as shown in Figure 3.3. The tops of the folds are penetrated by shrinkage cracks and cut by an erosion surface. The deformed sediments are composed of calcareous mudstones and lenticles and laminations of siltstones and very fine sandstones (Mayall, 1983). (Visitors may find the bed obscured by rock falls.)

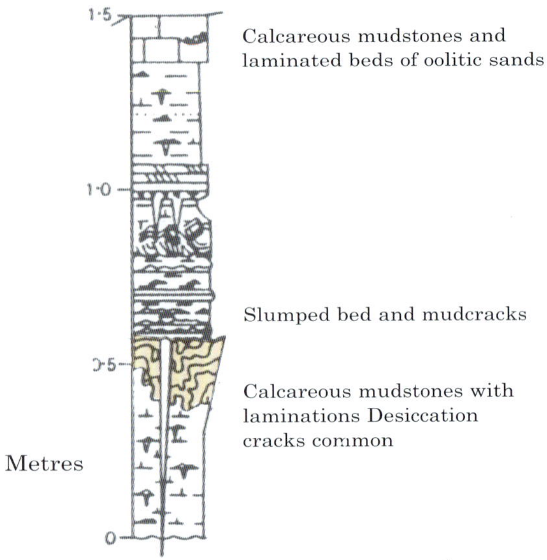

(Based on Mayall, 1983, by permission of the Cambridge University Press).

FIG. 3.3 Section through the Cotham Member showing the position of the slumped beds

Mayall suggests undulating ground motion caused liquifaction in the saturated sediment; the sudden loss of porewater would cause the sediment to lose its strength. The erosion surface and shrinkage cracks suggest that this episode was followed by elevation and exposure of the seabed. A bed with similar features dated to this time has been found from east Devon to Cheshire and this would indicate a widespread event. Elsewhere we mention blocks of Blue Lias at Taunton Castle and Staple Fitzpaine which contain numerous small brachiopods (Calcirynchia calcaria) scattered through the rock and usually in an unabraded state. Presumably these creatures were once attached to the seafloor. Did they suffer sudden upheaval and burial as a result of earth tremors or were storms the cause?

Recent detailed mapping by the British Geological Survey, including geophysical surveys, have shown that some sedimentary formations in the Wincanton-Shaftesbury area vary in thickness either side of a fault thus suggesting deposition more or less contemporaneous with movement on the fault (see Bristow et al., 1995 and Barton et al., 1998 for examples).

The study of earthquakes leads into many areas of geological and human concern and has recently extended to the planets. A wide range of related topics are covered in a popular publication from the British Geological Survey entitled *Earthquakes: our trembling planet* (van Rose and Musson, 1998).

Chapter 4
Building Stones

Recognition of the characteristics of the various rocks is important, not only for deciding how each was formed, but also for beginning to understand how and where they are used for building purposes. A select list of further reading is given in the Reference Section. The Taunton Rock Trail (chapter12) makes a good introduction for the reader to a great variety of building stones.

Properties and uses of building stones

Rocks with special qualities e.g. durability, ease of working or decorative appeal could stand the extra cost of being transported longer distances e.g. stone from Bath, Beer in Devon, Doulting and Ham Hill. The latter, from near Yeovil, is used for dressings in a high proportion of the local churches. Permo-Triassic Otter Sandstone may be seen in many doorways and windows. Large Blue Lias slabs were used extensively for flooring ('paviours') and church monuments.

A second group of building stones are those which are difficult to dress; examples are the Upper Westleigh Limestone, Devonian sandstones and Blue Lias. Cecil Somerfield, a retired stone mason living on the edge of the Brendon Hills, summed up the local stones succinctly when interviewed for the Somerset Magazine (Ruthven, 1998):

> I love working with sandstone. You can't dress shillet stone like you can sandstone-it's so hard that you have to put it into the wall as it comes out of the quarry.

The terms 'shillet' and 'ragstone' are everyday words for stone that was not generally sawn. 'Monkton Rag' refers to the sandstones that were once quarried at West Monkton in the Devonian Morte Slates formation. 'Shillet' also refers to the stony brash seen in arable fields and to commercially available broken stones used as an aggregate. These rocks were used for the roughly coursed walling seen in many of the older buildings in the Quantocks and Brendon Hills.

Hard-wearing stones such as chert, flint, certain sandstones, quartz pebbles ('popple stones') and granite have been used for roads and paths. Cornish granite sets have been used in the recent remodelling of the centre of Taunton.

The 20th century shop fronts in the towns display a range of exotic stones from elsewhere in Britain and overseas. Improvements in transport mean that we not only get tomatoes from South Africa but also flooring-slate from China. At the same time, more tourists and planners are beginning to appreciate the importance of local stones in creating local distinctiveness. Local stones tend to be the 'unsung heroes' when conservation schemes and listed buildings are under review. The geological variety in Taunton Deane is reflected in its buildings and it is important that even old walls are preserved wherever possible.

Some rocks weather more badly than others. Finely disseminated pyrite (iron sulphide) in the Blue Lias reacts with water and air causing the stone to break-up, especially the darker blocks. The Blue Lias in the Taunton area seems particularly susceptible to weathering, possibly also owing to a lower content of calcium carbonate which acts as a cement. The latter reason may explain the poor weathering properties of some of the red sandstones, especially in the Bishop's Lydeard area. Porous sandstones are at risk from the disintegrating effects of frost. Cements that bind rock particles together may be dissolved and drawn out by surface evaporation.

It is no surprise that the older walls often have a great mixture of stones, as at Taunton Castle and Cheddon Fitzpaine church. Many stones have been recycled more than once as is shown by the isolated blocks of reddened, burnt stone. The colour, variety and richness of a wall containing blocks of red sandstone, grey Blue Lias, Devonian sandstone and golden Ham Hill Stone, as seen at the Somerset Cricket Museum, may look crude yet these are surely features to treasure. A rough weather-beaten old wall of varied composition can have a friendly charm which is lacking in a clinical, neat wall of modern brick.

> *the lichen'd wall whose lizard hues are painted by slow Time*

New buildings and the restoration of older buildings have created a demand for supplies of local building stones which will harmonize with existing buildings. Freshly quarried, high quality Blue Lias from the Somerton area is now widely used. However, there are problems in matching the building materials: the older houses in the Blue Lias belt between Staple Fitzpaine and Somerton have a great variety of faces: pale grey, dark grey, buff yellowish-brown, smooth-faced, rough-faced, massive, shelly, laminated, weathered and unweathered rock fresh from the quarry!

Blue Lias quarried from near the surface tends to be yellowish-brown where weathering along the bedding and joints (cracks) has oxidised the iron compounds. However, this is usually a superficial feature and the interior of the split stone is grey as is stone hewn from more deeply buried beds. Some builders are presenting both the blue-grey and yellow-brown faces on the outsides of buildings, thus producing a chequer-board pattern which is not to

(Courtesy TDBC).

FIG 4.1 Medieval Priory Barn which now houses the Somerset Cricket Museum in Taunton

everyone's taste. Planners, architects and owners might wish to consider the aesthetic aspects of having one or two colours on the same wall. An added complication is that White Lias has been quarried in the past in the same area.

White Lias lacks the iron content of the Blue Lias and thus yields a whitish stone characteristic of rocks with a high content of calcium carbonate.

It is increasingly difficult to find sites with suitable stone to quarry and which are acceptable to planners and local residents. The alternative is to use artificial stone but this is not always easy. Does the architect try to match the local stone or complement it? There are some interesting 'experiments' to look out for in villages on the red Permo-Triassic formations. All of this is quite apart from the mix of styles e.g. squared or rubble stones, regular or irregular courses.

Sources and transport

It is difficult to be precise as to the actual sources of the various rocks without written records except where there was only one source as with Ham Hill Stone. Hummocky ground sometimes shows where the Upper Greensand was dug for chert in the Blackdown Hills. There are many disused slate, sandstone and limestone quarries in the Quantocks. The quarries around Westleigh supplied a great deal of drab building stone. Colourful red Permo-Triassic sandstones and conglomerates were extensively quarried west of Taunton, as at Bishops Lydeard. The Blue Lias was worked in many small quarries from Corfe, south of Taunton, to Langport and beyond. North Curry Sandstone was dug at Hele and Norton, west of Taunton, and at Knapp and North Curry north-east of Taunton. No one stone dominates Taunton, unlike Bath where the local oolitic limestones are used in a high proportion of the buildings.

The Pipe Rolls of the Bishopric of Winchester for 1245 to 1249 give an interesting insight into how Ham Hill Stone travelled from Ham Hill to Taunton (Hunt, 1971):

Dr Dunning (pers. comm.) suggests that the 'Monk's Meadow' may have been on the east bank of the River Parrett; there was a late-medieval wharf at Thorney. The 6 miles by road from the 'the foot of the hill' to Thorney cost nearly twice as much as the 15 miles by river to Ruishton. The cost of transporting stone was, and is still, an important constraint upon the use of stone. Today the cost of road transport doubles roughly every 30 miles for aggregates from Mendip quarries. In addition, the Pipe Rolls provide details of the costs of carts, quarry tools, workmen, masons and other building materials.

The Pipe Rolls of Winchester for 1207-8 refer to the need for mortar for building operations undertaken at Taunton Castle by Bishop Peter:

> In making a lime-kiln this year on the Quantocks and in removing the limestone and raising it from two cuttings, £2 12s.2½d. In hauling 281 quarters of lime, £1 12s. 3½d (Vivian-Neale and Gray, 1941).

The Permo-Triassic sandstones in the walls of Halse parish church could have come from a number of quarries. Luckily, the churchwarden's accounts for 1451-2 are specific:

> payd to the same Rychard for iii dayes worke of ye wch one of the' he worked at Lydyerd upon the stone..xix/d.
> payd to Cowlyn for caryeng of a stone frome Lyderd ....ii.d.

The Pipe Rolls of the Bishopric of Winchester for 1245 to 1249

	£	s	d
1245-46			
Carrying 600 stones from the foot of the hill to the water	*1*	*0*	*0*
Bringing the same stones by water to Riston (Ruishton, where there was a ford).		*9*	*0*
1246-47			
Carrying the stones from the foot of the hill to the water	*1*	*2*	*3*
Bringing the stones by water from the monk's meadow to Riston	*1*	*9*	*8*
Stipend and food of two servants hauling large stones with a cart for 14 weeks		*7*	*4*
48,000 stone tiles purchased for roofing the hall	*1*	*8*	*0*
1247-48			
641 stones purchased from Hamdon	*1*	*0*	*0*
Carrying these by water	*1*	*16*	*5*
50 cartloads of stone purchased at Hestercombe		*2*	*3*
1000 hard stones (slate?) purchased for the salt house			*7*
1248-49			
200 stones purchased at Hamdon		*5*	*9*
Carriage of 971 stones by water	*1*	*19*	*11*

The location of the quarries and the movement of building materials in the middle ages is a fascinating topic and there is a need to draw together all the documentary evidence for Somerset. Further information on the sources and movement of stone would be welcome *(see below)*.

Churches and churchyards

The local parish church is usually a good place to discover the local building stones and thereby something of the local geology. There is access to the outside walls even if the doors are locked for security as is frequently the case nowadays. The stones and architecture may represent some thousand years of quarrying, building and rebuilding. There is usually an informative guide for sale along with the latest edition of the parish magazine. You and your contribution to the upkeep of the fabric will be warmly welcomed. There will be something of interest whether the building be St Mary Magdalene in the centre of Taunton or tiny, lonely Raddington in the high hills west of Wiveliscombe.

In general quoins and buttresses tend to be large square-cut blocks e.g. Ham Hill Stone, Blue Lias and Permo-Triassic sandstone. Sandstones and Ham Hill Stone which can be more readily worked have been used for the thin mullions and tracery of windows and other dressings. These tend to be more exposed to weathering on several sides and many windows show piecemeal replacement of parts with Doulting Stone, Bath Stone and Ham Hill Stone. Some of the walls appear to be a bizarre mix of whatever the builders could lay their hands on. The orderly regular additions and replacements by the Victorians sometimes seem a trifle dull in contrast. Each must tell a story of fashion, need, cost, funds and availability of materials which are all worthy of more research. The parish church of Wellington, illustrated in Figure 33.1, exemplifies many of these aspects.

The churchyards should not be overlooked. The rocks used for the gravestones and tombs tend to be similar within a particular region; clearly, they were produced on a commercial scale. One can usually find Blue Lias slabs with beautiful engraving but badly weathered surfaces. In addition there are Ham Hill Stone table tombs, sandstone slabs and polished granite monuments which contrast with the older weather-beaten sedimentary stones. Fashions change and visitors can note the earliest dates on the granite and other more exotic gravestones. Do the Blue Lias, or the Ham Hill Stone slabs date from specific periods? Which stones are used, or indeed, allowed today?

> *Behold the moon slow rising up the sky.*
> *Throws on the tombs her mildly glowing beams;*
> *Say, canst thou trace with close attentive eye,*
> *Their sev'ral records, and discern their names?*
>
> Thomas Shoel of Montacute 1819

Increasingly, the rich wildlife of churchyards is being recognised: meadow flowers, lichens in abundance, ants' nests, butterflies, and old stone walls with the crevices crawling with wildlife. In high summer the afternoon is alive with the buzz of insects. The Living Churchyard Project (Robinson, 1992) has done much to encourage the sensitive conservation of churchyards and highlight the interest to be derived from studying the building stones and gravestones.

The 17th Century alabaster church monuments are of interest. Alabaster is a form of gypsum (calcium sulphate). Dr R. J. Firman, of Nottingham University, has mapped the distribution in the West Country of memorials made from East Midlands and Somerset alabaster (Firman, 1989). The visitor can compare both types in the churches at Pitminster and Burlescombe. The Somerset material has more impurities giving it a veined, blotchy or wispy appearance. Colours range from ivory, yellow, brown, grey to almost black. The East Midlands' gypsum tends to be colourless or have orange or red tints. The gypsum can be seen in the cliffs west of Watchet Harbour. The present-day cliffs provides much smaller samples than those to be seen in the church monuments. Cliff erosion may have removed the source of the larger blocks.

The regional pattern of building stones

The author has been struck by the variety of building stones used in the construction of the local parish churches in west Somerset. Is it possible to see a regional pattern? Appendix G lists, in a form of shorthand, the building stones used for the walling in the local churches. Capital lettering implies a significantly large proportion for a particular stone; lesser amounts are shown in small case. Dressings used around doorways and windows have been omitted in order to simplify the data. The amounts of each stone were estimated. For example, the walls of the parish church at Wellington (78 in the list) have significant amounts of chert and North Curry Sandstone but lesser amounts of Permo-Triassic rocks and Ham Hill Stone. Thus it can be summarised as CH/NCS/pt/hhs. Figures 4.2 and 4.3 presents this information in map form.

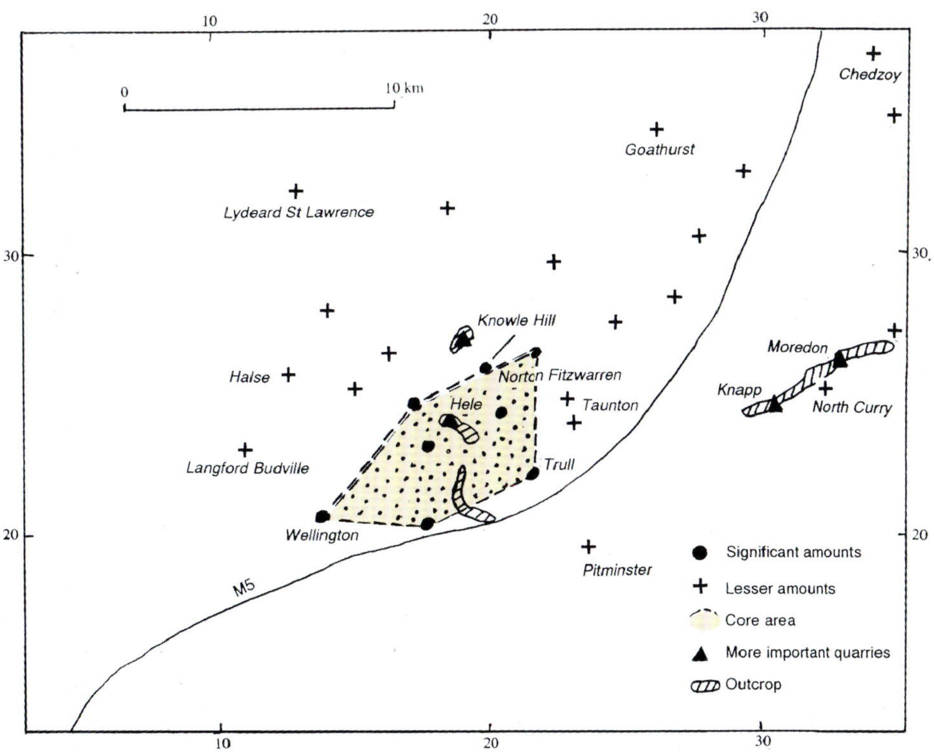

FIG 4.2. Distribution map showing churches which incorporate North Curry Sandstone.

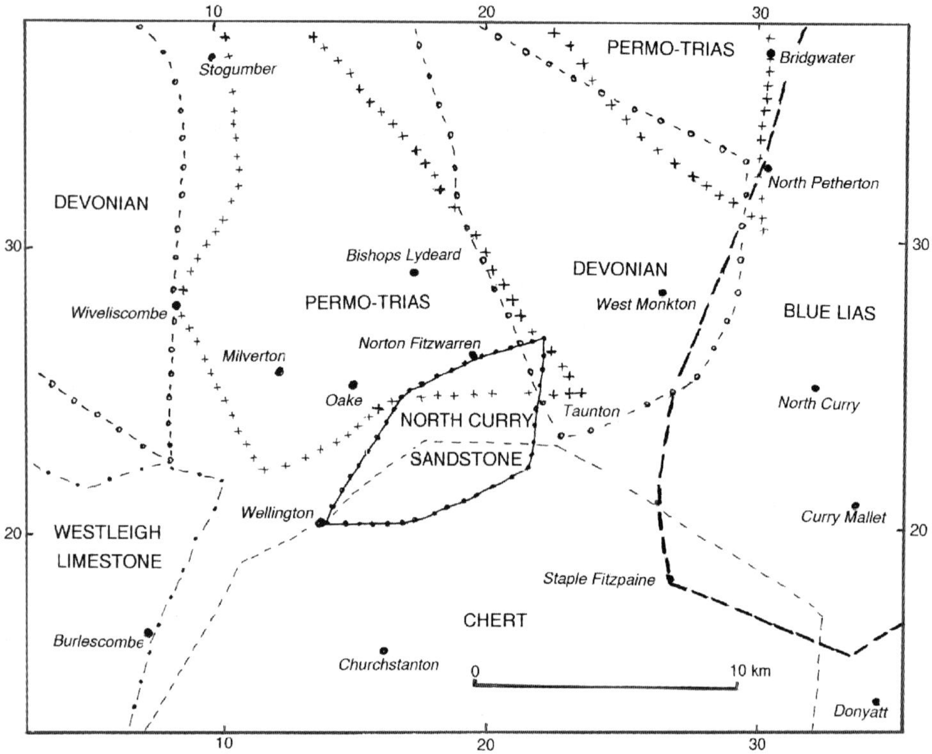

Fig. 4.3 Generalised distribution map showing building stone core areas

We immediately note that some churches are constructed of but one stone whilst others, such as those at Cheddon Fitzpaine (17) and North Petherton (55), have five. Secondly, there appear to be regional variations. For example, Westleigh Limestones (WL) figure to the southwest whilst Blue Lias (BL) predominates in the east and chert (CH) to the south.

The information may be simplified in two ways. Figure 4.2 shows the distribution pattern for the churches which incorporate North Curry Sandstone. The 'core area' has been constructed by connecting the outermost examples of churches showing significant amounts of North Curry Sandstone in their fabric and is represented by a dotted pattern within the broken line. Beyond this area is a peripheral area where the sandstone was only a minor element. Norton Fitzwarren church is almost entirely built of North Curry Sandstone. Elsewhere, especially in the peripheral area, it is seen as large blocks mainly in the towers, quoins and buttresses. This pale greenish-grey, coarse sandstone incorporates pebbles and grey silty flakes with good examples of cross-bedding. It is curious that very little found its way to the south east of what is now the line of the M5. Figure 4.3 to which we now turn, suggests that the Blue Lias was preferred.

Figure 4.3 has been constructed by connecting the outermost examples of churches showing significant amounts of each the rock types as was done for the North Curry Sandstone. For example, the edge of the Blue Lias 'core' area is shown by a line joining North Petherton (55), Ruishton (62), Stoke St Mary (69), Thurlbear (74), Staple Fitzpaine (66) and Ashill (4).

The building stones used in the parish churches represent some thousand years of building and rebuilding. For most of that time transport costs ruled that heavy, bulky, low value per weight materials should be obtained from local sources. Water transport, whether by canal or river would have distorted the pattern as this provides lower costs per mile. The coming of the railways and modern road transport facilities have extended the availability still further.

The map not only confirms our everyday experience that older buildings in settlements reflect the local geology but it also provides the building conservation officers in local district councils with an objective regional summary.

Generally, their aim is to maintain local distinctiveness and harmony.

Readers might care to compare Figure 4.3 with the summary of physical landscape types shown in Figure A1 (Appendix A)

We can recognise ten core areas:

(a) Two areas of Devonian sandstone drawn from the Brendon Hills and the Quantocks with variable surface textures and often tinged red.
(b) Grey Westleigh Limestone in the southwest which is somewhat drab in character.
(c) Two areas of Permo-Triassic sandstones and conglomerates to the west and east of the Quantocks providing rich red colouring but indifferent weathering quality.
(d) North Curry Sandstone in a concentration to the west of Taunton and quarried mainly in the Norton-Hele area but also perhaps from the North Curry-Knapp area. Note that there was another source of North Curry Sandstone to the east of Bridgwater.
(e) The southwestern tip of a belt of Blue Lias settlements extending north east to the Poldens, Mendips and beyond.
(f) Chert from the Upper Greensand which forms an important building material, along with flint, in much of the Blackdown Hills.

These are the core areas and it will be understood that the stones were also used beyond the core areas. The data in Appendix G could be used to plot the peripheral areas which surround the core areas where each stone was used. Many of the boundary lines of the core areas are close to that of their neighbour. Note how the Blue Lias zone extends westward away from the outcrop containing the quarries so as to serve areas lacking much good building stone which in this case is the Mercia Mudstone. The latter, along with the Lias Clay Vale, is brick country.

As has been stated above, Taunton has a remarkable variety of building stones as is demonstrated on the geological trail in the town centre. Figure 4.3 reveals the reasons for this sumptuous variety. Five core areas converge on the County town: Devonian, Permo-Triassic, North Curry Sandstone, Blue Lias and Upper Greensand chert. The Westleigh Limestone may well have come in via the Bridgwater and Taunton Canal or railway in the 19th century both of which passed close to the quarries.

A distribution map showing the various building stones used for window and door dressings would show additional use of Ham Hill, Bath and Doulting Stone, especially in 19th century additions and rebuilds.

Modern human geography concerns itself very much with the study of the individual decision-making that contributes to spatial patterns. Here is an area for research with great potential: we need to know the precise locations of the quarries which supplied particular churches. We also need to bring together historical records so as to understand the motivations that led to the use of particular building stones in this or that place: the master masons might have had their own motives for asking for particular stones; the benefactors would have been keen to get value for money at least - cost and perhaps increase their prestige by using certain stones; the abbots and diocesan authorities may have owned quarries.

There have been a number of recent publications concerning building stones of interest to architects, builders, planners, geologists and tourists ; these are listed in Appendix G.

Chapter 5
Soils and Farming

Many writers have remarked upon the association of rocks, soils and farming in Taunton Deane. De la Beche wrote in 1839 as follows:

> Excellent grassland is often seen on the lias, as also many good orchards; but in general the arable land upon it seems not very remarkable for abundant produce. Oaks, as might be expected, often grow well, particularly upon the marly or clayey parts...Taken as a whole the area occupied by the red sandstone series is one of considerable fertility, especially when uncovered by transported gravels.The red marls, with their higher variegated parts adjoining the lias, would appear very favourable for the growth of apples; and cider obtained from their range is commonly found to be very excellent, when sufficient attention is paid to the mode of making- an attention not so common as could be desired.

Dr Buckland mentioned soil fertility in his address to the first annual meeting of the Somerset Archaeological and Natural History Society in 1851:

> In the vale of Taunton Deane and at Bridgwater the land was too fat, and afforded not to the well-fed farmer sufficient work...where farmers had to do nothing but buy a few Welsh cattle-turn them into the Bridgwater meadows to walk about and get fat. Let gentlemen buy their estates... on the red marl.
>
> (Buckland, 1851).

Ackland, (Ackland and Sturge, 1851), in writing about the stony soils of the 'mountainous' parts of western Somerset had this to say:

> The stone rag is a soil composed of finely laminated layers of clay-slate, which have a tendency to rub down into clay and to hold moisture. The stone rush is a soil in which irregular portions of stone work up to the surface, where they are slow of decomposition. As a general rule, the stone rag is more favourable to the growth of grass, and is considered as worth from 5s to 10s an acre more than the stone rush which is apt to suffer from drought The stone rush is also an unsuitable soil for the action of any agricultural implements which are liable to be damaged or impeded by stones.

Sturge, in a separate essay, (Ackland and Sturge, 1851), added the following:

> On the tops and the steep sides of the hills this (the rag or stone rush) is thin and weak; lower down the soil improves, the best being found at a little height above the valleys, where the sides of the hills are not so steep as to cause it to wash away with the heavy rains.

William Ussher, in his report *Geology of the Quantock Hills* (1908), wrote:

> The only part of the area that can be termed barren is the Lower Devonian grit district forming the northern and higher portion of the Quantocks, and this is renowned for the growth of whortles or whortleberries......For arable or grazing, however, the Keuper Marls (=Mercia Mudstone) form the best soil and have given to Taunton Deane a widespread reputation for fertility. The Rhaetic and Lias limestones and clays afford heavy, and moderately heavy, land suitable for certain roots and cereals, and fair grassland.

The whortleberries grow on acidic soils which are the norm on the non-calcareous Hangman Sandstones, especially where there is a high rainfall which leaches bases from the soil.

Clearly, the varying bedrock, soils, topography and climate influence the productivity of the land. Sturge (Ackland and Sturge, 1851, p126-7) quoted the annual value of land per acre based upon the assessment to the county rate, as published in Spackman's Statistics of the British Empire (1843). Spurge also adds the principal rock type in each parish:

Permo-Triassic rocks:			**Devonian slates and sandstones**		
	s	d		s	d
Milverton	48	5	Clatworthy	18	0
Trull	43	7	Huish Champflower	18	4
Halse	43	1	Withial Florey	10	6

Withial Florey was the lowest value in the County. The highest value was Mark, east of Highbridge, situated on alluvial silts (57s 3d).

Unhappily, Somerset shows some of the worst soil erosion in Britain: the light soils on the Yeovil Sands near Ilminster, and the red Permo-Triassic sands in west Somerset, lack the cohesion and stability of the heavier clays. They suffer compaction, develop hardpans and surface crusts. The bright red colour of the soils on the Permo-Triassic rocks is partly a result of the loss of dark humus and erosion of the topsoil.

The results of heavy rainfall are seen in the spreads of sands in the country lanes. The latter are often lowered well below field level owing to centuries of traffic and the erosive effects of intense surface run-off. Field boundaries across hillsides often show a build-up of sediment on the upside and erosion on the downside; the height difference can be up to 3m in some instances.

Ploughed fields are more at risk of erosion than grassland; they have less infiltration, evaporation and transpiration and therefore greater run-off. Other factors are soil structure and particle size, humous content,slope gradient, crop type and cultivation practices. There has been a steady increase in the percentage of land used for arable cultivation since the 1930s. The Environment Agency is keen to promote a greater awareness of these problems in Taunton Deane. The River Tone Catchment Project is a collaboration between the Environment Agency, the Farming and Wildlife Advisory Group and the Somerset Wildlife Trust.

There are soil maps at the scales of 1:63,360 and 1:25,000 on the periphery of Taunton Deane which are listed in Appendix E. The primary reference to local soils is the 1:250,000 Soils of England and Wales: Sheet 5 South West England. It has a companion text with a wealth of detail (Findlay et al., 1984). Figure 25.3 is a block diagram taken from the text to show the soil associations on the East Devon Plateau. It illustrates the general arrangement of the geology together with the overlying soils. Note how the soils vary according to the nature of the underlying rocks and their topographical location.

A regional summary of soil types in Taunton Deane can be found in Appendix A.

Chapter 6
Hydrology and Water Supplies

ROCK GROUP	Run-off	Infiltration	Ground Water (Aquifer)	Quality
UPPER GREENSAND		▲	▲	Soft
RHAETIC AND LIAS LIMESTONES AND CLAYS	▲			Hard - some chalybeate & petrifying springs
MERCIA MUDSTONE	▲			Hard - some saline water
BSP BEDS AND OTTER SANDSTONE		▲	▲	Hard
DEVONIAN SLATES AND SANDSTONES	▲			Soft
FLOOD PLAIN DEPOSITS	▲	▲	▲	Tend to be polluted

FIG 6.1 Hydrological aspects of the main rock formations. ▲ Indicates characteristic feature.

The average annual precipitation over the Tone basin ranges from over 1100 mm/year on the Brendon Hills to under 700 mm/year along the lower Tone. The table below shows that precipitation spread out over the basin averages 914 mm/year of which 52% is lost by evapo-transpiration. Of the remainder, 11% is lost by surface run-off and 36% infiltrates underground.

Hydrology of the River Tone catchment (mean values).

Rainfall	914 mm
Evaporation	482 mm
Surface run-off	101 mm
Infiltration	330 mm

(Sherrell 1970).

The nature of the underlying rocks, along with land use, are important in determining whether there is surface run-off or infiltration. Figure 6.1 summarises the hydrogeology.

Upper Greensand

De la Beche observed; We know that such a thing as a spring of pure water can nowhere be obtained, all being more or less impregnated with foreign matter in solution. While some of these springs may rise through faults from unknown depths, and bring this foreign matter with them, others are certainly formed (such, for instance, as those which flow from beneath the green sand of the Blackdowns, and other places where similar conditions prevail) by the percolation of rain-water through rocks, until thrown out by beds sufficiently impervious.

(De la Beche 1839).

The porosity of the Upper Greensand, together with the gentle slopes of the plateau, allow water to pass through the sandy beds where the water is temporarily stored underground. The escarpment south of Taunton, and the sides of the valleys farther south, are ringed with springs and see pages where the ground water emerges on the hillsides. These springs are important in maintaining stream flow during summer months. The wetness around the springs has encouraged landslides aided by stream undercutting. These conditions were magnified during Pleistocene cold phases with the result that there were landslips on a massive scale especially on the steeper slopes.

The rising demand for good quality water was felt in Taunton in the 19th century. Jeboult (1873) records that 'Although Taunton was far better off than most towns, it was felt by many of the more enterprising inhabitants that it required a larger, better and more copious supply of water than was furnished by wells, cisterns, and streams. Accordingly public meetings were called, and much discussion arose on the subject as to the best method of obtaining it.' Trial borings were made on Leigh and Blagdon Hills and the water 'found to be of unusually good and suitable quality, and great care was taken by the company not to incur any improper or unnecessary expense.......Several tunnels, adits, wells and shaft-holes were constructed.' The water was collected in reservoirs and conveyed to the town in cast-iron pipes. The price allowed 'its use even amongst the lowest-class cottages, the rent being but one penny per week for this class of property'. As the reservoirs stood 'a very considerable height above the town the pressure was great, and in case of fire proved most serviceable'.

The reservoirs formed the background of Taunton's water supply until Clatworthy reservoir was opened in 1961.

Permo-Triassic sands, breccias and conglomerates

The porosity of the Budleigh Salterton Pebble Beds, Otter Sandstone, Vexford Breccias and Wiveliscombe Sandstone (Figure 13.5) is high enough to facilitate the movement of water through the strata. However, the porosity in the first two is limited by the presence of calcium carbonate cement between the sand grains and cobbles. The usefulness of these aquifers for water supply is also limited by the fact that E-W faults have broken-up the strata into small compartments.

These rock formations produce light, free-draining soils much favoured for improved grassland, maize and potato growing. The demand for water, especially for spray irrigation, is met by abstraction from shallow boreholes and adjacent streams. Spray irrigation represents a net loss of water by evaporation and transpiration when demand is greatest during the summer and river flow is at a minimum.

Mercia Mudstone Group

These silty mudstones have a close texture which leads to surface run-off rather than infiltration and which increases the risk of flooding in the lower parts of the Tone basin.

Devonian slates and sandstones

These are relatively impermeable although joints and fissures allow the passage of some ground water. The widespread cover of stony, sandy head may lead to local infiltration. Water from the Brendon Hills is stored in Clatworthy Reservoir.

It will be apparent that water resources are scattered unevenly in the Tone basin and, on the larger scale, in the area served by Wessex Water. At the same time there is an uneven geographical and seasonal demand for water. The result is that the transfer of water eastward from the Brendon Hills is becoming more important.

Water supplies in the Tone Catchment are predominantly from reservoirs. Natural flows into some of these reservoirs are supported by abstraction from rivers. A number of borehole and spring sources have a low and unreliable output especially during extended dry periods. Consequently some of these sources are not now used.

The recent run of dry years in the 1990's the emphasised the problems of water supply, especially in southern and eastern England. Regional planning policies are beginning to take into account the provision of adequate supplies of water at reasonable cost. Some major flood events have also drawn attention to the problems of excess water. Changing land use patterns must be considered alongside precipitation, topography and the underlying geology For example, increases in forests and grassland tend to reduce run-off and soil erosion; arable cultivation, especially autumn sown cereals, roads and the building of housing estates tend to increase run-off and erosion.

Readers are recommended to consult the River Tone Local Environment Action Plan (LEAP) which gives a wealth of information about the Tone catchment.

Chapter7
Radon

Radon is a natural radioactive gas produced by the decay of uranium and thorium in rocks and soils. Its distribution in the environment is related to both the underlying geology and the presence of transport pathways through rocks and soils. At high concentrations, radon and its daughter products can significantly increase the risk of householders contracting lung cancer. Most damaging are alpha particles which may accumulate in the lungs (Heath 1991).

Figure 7.1 below is taken from the Radon Atlas of England published by the National Radioactivity Protection Board (NRPB). It shows the estimated proportions of homes exceeding the Radon Action Level in each 5 km grid square of Somerset. The Action Level is set at 200 Bq m^{-3} averaged over a year and is used as an indicator of the need for householders to take precautionary measures to reduce radon levels in the home. The map indicates that the highest readings in west Somerset are concentrated in the Brendon Hills running north from approximately Clayhanger to Clatworthy and westward to Upton.

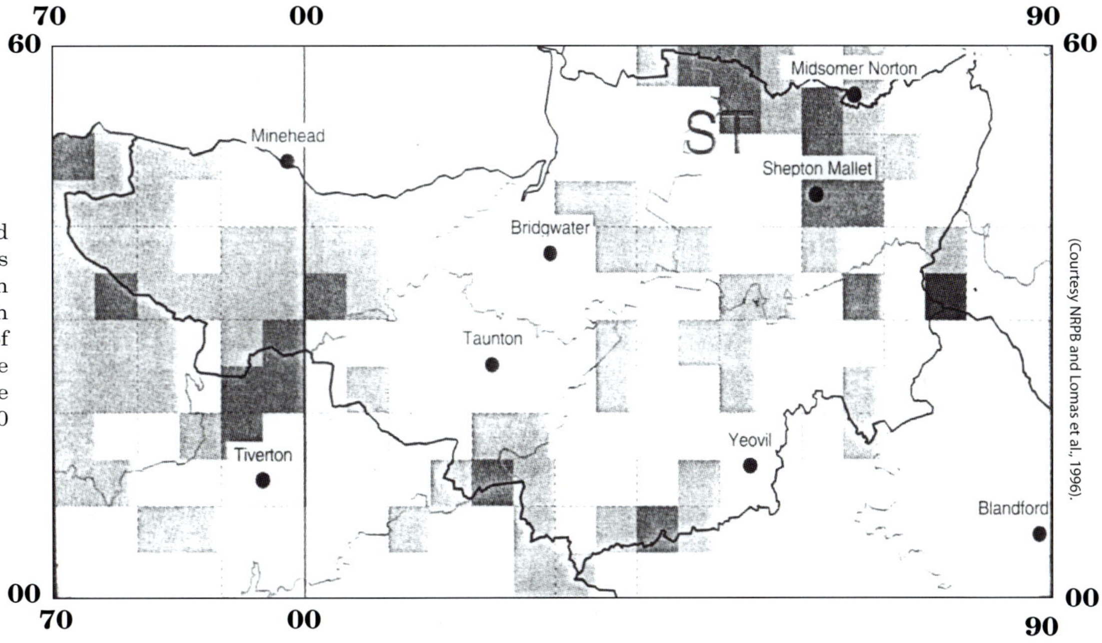

FIG. 7.1 Estimated proportions of homes exceeding the Radon Action Level in each 5 km grid square of Somerset, the shadings graduate from < 1 to >30

Whilst some of the highest readings in Southwest England are associated with the presence of granite, it does not follow that granite is the only source of radioactive emissions. Most rocks are radioactive to a greater or lesser extent. The Jurassic Inferior Oolite, in the east of the County, contains a bed with above-average levels of radioactivity.

Rising ground water and fractures in the rocks are associated with the outgassing of radon. The brittle Devonian rocks of the Brendon Hills and the Quantocks are highly fractured as a result of compression, wrenching and stretching at various times. The Carboniferous Limestone in the Mendips is especially prone to high radon generation because of the high karstic permeability and low water table. Radon concentrations can be very high in caves.

On the other hand, the close-textured Mercia Mudstone Group of silty clays around Taunton and the Lower Lias clays towards Ilminster form a less permeable blanket; these areas do indeed show much lower radon values. Readers are referred to Miles et al. (1992) and Lomas et al. (1996).

Chapter 8
Limekilns and Lime Burning

Many of the soils in west Somerset are developed on non-calcareous rocks and tend toward acidity, especially those on the Devonian slates and sandstones. There was a growing awareness in the C17 that the application of lime improved both the soil and crop yields. Limestone was eagerly sought and the distribution of limekilns, in general, reflects the various outcrops of limestone. Figure 8.1. shows the location of limekilns associated with the Budleigh Salterton Pebble Beds (BSPB). The production of lime is an example of an industry situated near heavy, bulky raw material.

John Strachey has left a manuscript, dated about 1730, in which he discusses various aspects of Somerset geology including limeburning:

> Limestone. There is a great quantity in almost all parts of this County the Marsh excepted.....They burn it altogether in round kilns built about 12 feet in height, & Closing Coniccall in their bottom, where they draw forth the lime at an Eye or two. They burn it with pit Coal, laying that with the stone stratum super Stratum to the top. They make lime also of blew & white lyas, of Marble & in some places of freestone. (Webby 1966a).

De la Beche, writing in 1839, adds further details concerning the BSPB quarries as a source of lime:

> Much lime is supplied, chiefly, however, for agricultural purposes, by the conglomerate, with a calcareo-magnesium cement, of the red sandstone series, extending from Williton, by Stogumber, Lydeard St Lawrence, Fitzhead, Milverton, and Langford Budville, to Thorne St Margaret. This material varies

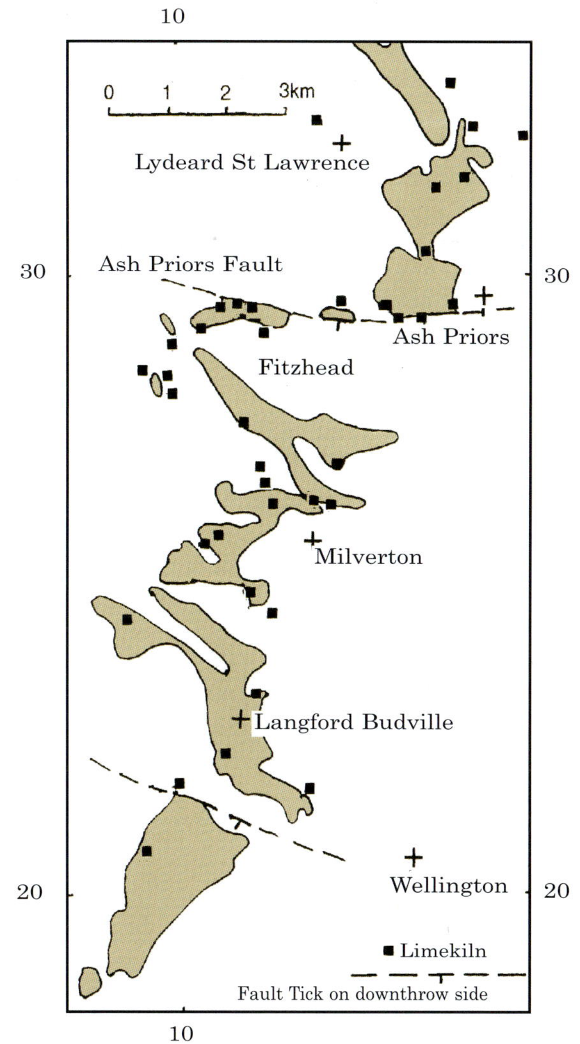

FIG. 8.1 The outcrop of the Budleigh Salterton Pebble Beds and the distribution of limekilns.

much in quality, as might be expected, but is best where rolled pieces of grauwacke* limestone form part of the conglomerate. In breaking up the stone the siliceous pebbles are separated, so that as much of the cementing matter may be burnt pure, except in the case of the limestone pebbles as above noticed, as can be managed. Extensive works are carried on near Wiveliscombe and Milverton to supply the country on the east and west.

The Bulletins of the Somerset Industrial Archaeological Society contain a useful collection of articles on limekilns (e.g. Daniel, 1988 and 1990). Good examples of limekilns are to be seen west of Ash Priors (see Ash Priors chapter below for further details). The Sites and Monuments Record (SMR) held by Somerset County Council includes information on limekilns in Somerset. Figure 8.3. shows the distribution of limekilns recorded for west Somerset. One can pick out the BSPB group extending from Williton to Wellington. To the west is a line of kilns located on Devonian limestones which cross Exmoor; the same beds supported kilns to the north of Taunton in the southern Quantocks. The belt of kilns south and east of Taunton mark the outcrop of the Blue Lias. Those around Chard are near outcrops of Chalk and very interesting details of the history of limeburning are given in the Chard History Group's publication *Number 3 Chard: a geological survey.*

One such kiln has recently been restored at the Somerset Wildlife Trust's (SWT) reserve at Bishopswood Meadows (ST 2542 1314). Details of access from SWT.

Lime mortar is still needed especially for the restoration of buildings.

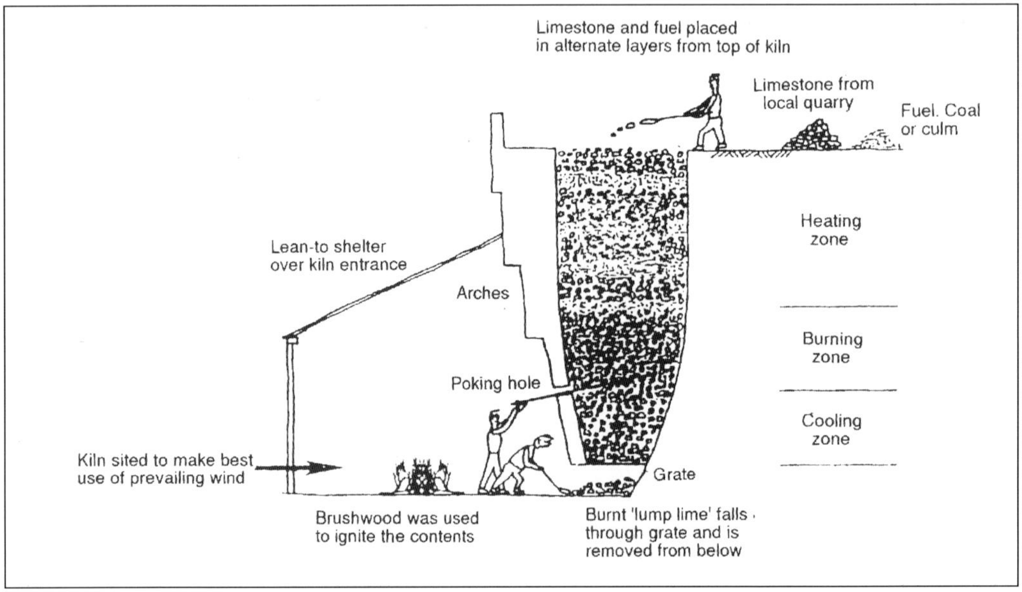

FIG. 8.2 The production of lime in a working kiln (courtesy Peter Daniel).

The limestone pebbles were selected by hand from the BSPB. The non-calcareous stones were used for surfacing roads. Beds that were well-cemented with calcium carbonate could be used as building stones. The stone was dug from the hillsides for ease of working. The abandoned quarries are an important feature of the west Somerset landscape and havens for wildlife. It is important that the best are not obliterated with landfill.

The following comments by De la Beche on the marketing of lime were written in 1839 at a time when kilns were still in operation:

> The quarries of Holcombe Rogus and Westleigh supply large quantities of lime to the non-calcareous country around them. On the south of Taunton the Lia country in the direction of Staple Fitzpaine, Hatch Beauchamp, Curry Mallet, Fivehead, Ashill and Broadway, is of course well furnished with this necessary material, and supplies it to a part of the district formed by the red sandstone on the north and to a portion of the Greensand country of the Black Down Hills which rise above it.

(The distribution of lime kilns is courtesy the Sites and Monuments Record at County Hall.)

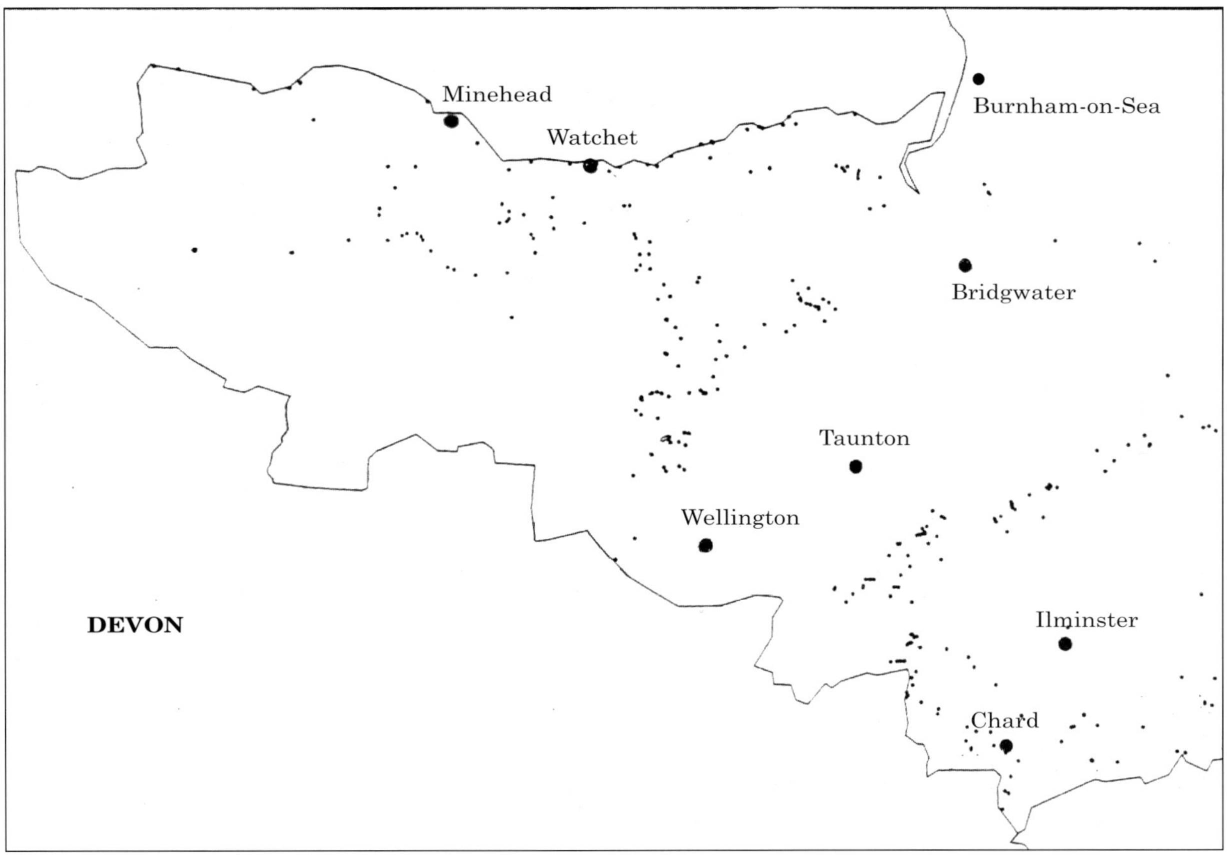

FIG. 8.3 Distribution of limekilns in west Somerset.

Chapter 9
Conservation

Geological conservation

There is an increased need to retain the good things from the past in our rapidly changing world. Rock exposures take their place alongside archaeological sites, historic buildings and rare plants. The importance of geological conservation is highlighted in *TDBC's Nature Conservation Strategy,* published in 1997.

Somerset has been surveyed for Regionally Important Geological Sites (RIGS) which are sites of geological importance not included in the Sites of Special Scientific Interest (SSSI) category. They are the equivalent of County Wildlife Sites. Details about geological sites of importance are kept at the Somerset Environmental Records Centre. Brief details of sites are listed in the Taunton Deane Local Plan and at the end of the chapter.

The large quarry at Triscombe has the potential to provide opportunities for a combined geological and wildlife conservation area. The old working face can become the haunt of peregrine falcons and provide rock faces for geological study. It will provide a nutrient-poor, acidic habitat for wildlife. The sheer size of the quarry at Triscombe can be compared in scale with the gorge at Cheddar.

Geologists are for ever using new techniques and applying changing concepts in studying the history of the Earth as for example with regard to radioactivity, microfossils, rock deformation, dating, ground water and palaeomagnetism. Old quarries and brickpits are also of interest to industrial archaeologists. It is important that old pits and quarries are seen as a valuable scientific resource and not just depositories for waste materials.

There are many other abandoned quarries which have developed into peaceful wildlife sites such as the Devonian limestone quarries that extend from the east side of the Quantocks via the Brendon Hills to Exford. The old pits in the Budleigh Salterton Pebble Beds from Langford Budville to Williton are sanctuaries for wildlife and compensate for the effects of the more intensive forms of landuse even if they may not contain exotic and rare species. One such old pit lies to the west of Ash Priors (ST 136295); details are to be found in the Ash Priors chapter below.

Wildlife conservation

Figure 9.1 is taken from the *Taunton Deane Biodiversity Action Plan* (May and Butcher, 1997) published by TDBC. It combines measures of species diversity and habitat extent to indicate prime biodiversity areas with the best potential for conservation. The scores are a measure of the richness of each 2km x 2km grid square (tetrad); an average tetrad would score 200.

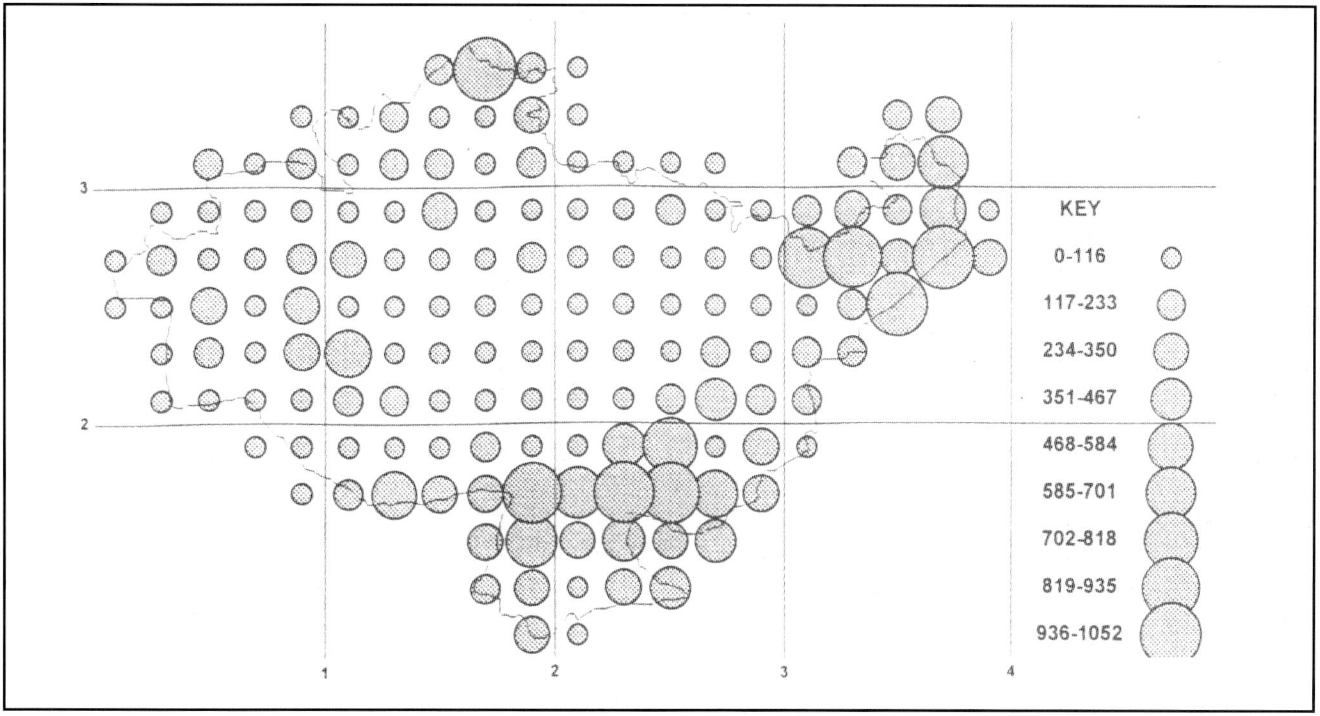

FIG 9.1 Biodiversity scores in Taunton Deane. (May and Butcher, 1997).

It is interesting to compare Figure 9.1 with the Physical Landscape types in Figure A1 (Appendix A). It is to be expected that the various combinations of slope, aspect, altitude, soil, drainage and rock will result in variations in landuse and therefore present-day biodiversity. There follows a brief summary of the more important areas:

(a) Blackdowns

Springline mire plant communities and species-rich wet alder woodland. Some heathland remains as at Sampford Common south-west of Wellington. Extensive tree cover. Unimproved grasslands. A large number of SSSIs and wildlife reserves.

(b) Flood Plains

Wet grassland and grazing marshes. Extensive freshwater rhynes and ditch systems. Important feeding grounds for wild fowl. Upper reaches of streams have a variety of channel forms and habitats. A number of SSSIs.

(c) Blue Lias Escarpment and Dip Slope

Extensive woods. Species-rich calcareous grassland. Several wildlife reserves including the worked out area of old quarries at Thurlbear.

(c) Morte Slates

High Hills (Quantocks) Heathland especially on outcrops of sandstone. e.g. Cothelstone Hill. Variety of woodlands.

A detailed account of nature conservation and resources in the Taunton Deane District is available in their Nature Conservation Strategy (TDBC, 1997).

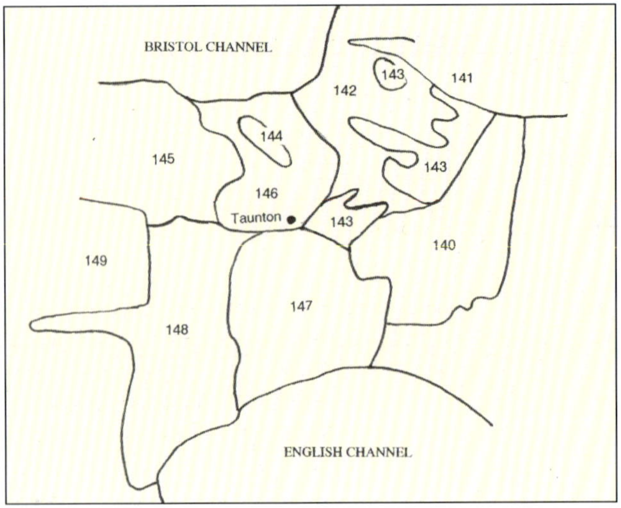

(based on map in 'The character of England: landscape, wildlife and natural features' issued by the Countryside Commission and English Nature, n.d.).

FIG 9.2 Natural Areas in and around Taunton Deane

140 Wessex Vales 143 Mendip Hills 142 Somerset Levels
143 Mid Somerset Hills 144 Quantocks 145 Exmoor
146 Vale of Quantock and Quantock Fringes 147
Blackdowns 148 Devon Redlands 149 The Culm

The Natural Areas concept

The Natural Areas approach is an initiative of English Nature which is the government agency given the task of overseeing and promoting nature conservation. To help achieve this task they have crystallised the landscape into a number of areas based upon the physical landscape, wildlife and landuse. Each area has its own particular set of characteristics which reflect local distinctiveness. Natural Areas provide a framework and setting for a more integrated approach to wildlife conservation.

The concept of Natural Areas is used very effectively in *Birdwatching in Taunton Deane* by John Clare (Clare, 1998). This is a delightful and readable guide which associates the various bird communities with Taunton Deane's varied landscapes.

Profiles of Natural Areas are being published which are designed to describe and evaluate the wildlife and geological features, and identify the most meaningful areas of actions that need to be taken. Important habitats, species and physical features within the Natural Areas are identified and described, and objectives set for their conservation.

Figure 9.2 shows the Natural Areas around the Taunton area. They help the general reader form a mental image of the landscape. They are on a smaller scale than the units listed in Appendix A (The Physical Landscape). Both offer generalisations and summaries of the features. The influence of the rocks and soils shows through very strongly. Geographers may care to note that the Natural Area concept marks a return to the kind of descriptive regional geography taught in schools during the first half of this century.

Selected Regionally Important Geological Sites (RIGS)

Broomfield Quarrylands ST 2210 3237 Morte Slates Ch. 16

Castle Neroche ST 2418 Escarpment and landslides Ch 28

Clatworthy Reservoir and Nature Trail ST 0438 3150 Monolith and Morte Slates Ch 15

Cushuish Lane ST 1975 3031 to 1952 3089 Otter Sandstone, Morte Slates and tectonic features. Ch 19

Hestercombe Intrusion ST 2428 2928 Intrusion of diorite Ch 20

Hestercombe Overflow car park ST 2406 2920 Cooled margin of diorite plus Morte Slates Ch 20

Hoccombe Stream ST 1131 2980 Stream channels and flood plain Ch 14

Langley Hollow ST 0800 2890 to 0805 2930 Wiveliscombe Sandstone Ch15

Morden House Hollow ST 3250 2601 to 3249 2623 North Curry Sandstone Ch 22

North Newton Hollow ST 294 309 Otter Sandstone (calcretes) Ch 32

Northway Quarry ST 1363 2950 Budleigh Salterton Pebble Beds Ch 13

Norton Fitzwarren Church ST 1972 2598 North Curry Sandstone Ch 23

Nynehead Hollow ST 1410 2290 Otter Sandstone Ch 24

Otterhead Pit ST 224140 Upper Greensand and Head Ch 25

Pepperhill Quarry ST 1898 3722 Devonian limestone and overturned syncline Ch 27

Staple Fitzpaine ST 2645 1845 Group of sarsens Ch 28

Thurloxton Hollow ST 2753 3040 to 2753 3021 Terminal curvature in Morte Slates Ch 32

Waterrow Viaduct Quarry ST 0550 2458 Pilton Shales Ch 29

Chapter 10
Exploring the Taunton Area

Introduction

The adjacent sketch is taken from the *Geology of England and Wales* by the late-19th century geologist Henry B. Woodward. It neatly sums up the spirit of this geological guide to Taunton Deane. The geologist has an air of anticipation. He is looking at the landscape ahead of him rather than burying his head in a book! He has his sights on what looks like a rocky outcrop. There will be a notebook, hammer and some bags for specimens in his rucksack. He may well have looked in at the church to examine the building stones.

FIG 10.1

Twenty contrasting areas have been selected where a day or half-day may be usefully spent exploring the Taunton area. These are shown in Figure 10.2. The accounts provide loosely woven descriptions for the visitor to use as desired. Two exceptions are the self-guided trails: one in central Taunton and the other in the southern Quantocks. The details for each venue are selective and should not be looked upon as definitive descriptions and explanations.

The OS 1:50,000, or better still, the 1:25,000 map series are essential for making the best use of the network of footpaths and lanes. A hand lens will reveal some of the finer details in the rocks. The Wellington and Taunton geological maps are good investments. Needless to say, this is excellent walking country.

Without doubt, building stones are the most accessible material for studying rocks, apart that is, from the coastline. Hence most chapters mention the stones used in the fabric of the local church. There is open access at least to the outsides and they contain much of artistic and historical interest and are often well- researched.

Taunton Deane Borough Council (TDBC) have produced some excellent leaflets which are listed in Appendix F and available from Deane House and Tourist Information offices: *Taunton Deane Church Trail, Bench Ends and Pulpits, Towers and Hunky Punks and The West Deane Way* are very useful guides. The *West Deane Way* is a circular walk which touches on a number of places mentioned in the book (details can be found in the Appendix F).

The centre of Taunton provides an exceptionally rich display of building stones and is highly recommended: the experience will enable you to recognise Blue Lias and Devonian sandstone and compare Bath Stone with Ham Hill Stone and many more.

We start with a splendid word picture of a late-18th century traveller from the days long-before the advent of the audio cassette. When did you last meet lime carts or see a string of oxen at work in the fields?

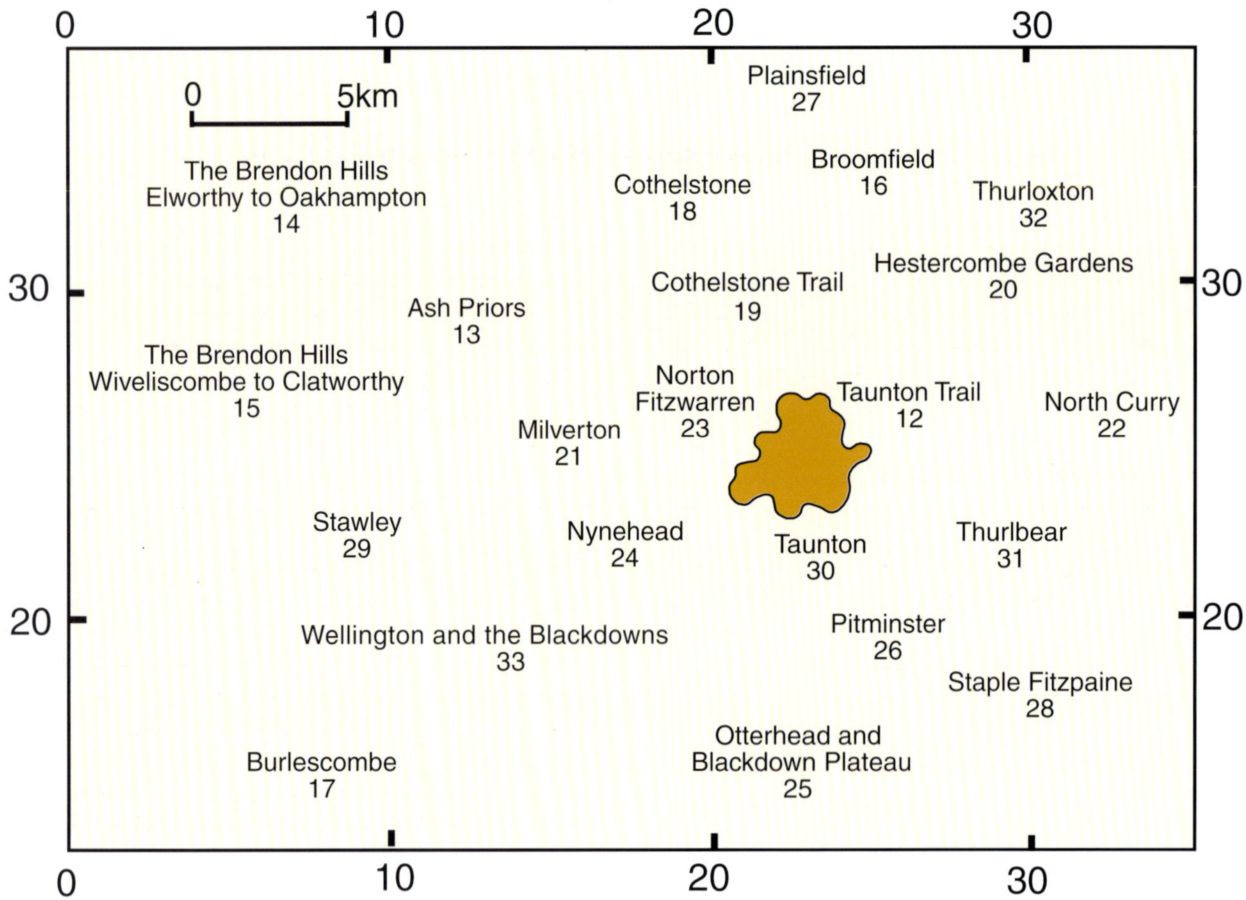

FIG 10.2 Chapter numbers of the regional studies.

The great vale of Taunton Deane, seen distantly from Wills Neck or the lower Quantock slopes, is not easy to forget. A landscape both spectacular and serene reaches south to the long line of the Blackdown Hills, west to the Brendon foothills, and east, beyond the towers and spires of Taunton itself, to the levels of central Somerset. This is the 'paradise of England' described by John Norden in 1609, the land of meadows, orchards and 'rich redd earth' which Thomas Gerard discovered a generation later, the 'golden vale' so often praised by sentimental Victorians.

The Vale of Taunton Past by Tom Mayberry.

Chapter 11
A View of the Countryside in 1794

A journey from Tiverton to Somerton and beyond

William Marshall travelled extensively at the end of the C18 in order to report back to the Board of Agriculture on the state of agriculture and the countryside (Marshall, W. 1796). The following extracts are those which have a geological connotation; they provide a vivid word picture of the landscape at the time.

Tiverton to Taunton ***Friday 19th September 1794***

The Blackdown hills, with mountain features, appear in front, and at hand.
Meet more lime carts, and some waggons.....
Pits of red gravel, by the side of a good road. (=Budleigh Salterton Pebble Beds)
The subsoil-a seam of waterworn gravel, and rough pebbles.
A deep white sandy substratum, and sandy roads.
Sandy road, and holloway: the substratum red sandy rock. (=Otter Sandstone.)
Six oxen stirring a fallow of strong red land.
Meet a string of culm carts; on their way, from the Taunton Navigation, to the Limeworks.
Lime compost, on headlands, as in Devonshire.
Subsoil variegated: streaks of red and white.
Leave the red land: the soil and subsoil, now, of a light brown color.

Taunton to Somerton *Saturday 20th September, 1794.*

Much arable land: soil mostly a strong red loam.
The under stratum appears in seams of red earth, and a sort of white stoney substance.
Cross a dip of cold weak land (5 miles).
quarry of blue building stone (Blue Lias).
The soil and subsoil still red.
Good limestone road.
Ascend the limestone heights (Blue Lias escarpment?).
Carts and waggons, at the lime kilns: no pack horses.
A broad view of South Sedgemore.....
Thin limestone land; and more lime kilns.
Continue upon cold limestone heights.
Pass Burton Pynsent.
Leave the limestone heights, and descend towards Langport.

Marshall's journey continued beyond Langport to Somerton:

The tops of the swells are dry-stone to the surface.....the country now more open....Large limestone flags-or coarse marble slabs-raised near the road.....another mean market town (Somerton): the suburbs in ruins. The building materials limestone and thatch. The stones neatly formed, as in the Vale of Pickering.

Many men at work; and teams waiting. Mostly raised in large slabs, six or eight inches thick, and several feet in dimensions. Lie horizontally, and near the surface of level ground. Men employed in polishing them. The color a blue grey. Village buildings of stone and pantile.

The soil a cold crumbling clay; like that over the claystone of the Vale of Glocester. Elm trees and pollards, scattered over the grass inclosures. Still a cold flat Vale District.The fields blue with Devilsbit (Scabiosa succisa). The grass inclosures intersected with surface drains. A very cold plot of country: weak and languid, even at this season of the year. Adapted to the cheese dairy, and rearing of cattle. A plot of woodland, well-timbered: much of the land of this Vale is well-adapted to oak timber. The whole in a state of grass: no arable land seen from the road.

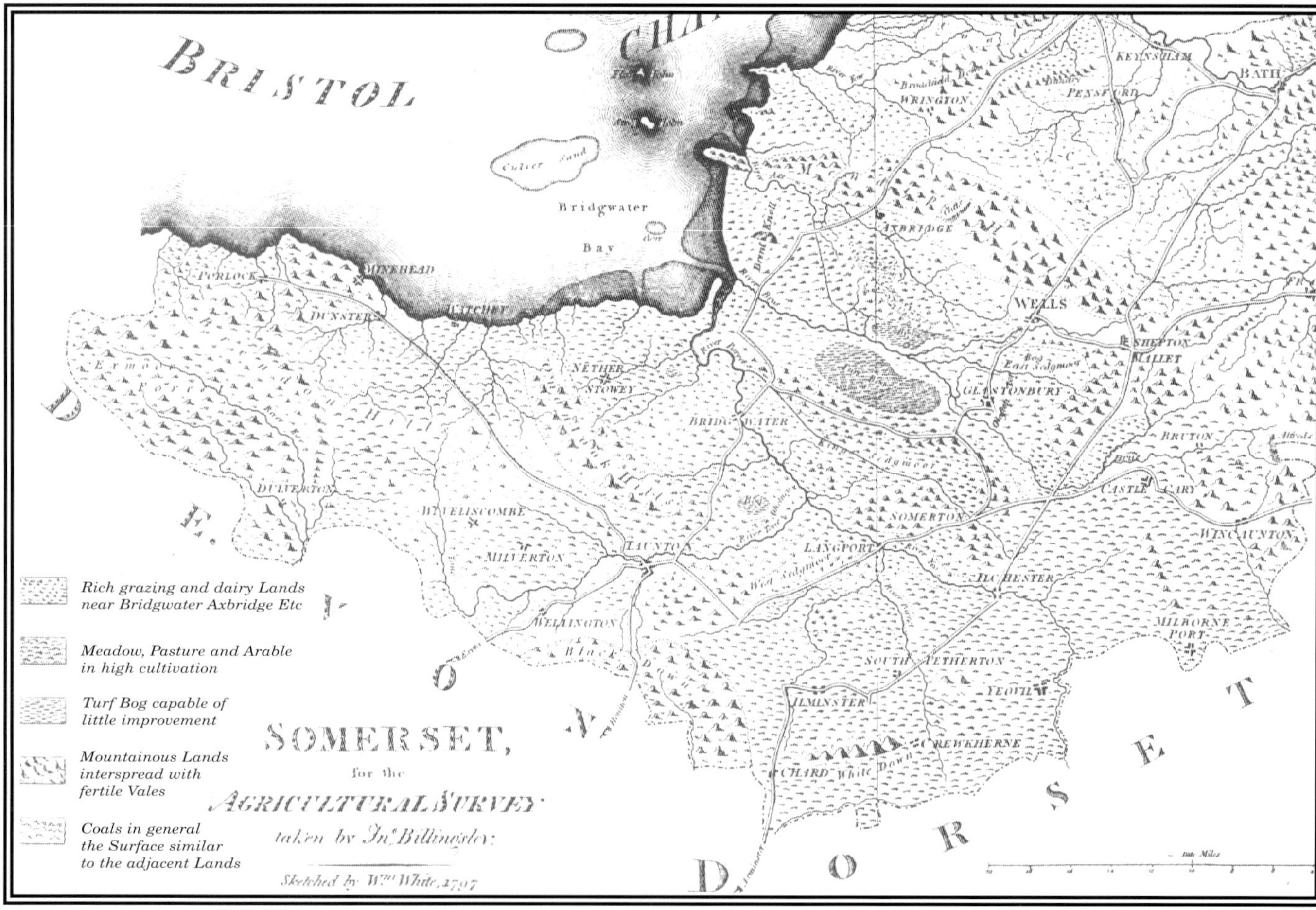

FIG 11.1 This very early example of a land use map was prepared for Billingsley's *General View of the Agriculture of Somerset* published in 1797. One can pick out the route taken by Marshall reported a year earlier.

Today's traveller cannot fail to notice the contrast between the aforementioned limestone-rich Blue Lias hills around Somerton and Keinton Mandeville, and the low-lying clay vale especially when travelling along the A37 from Ilchester to Shepton Mallet near Hornblotton.

The kind of features that Marshall mentions form part of the mental map of every motorist: the straight, level stretch of road from Taunton to Burrowbridge across the moors; the climb and sharp bends as one heads westward away from the red soils around Wiveliscombe toward the slate country of the Brendon Hills; the switchback across the vale and scarp country on the road from Taunton to Ilminster; the steep winding roads that climb the Greensand escarpment from Taunton and which lead to the remarkably level roads that cross the plateau ridgetops.

The chapters that follow explore this rich variety.

Chapter 12
Taunton Rock Trail

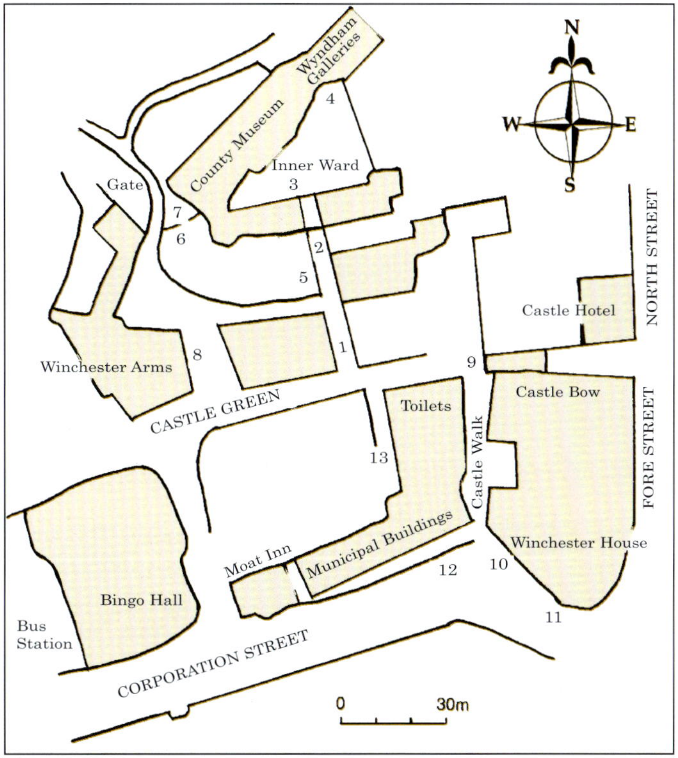

FIG. 12.1 Trail plan showing the location of main stopping places

The science of geology has been built upon the study of rocks. Hence, we recommend as a first step, a short tour of the building stones that can be seen close to the County Museum. Here we concentrate mainly on what the stones look like as this is the basis for understanding them. More details of the stones are provided in Appendices B and D and the index. An * indicates a reference in the glossary. A x10 hand lens will reveal finer details of the rocks..

The trail starts at the entrance to the County Museum. The locations are numbered and shown on the street plan Figure 12.1 . Please check the opening hours of the Museum and its courtyard. The Museum has a bookshop and various displays with a geological connotation. The booklet about Taunton Castle by Bush (1988) is recommended. The Trail can be undertaken in less than two hours.

ACCESS FOR THE DISABLED The trail crosses no roads and uses paths. Pass through Castle Bow into Fore Street in order to avoid steps by Winchester House.

1. Driveway

Study the stones in the walls driveway.

(Barrett, 1894).

FIG 12.2 Localities 1 & 2
Gateway to County Museum

The wall on the left is composed of a hard, siliceous, massive, crystalline rock varying from grey to brown in colour. Contrast the smooth broken surfaces with the rougher, weathered outer surfaces.
UPPER GREENSAND CHERT

2. Gateway

Locate the stones on the left-hand wall in front of the gate with the help of Figure 12.3. Use a hand lens, if available

HHS Yellowish-brown mass of broken shell debris cemented with calcium carbonate and limonite (hydrous oxide of iron); the latter gives the stone its golden colour The short, sloping beds of irregular thickness are examples of cross-bedding* where weathering has picked out the weaker beds.

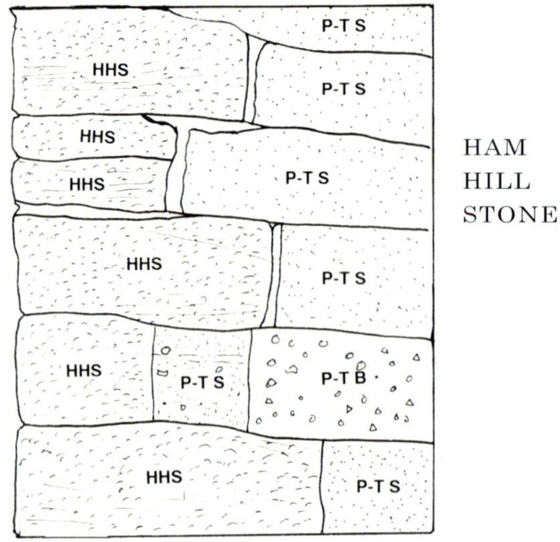

FIG 12.3 Locality 2 Wall on left of Gateway.

P-T S Red sandstone with a variety of rounded and angular quartz sand grains. Iron oxide (haematite) gives the red colour. Some blocks have a few small pebbles.
PERMO-TRIASSIC SANDSTONE

P-T B Red sandstone with angular rocks/ fragments
PERMO-TRIASSIC BRECCIA

Step back and note the use of the various stones higher up in the front of the Gateway including the Ham Hill Stone shield (c1495). Proceed through to the Museum courtyard if open.

3. Inner ward

The wall immediately on the left consists of grey, calcareous* mudstones, with traces of horizontal and wavy, laminations. Some weathered surfaces tend to be yellow as a result of the oxidation of iron compounds. The grey colours indicate iron in its reduced state. The stones are flaking badly. The many parallel vertical cracks indicate that the rock has been stressed at some time in the geological past. Some blocks contain the small fossil brachiopod* *Calcirhynchia calcaria*. Please resist the temptation to remove these fossils.
BLUE LIAS

The yellow stones in the parking area are mainly water worn, or frost-chipped, flints.
VALLEY GRAVEL

Lord Harding is mounted on a plinth of a stone composed of ooliths* and shell fragments set in a calcareous matrix*.
PORTLAND STONE

4. Wyndam Galleries

(Newer building to the right)

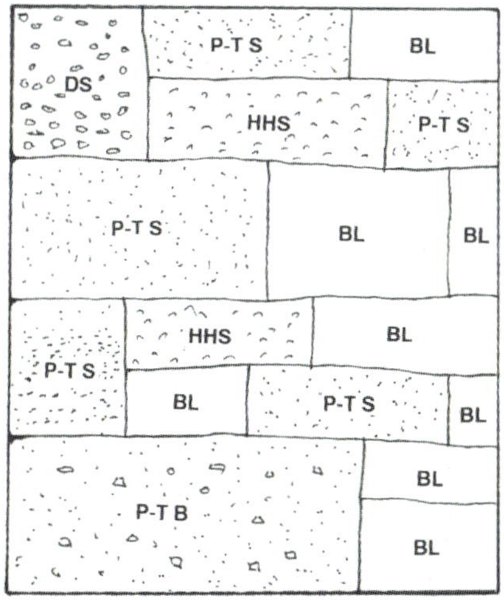

FIG 12.4 Locality 4 Corner of the Wyndham Galleries in the Courtyard built in 1932.

The mix of colourful dressed* stones was surely designed for their decorative appeal and as a geological display. Use Figure 12.4 in order to identify the stones. The back of the Wyndham Galleries can be examined at the rear of the Museum (location 7) if the courtyard is shut.

HHS Golden-coloured stone composed of broken seashells.
HAM HILL STONE

DS Greyish stone composed of crinoid* debris and shell fragments.
DOULTING STONE

P-T S Vivid red, thinly laminated sandstones, plus fine-grained, pale cream sandstones. Some pebble inclusions.
PERMO-TRIASSIC SANDSTONE

P-T B Coarse sandstone with a variety of rock fragments including black chert and red sandstone.
PERMO-TRIASSIC BRECCIA

BL Pale grey, muddy limestone with bivalve shells and crinoidal* debris. (Use hand lens.)
BLUE LIAS

The green rock is COCKERCOMBE TUFF from the Quantocks: volcanic ash containing the green mineral chlorite*. Note the sandstone paving slab with asymmetrical ripples.

Note the variety of rocks seen in the courtyard walls before returning through the Gateway to the large stone and sword at the entrance to the driveway.

5. Excalibur Stone

(Courtesy TDBC).

FIG 12.5 Locality 5
The Excalibur Stone

A very hard, massive, grey limestone of Carboniferous age. It is difficult to make out the composition of the rock, even with a hand lens as there has been partial recrystallisation but it may contain ooliths* and crinoidal debris. Crystalline pinkish-white calcite (calcium carbonate) fills gaps where the rock has fractured; note the cross-cutting veins implying several occasions of splitting and vein formation.

Follow the path around to the right and view the large rock in the Castle gardens.

6. Sarsen

This massive block of quartz grains and small pebbles in a siliceous cement was brought from Staple Fitzpaine and set upright in the Castle grounds (Cameron, 1909). It is similar to the sarsens at Avebury and Stonehenge. The gate to the garden is normally locked.

Continue to the right up to the Castle walls

7. Castle Walls

This really is a random rubble wall but it is said to be 12th century (Bush, 1988). Pick out, from Figure 12.6, three types of rock seen previously. (Blue Lias **BL**, Chert **Ch**, Permo-Triassic sandstone **P-T S**). In addition, there is a reddish-brown, Devonian quartz-rich sandstone cobble (?Pickwell Down Sandstone **PDS**). The sand grains are welded together and are not as easily distinguished as in the red sandstones seen previously. This is a sandstone that has experienced the high pressures and temperatures found deep below the earth's surface. Similar rocks are found in north Exmoor and the Quantocks. It is worth comparing the degree of weathering of the various stones.

Proceed around the corner to the right.

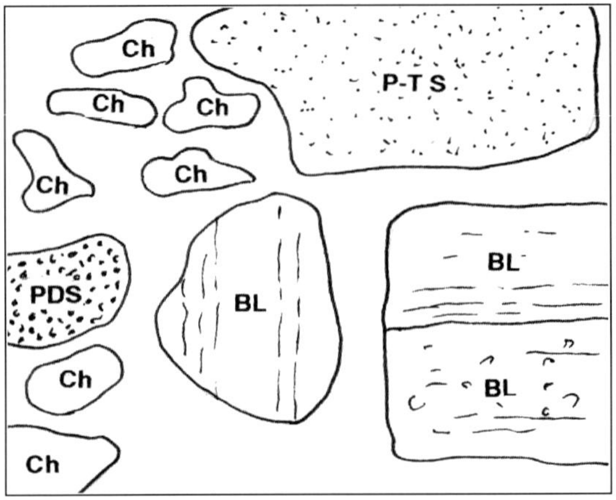

FIG 12.6 Locality 7 Wall on southwest side of Museum.

Red Permo-Triassic sandstones contain pebbles which are similar to the Devonian cobble. The scatter of reddened, burnt blocks of Ham Hill Stone suggests that many of the stones have been recycled. The pale cream pillars either side of the path are oolitic* Bath Stone.

Return along the path to Castle Green and examine the walls of the Winchester Arms.

8. Winchester Arms

Most of the front and side walls are built of pale brownish-grey, sands with grey, fine-grained rock fragments. The finer-grained sediments show ripple-lamination* whilst the coarser-grained material has similar, but larger-scale cross-bedding*.
NORTH CURRY SANDSTONE

Walk past the front of the Museum to the stone archway ahead of you. Note the hard-wearing squared sandstone paving blocks, imported second-hand from Yorkshire.

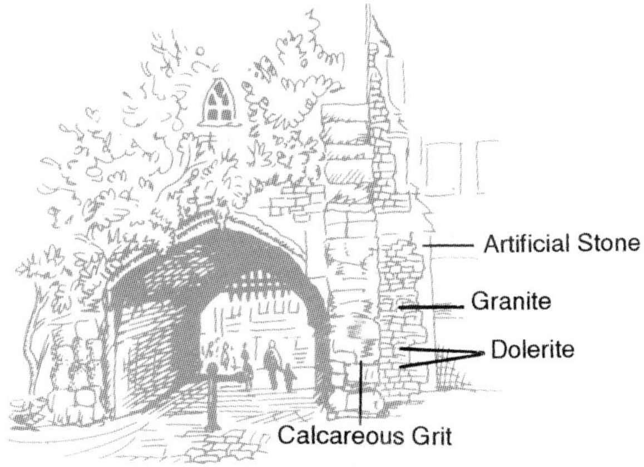

FIG12.7 Locality 9 Castle Bow

9. Castle Bow (Eastgate)

CALCAREOUS GRIT

The front buttress shows cream fine-grained, calcareous sandstone; the black specks are glauconite*. Used for quoins and buttresses in many churches in the Blackdowns.

GRANITE

A whitish, speckled rock with three types of interlocking crystals: off-white=feldspar, grey=quartz and dark grey=mica.

DOLERITE

A darker rock composed of minerals with less silica (49%) but more iron and magnesium than the granite.

The last two rock types have formed as result of melted rock (magma) cooling with the consequent growth of interlocking crystals.

ARTIFICIAL STONE

This would not conform to modern ideas of conservation in historic settings yet how many people notice it?

The right-hand side of the buttress has several blue-grey blocks of Blue Lias; scattered shell debris can be seen with a hand lens.

Turn right along Castle Walk to Corporation Street noting the Blue Lias at the front of the ladies' toilets.

10. Winchester House

An orange-brown limestone from the Cotswolds. Best seen with the hand lens; note the shelly, crinoidal debris with ooliths in a calcareous, ferruginous matrix. Acid rain appears to have bleached the upper projecting surfaces. GUITING STONE

11. TSB Bank

A pale cream, smooth-faced limestone with ooliths supported in a lime-mud matrix.

BATH STONE

FIG 12.8 Locality 12 Municipal Hall.

12. Municipal Hall

DEVONIAN SANDSTONE (MORTE SLATES)

Old Grammar School c1520
The front and side walls show rough-faced, sharp-edged, grey siltstones and sandstones from the Quantocks. Some blocks have diagonal irregular slaty cleavage.*

HAM HILL STONE
The golden stone is the only one of the three stones that can be readily dressed for windows and doorways.

UPPER WESTLEIGH LIMESTONE
Walls next to the pavement show a banded, well-bedded rock with (a) pale and dark brown, calcareous sandstones, and (b) black, smooth, very hard chert quarried to the west of Wellington. The beds are best seen in the end walls of the Moat Inn. Also look for thin laminated beds and pebbly inclusions.

Across the road is the old library in red Permo-Triassic Otter Sandstone. It is interesting to compare the aesthetic appeal of the various types of stone.

Follow around to the right into the car park and make for the wall on the left of the public toilets.

13. Car Park Wall

The wall provides a test piece of the rock types already seen on the Trail. How many different rocks are represented in this wall?

Retrospect

The variety of rocks on the Trail reflects the diversity of rocks to be found within a few miles of Taunton. Secondly, the properties of the various rocks has affected how and where they have been used. Thirdly, improvements in transport have improved the availability of building stones and widened the choice. Pre-railway era buildings often feature recycled stone as is shown by the odd blocks of Ham Hill Stone reddened by fire. Later buildings and walls tend to use one, or at most, two types of stone. Examples which illustrate these points can be readily observed.

Please refer to Chapter 30 entitled 'Taunton' for additional buildings of interest in Taunton which are not included in the Trail.

Chapter 13
Ash Priors

(ST 1529) Church-Budleigh Salterton Pebble Beds-TDBC Walk Geological structure between the Brendon Hills and the Quantocks-Ash Priors Fault

From Ussher, 1908

FIG 13.1 Old quarry in Budleigh Salterton Pebble Beds near Ash Priors

Church

The church of Holy Trinity is mainly a 19th century rebuild using red sandstones, some of which show inclusions of pebbles of rock clearly derived from the Quantocks or the Brendon Hills. The massive blocks on the corners contrast with the rubble walling which uses stone of lesser quality. Baynham (1908) quotes a Mr Spencer regarding the reredos:

> The reredos, formed of fine Corsham Stone, Ham Hill Stone, White Lias and marble, consists of three canopied compartments with stone diaper on each side and below. In the central compartment there is a black marble cross. The pulpit is octagonal, formed of similar stone and marbles supported by a clustered column of Devonshire marble.

These features clearly reflect Victorian architectural tastes and the wider availability of decorative stones.

Budleigh Salterton Pebble Beds (BSPB)

These beds are up to 30-35 m thick. They include cobbles 50 cm across. The cobbles are rounded to sub-angular in shape which suggests wear from traction in braided river channels. Confirmation comes when the bedding structures are examined as, for example, those in Figure 13.1; the beds thicken and thin with upper beds cutting across and down into lower beds. Cross-bedding can be seen to the left of the lady.

This type of accumulation is to be seen in Alpine and semi-desert river beds where a lot of rock waste moves down the steep hillsides. River systems become choked with rock waste and are unable to transport all of the load. The result is the kind of gravel accumulation seen in the local BSPB quarries. It is possible that the BSPB accumulated at a time of earth movements accompanied by earthquakes causing rockfalls and landslides. An increase in rainfall intensity would have increased both mass wastage of hillsides, debris flows and peak discharges.

Baker, in 1851, wrote of these pebbles, in the first volume of the Somerset Proceedings, as follows:

> In the western district, many of these rocks contain pebbles of limestone in great abundance, and are called popple rocks; they are extensively worked for lime in many places. In the neighbourhood of Milverton and Wiveliscombe, the limestone in the conglomerate beds is much worn by abrasion, and they contain such fossils, and have such other characters, as may lead geologists to look to the spaces between the Mendip Hills and the Holmes, as the localities from which these water-worn pieces of Carboniferous Limestone rock were derived. (Baker, 1851.)

Martin re-examined the conglomerates and produced the map in Figure 13.2 which suggests that present-day outcrops of Carboniferous Limestone may have been possible source areas for some of the limestone cobbles. A recent reinterpretation of geophysical observations in the Bristol Channel has suggested that Carboniferous Limestone may underlie parts of the Bristol Channel. It is possible that some of this may have contributed to the limestone content found in the BSPB (Smith et al., 1999). It should be understood that this was long before the existence of the coastline and hills as we know them today.

(From Martin, 1909)

FIG 13.2 The probable directions of the currents which transported the pebbles in the BSBP

The lithology of the cobbles changes to the south of Langford and a comparison of the lithology and fossil content of the cobbles with the nearby rock outcrops suggests that rivers were carrying rock waste from the west as well as from the south in this area (Martin, 1909).

The character and distribution of various rock types help geologists to reconstruct past landscapes and geographies. The search for the reasons underlying changes in rock type is fundamental to our understanding of earth history.

(Courtesy of TDBC.)

Walk 3 Ash Priors Common - 5 Miles

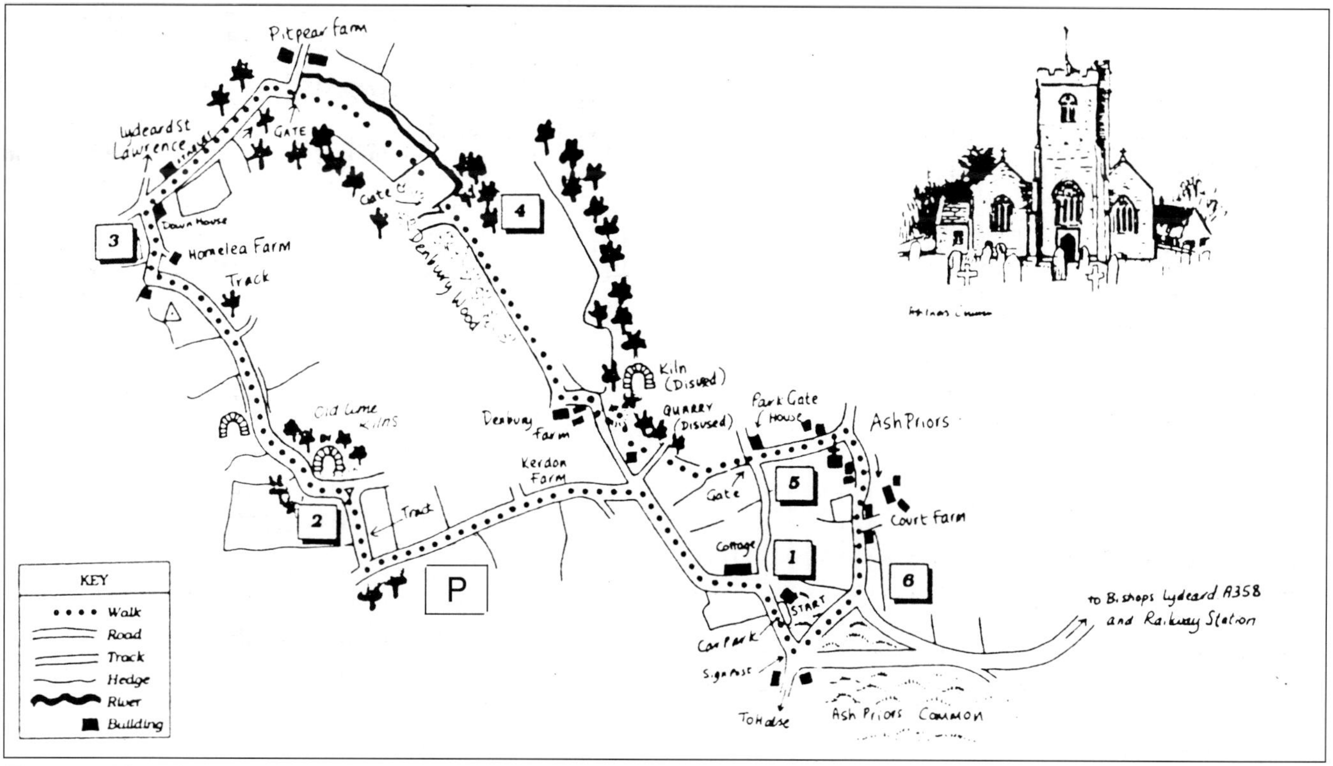

FIG 13.3 Map showing route of Taunton Deane Borough Council's *Country Walks Around Taunton Set 1* (No.3 Ash Priors Common.)

TDBC Walk

This walk passes a group of worked-out quarries owned by Somerset County Council, some 4 km west of Ash Priors (Regionally Important Geological Site). Use the map in Figure 13.3 for the route. For those in a hurry the best place to park (P on map at ST 1400 2921) is on the grass verge some 200 m along the lane toward Kerdon Farm; on no account should cars be parked where they might obstruct wide agricultural machines, milk lorries, or in passing places. A rough track leads north from the lane to Location 2 .

Note the exposure of red silty Mercia Mudstone at Location 2 where the track divides; its significance is given below.

The two limekilns should be approached with care. The OS map for 1904 shows the area was wooded at that time and the quarries and limekilns abandoned (Figure 13.4).

Peter Daniel, a member of the Somerset Industrial Archaeological Society has commented as follows (pers. comm.):

> My view is that local burning of lime for agricultural use in western Somerset gradually ceased over the period 1870-1900 as artificial fertiliser became available, crushed limestone also became available as a source of lime and farming entered a depression. There are no limeburners listed in trade directories for Ash Priors or Halse and almost certainly these kilns were operated as farm or estate kilns.

The diagram in Figure 8.2 is based on the typical west Somerset style of kiln with 2 or 3 arches and a lean-to front.

A signposted path leads into the old quarry workings a few metres before the end of the woods on the north side of the track. You are requested to keep to the path to the quarry and not to wander off into the woodland; the area is very overgrown and uneven.

Health and Safety considerations and geological conservation require that there is no interference with the rock face. Pebbles can be examined in the trackway. Compare your observations of the rock face with Figure 13.1 and the description of the beds given above. In addition, there are north-south lines of joints* where the rock is weakened and calcium carbonate has been both dissolved and precipitated. Many quarries in west Somerset show NNW-SSE and N-S joint faces. These result from stresses caused by compressive earth movements. It is also possible that there has been foundering of the strata as a result of superficial movements which have opened-out the beds (gulling*)

The whole area has been recolonised since the end of quarrying and is now a County Wildlife Site. It is also a reminder of what our countryside would look like if left to itself. It is reminiscent of the present state of the landslip areas between Lyme Regis and Seaton.

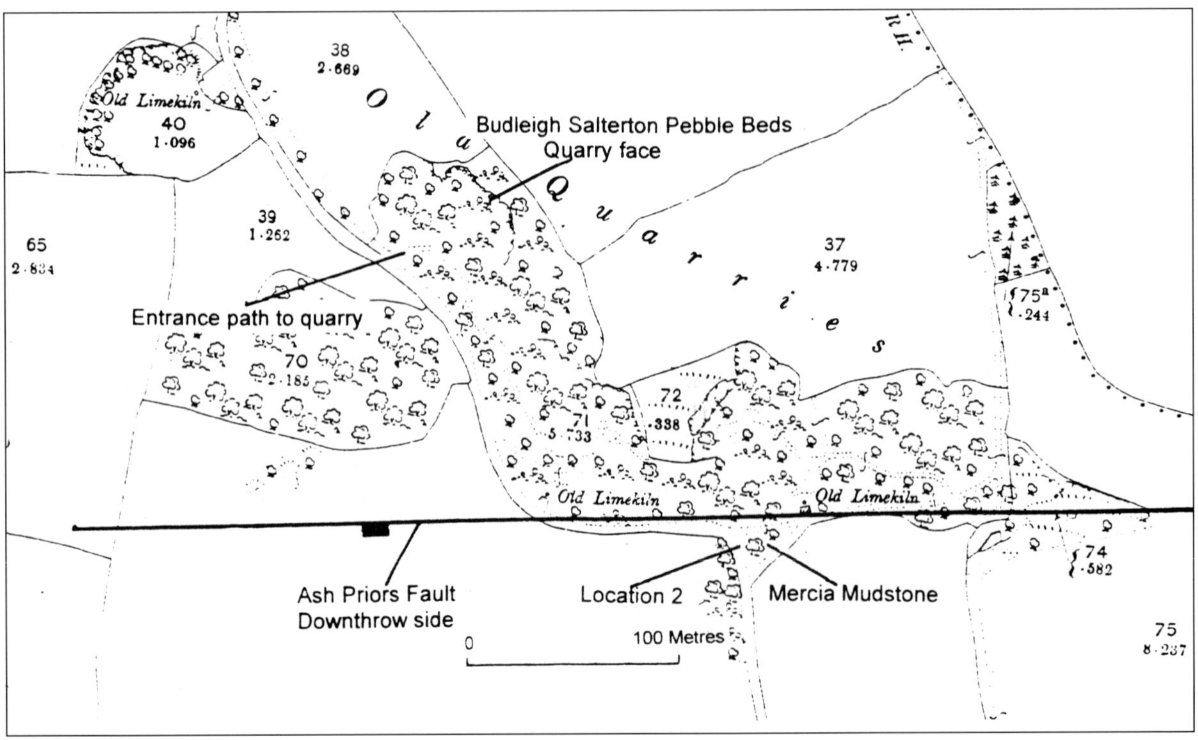

FIG 13.4 Old quarries and limekilns west of Ash Priors recorded on the OS map of 1904.

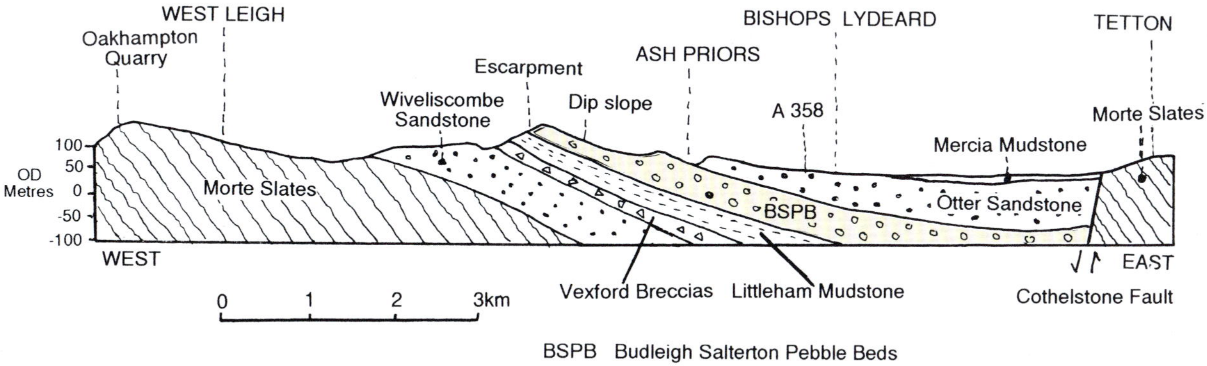

Fig 13.5 Geological section from Oakhampton to Tetton (Based upon Sheet 295 by permission of the British Geological Survey 'IPR/2-108 British Geological Survey " NERC. All rights reserved'.)

The BSPB is a relatively resistant formation and the visitor on the TDBC Walk will note how it is associated with narrow valleys and steep hillsides. Additional quarries in the same formation can be seen from the footpath on the TDBC Walk near Denbury Farm at ST 1464 2941; they are on the left after leaving the road and passing through a small gate. Please remember that they are on private land.

The geological structure between the Brendon Hills and the Quantocks

The section in Figure 13.5 below shows that the Permo-Triassic strata rest on the older Devonian Morte Slates to the west near Wiveliscombe and are faulted against the same rocks in the southern Quantocks near Tetton. The Permo-Triassic strata dip to the east between the Brendon Hills and the Quantocks which accounts for the north-south alignment of the outcrops.

The Permo-Triassic formations shown in the section are known collectively as the New Red Sandstone Supergroup (see Appendix C) although they are not all sandstones by any means; it is simply a historical term which has been retained. These beds were deposited at a time when the earth's crust in this area was being stretched and large fault-bounded blocks were subsiding. The climate appears to have been semi-arid but these sedimentary pebble beds and sandstones clearly indicate the presence of alluvial fans and ephemeral floods reworking braided stream channels. The sediments are rather unusual in that they were deposited on land as opposed to the many formations found in Somerset which are of marine origin. Recent research in the Crediton Trough has revealed much about events at this time (Edwards et al., 1997).

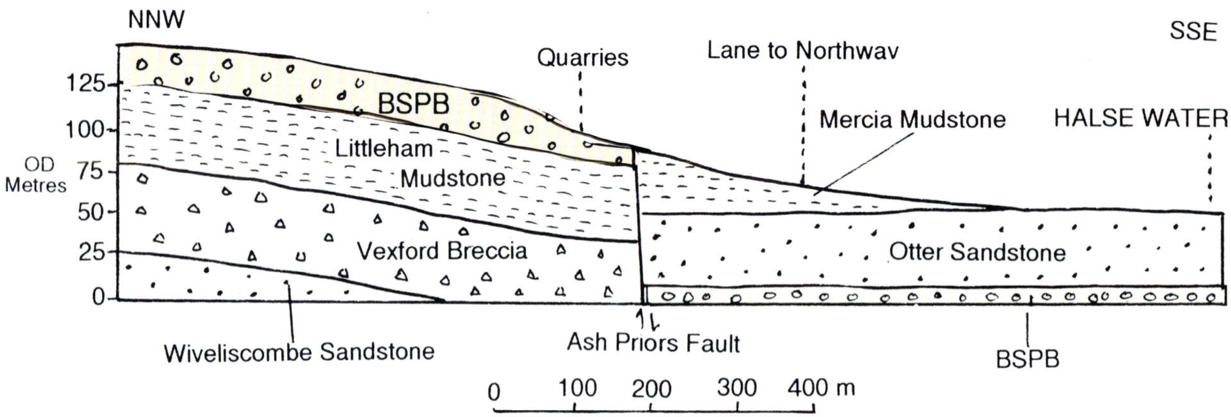

FIG 13.6 Geological section from Oakhampton to Tetton

Ash Priors Fault

Figure 13.6 is a NNW-SSE section through the line of quarries. Notice how an important E-W fault-the Ash Priors Fault-passes close to the south side of the quarries shown on the map in Figure 13.4. The rocks are let down on the south side of the fault. The vertical movement on the fault has juxtaposed strong beds of BSPB seen in the quarries to the north alongside weak Mercia Mudstone to the south The BSPB are less easily eroded than the Mercia Mudstone, hence there is higher ground to the north and lower ground to the south. The change in height is the result of differential erosion and is not a direct result of movement along the fault which happened a long time ago. The presence of red silty Mercia Mudstone (previously noted above) in the bank at the edge of the track at Locality 2 means that the fault must lie between this point and the quarry faces on the north side of the track.

East-west faults are an important element in the geological history of Somerset; differences in the thickness of sediments on either side of some of these E-W faults show that there was vertical movement on them when sediment was being deposited.

Chapter 14
The Brendon Hills
Elworthy to Oakhampton

Hill country - Hoccombe stream channels - Oakhampton slate quarries - Tolland and Elworthy Churches

Hill country

The country described in this section is served by the B3188 from Wiveliscombe to Monksilver and beyond. The high, rounded hills have slopes as steep as those in the Quantocks. The narrow combes have shallow, fast-flowing streams. There is a diversity of land use: woodland and pasture on the steeper slopes and arable on the gentler slopes. Choose a sunny day in spring for a visit so as to enjoy the primroses, daffodils and lambs.

The geological map (Sheet 295 Taunton) shows that the area is underlain by the Devonian Morte Slates which also underlie the southern end of the Quantocks. The black symbols with a triangle and number indicate the direction and steepness of the cleavage* which is mainly to the south-southeast at anything from 15° to 90°. A fault is suspected to run from the edge of the map, via Elworthy to Tolland and beyond. Note the curious outlier of Wiveliscombe Sandstone at ST 085 347 which may owe its preservation to having been let down by faulting and thus escaped being eroded.

Hoccombe stream channels

The 'bird' symbol on a yellow background shown on geological maps denotes silty alluvium deposited on river floodplains as, for example, at Halse Water Bridge (ST 144 283). It is worth following the valley up to Hoccombe (ST 1135 2986); one can park on the verge just before the footpath from Burrow Hill Farm meets the lane at a wide gate on the east side of the stream. Gain access to the stream via the public footpath.

Alluvium can be seen where the banks are being eroded. The stream channel has irregular meanders with alternating shallows (riffles) and deeps (pools) which tend to lie first on one side of the channel and then on the other. The stream will show upwellings and whirlpools at these locations when the stream is in flood at bankfull stage. At low water stage, which is the situation for most of the year, the stream neither carries fine sediment in suspension, nor drags debris along its bed. It would therefore seem that the riffles and pools are created at flood stage. On returning back along the footpath to the road, notice the abandoned curving channels in the meadow which are relicts from a time when the river stood at a higher level. There are also the remains of a mill leat.

Oakhampton Slate Quarries

Walkers may like to plan a ramble through the abandoned Oakhampton Quarries (ST 086 301) using public footpaths. There are panoramic views. It is suggested that cars are parked carefully on the grass verge alongside the B3188. Walk up the short lane and pass through Oakhampton Farm, follow the track to the left and then pass through the right-hand gate. Please close all gates.

Proceed along the path for about one kilometre (ST 089 301). Figure 14.1 shows a cross-section looking to the south. Sir H.T. De la Beche featured Castle Hill in his *Report on the geology of Cornwall, Devon and west Somerset* (1839); he describes the view and illustrates it with the section which has been redrawn so as to match the view from Oakhampton Farm. The wooded knoll to the left is Castle Hill; he refers to the rising ground on the right as Main Down although it is Maundown on the OS map.

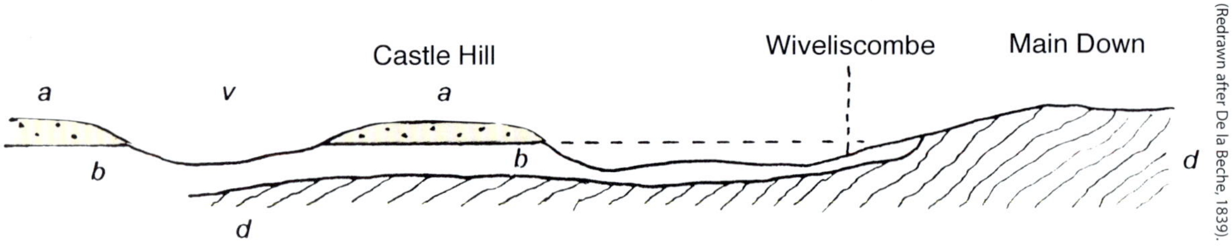

FIG 14.1 Geological section from Maundown (Main Down) to Castle Hill near Wiveliscombe

> This conglomerate (i.e. the Budleigh Salterton Pebble Beds), extensively worked for lime in the cementing manner, is well seen near Wiveliscombe occupying the higher parts of hills which are cut by valleys of denudation. The following sketch....will serve to exhibit the mode of occurrence of the various rocks, ***aa*** being the conglomerate, composed of portions of the adjoining and subjacent grauwacke* cemented by magnesio-calcareous matter; ***b b,*** red sandstone, which may be about 140 or 180 feet thick, and ***d d,*** grauwacke upon which the whole rests unconformably*. (De la Beche, 1839).

The conglomerate is now known as the Budleigh Salterton Pebble Beds (BSPB). It is a relatively strong rock and caps Castle Hill. Clearly, however, the conglomerate must have been more extensive in the past and formed a continuous bed, not only across the small 'valley of denudation' ***v,*** but probably between Castle Hill and the greywacke* of Main Down. Otherwise it is difficult to see how the pebbles derived from Main Down could have reached Castle Hill. In other words, erosion has removed the rock between the two hills to form a 'valley of denudation' to quote the phrase of De la Beche.

Oakhampton Farm is on the Morte Slates rock formation. To the east lie the red Permo-Triassic formations and, at the southern end of the Quantocks, the Devonian Morte Slates. The latter are composed of Devonian rocks similar to those that you are standing on. Figure 13.5 illustrates how the rocks are arranged. These formations constitute a tilted block (half-graben) that is let down principally by faults on the west side of the Quantocks (e.g. the Cothelstone Fault). Such tilted blocks, let down along faults, can result from crustal stretching and are an important structural feature elsewhere in Somerset e.g. at Porlock.

Figure 14.1 shows that the red Permo-Triassic sediments were deposited on the up-turned edges of the older Devonian strata referred to by De la Beche as 'greywacke' ***(dd).*** Notice the irregular surface. Clearly the Permo-Triassic beds will vary in thickness and become thinner near the edge of the basin as the basin fills. The lower Permo-Triassic sediments are coarse breccias, conglomerate and sandstones; the uppermost sediments (Mercia Mudstone Group) are silty mudstones. This can be interpreted as reflecting the destruction and burial of the mountainous terrain which followed the Variscan mountain building episode.

The view to the south, with its rolling hills, is along the outcrop of the lower Permo-Triassic formations with the Blackdown Hills escarpment (Upper Greensand), including the Wellington Monument, in the distance. To the southwest is the higher ground of North Down underlain by the more resistant Devonian slates and sandstones. The latter emerge from below the red Permo-Triassic formations as is shown in De la Beche's section (Figure 14.1). Knowledge of the geological structure helps to create a mental image and understanding of what might appear to be a chaotic landscape pattern.

The track from Oakhampton Farm passes over and down the old spoil heaps where rock samples can be sought. The larger slabs tend to be sandstones. There are glimpses of the old slate workings which now form a deep, steep-sided pit. Mark well the warning signs in red. The quarry seems to have stopped work just before the First World War (Tilley, 1992).

(Courtesy: Somerset Studies Library).

FIG 14.2 Tolland Church in 1845 by W. W. Wheatley

Jeboult (1873) had this to say about the products:

> Two colour slates are made at this quarry - blue, the most sought after; purple, considered the most durable. Slabs of large size are obtained, from which handsome mantelpieces are manufactured, which when varnished show the beautiful veins caused by the presence of oxide of iron. In addition to this, they are admirably suited for flooring, window sills, hearth-stones, water and beer cisterns, ejects, and, last but not least tombstones, since they resist the action of frost better than many of the harder stones.

Continue down the track and bear to the right; exposures of the slates can be studied where the tracks divide in the wooded area on the west side of the workings. The cleavage planes in the slates are inclined at 60°-80° in a south-easterly direction with the beds themselves inclined by similar amounts. The slates, which were once mud on the sea floor, break down into a brown stony clay loam. The soil often has a silky feel when rubbed between the fingers indicating a high silt content. Return to the B3188 directly or continue a circular walk via footpaths.

Tolland and Elworthy Churches

The church of St John the Baptist at Tolland (Figure 14.2) is built with a mixture of local red Permo-Triassic sandstones and breccias, plus Devonian siltstones and sandstones. Note the white blocks of quartz in the foundations and walls. It is a quiet and lovely setting enhanced by the presence of an area dedicated to wildlife (Living Churchyard Scheme).

An equally entrancing church is that of St Martin of Tours higher up the valley at Elworthy. The unbuttressed tower, of 13th century origin, is built of Devonian siltstones and sandstones as is much of the church. Note the slate steps. There are also blocks and dressings of local, red Permo-Triassic sandstones plus some Ham Hill Stone. The font is Watchet alabaster and provides a good opportunity to examine Somerset alabaster at close quarters. There is mediaeval and Jacobean woodwork and two charming 15th century stained glass figures of saints.

The church is in the care of the Churches Conservation Trust which looks after churches no longer in regular use for worship. Many served remote rural communities and thus often escaped restoration by the Victorians. Many are located in peaceful countryside. St Martin's is typical of many in the scheme in that it is small, intimate and full of interest. The church guide adds another dimension by recalling how the church has changed over the centuries with the changing fortunes in the countryside - changes which still continue (Dunning, 1987).

Chapter 15
The Brendon Hills
Wiveliscombe to Clatworthy

(ST 0827) - Wiveliscombe Church - Wiveliscombe Sandstone and Vexford Breccias - Raddington Church - Clatworthy Reservoir - Pickwell Down Sandstone.

Wiveliscombe Church

The pleasant parish church of St Andrew was rebuilt in 1829. The walls are mainly Permo-Triassic red sandstones and breccias*. The south wall has breccias with angular rock fragments set at all angles. The rock fragments look similar to the purple/red Pickwell Down Sandstone which outcrops on the west side of Wiveliscombe and forms the hilly country extending to Dulverton and beyond. Pickwell Down Sandstone can be seen nearby in the walls of houses in Rotten Row.

We can therefore surmise that the breccias are composed of rock fragments derived from what were, at the time of deposition of the breccias, nearby outcrops of Devonian rocks. The jumbled arrangement of angular rock of various sizes suggests that the rock was once a mixture of water and rock debris, namely a debris flow. Note that blocks containing thinner slate fragments tend to have the rock fragments sub-parallel; the flowing motion produces a preferred orientation of the long axes of stones parallel to the direction of flow, with the dip of the long axes downslope.

These features suggest the active destruction of a mountainous landscape composed of Devonian rocks. This mountainous landscape was the result of the uplift that followed the Variscan Orogeny. Rocks that were buried and crumpled at depth were subsequently raised as mountains. The present-day Devonian and Carboniferous rocks of west Somerset and Devon are thus the truncated stumps of those mountains.

The church has dressings of Bath Stone. The pillars inside the church are Ham Hill Stone and the monument to Humphrey and Margery Wyndham is in Somerset alabaster from Watchet.

Wiveliscombe Sandstone and Vexford Breccias

Wiveliscombe stands on the Wiveliscombe Sandstones-the lowest formation hereabouts in the Permo-Triassic succession; these can be explored in a lane north of the town as part of an enjoyable country ramble. Park carefully at the T-junction in Langley (ST 0800 2886) and proceed up the public footpath in the steep sunken lane. The latter shows how, over the centuries, carts and livestock have broken-up the friable sands which heavy rains have subsequently washed away. On 25-26 June, 1997, 180 mm (7") of rainfall was recorded locally. Channels were cut in the track, a lot of sand was washed down the cutting and soaking caused the sides to slump. The explanatory memoir to the Taunton sheet (p30) reports massive and thickly bedded red and brown sandstones dipping at 10º/090º (i.e. 10º to the east) plus friable, calcareous sandstone, stony lenses, breccia and a concretionary iron oxide.

Follow the lanes around to the right, noting the wooded spoil heaps of the old Oakhampton slate quarries in the distance to the north. Descend to Grant's Farms (ST 089287) and return to Langley noting on route the exposure of the Vexford Breccias in the road cutting (ST 0830 2889) where 3.5m of breccia overlies sand rock and pebble bed dipping at 15° to the east. Pebbles and rock fragments include quartz, sandstone. Carboniferous Limestone and chert. There is a small fault in the exposure.

These exposures of Permo-Triassic sediments, and the local building stones, record the beginning of the infilling of basins created by the stretching of the crust which followed the Variscan Orogeny. Similar breccias in the Crediton Trough and around Exeter record not only volcanic eruptions and lava flows but also evidence that some of the granite domes were being eroded. Clearly, the rock fragments in breccias are worth close study. (Edwards, 1997).

FIG 15.1 Raddington Church as it may have looked (Bond 1907)

Raddington Church

Westward from Wiveliscombe, the B3227 leads into shillet* hill country: deep, steep-sided valleys with less fertile soils. There are still unconverted old barns to be seen among the maze of narrow lanes which connect the many hamlets. Visitors on a church-crawl should include Raddington Church (Figure 15.1) which escaped heavy Victorian restoration and is reached by a footpath across a field (ST 020 260). The building stones include, Pickwell Down Sandstone, Morte Slates, red and whitish Permo-Triassic sandstones. Ham Hill Stone, Doulting Stone and a window with the central mullion made of Exeter Volcanics (cf. Burlescombe Church). White Beer Stone has been used for the window dressings. Slate and ancient tiles are used for the floor. Yet another atmospheric church where one feels the presence of congregations over the centuries.

John Betjeman has referred to church crawling as 'the richest of pleasures, it leads you to the remotest and quietest country, it introduces you to the history of England in stone and wood and glass which is always truer than what you read in books' (Betjeman, 1952).

Clatworthy Reservoir

Clatworthy Reservoir and Nature Trail are set in this hill country and make a nice excursion (ST 0431). There are toilets, picnic benches and a car park.

A large, dark upright stone, turned on its end, stands in the car park. The side with the plaque is the undersurface of the bed. Technically, the rock is a strongly lithified, fine-grained sandstone-siltstone with an abundant, original clay matrix. The bulbous protuberances represent erosional hollows cut into the underlying sediments and later filled by the sediment which composes the monolith. The erosional hollows are the result a turbidity current* flowing across a muddy sea floor and are known as sole marks. The steep, bulbous noses would have pointed upstream. Turbidity currents often carry a mix of fine- and coarse-grained sediments which are deposited in a fining-upwards sequence. A turbidity current off Newfoundland once cut undersea cables and is reckoned to have flowed at 60 mph.

The features suggest an 'Upper Culm', probably Crackington Formation, origin and the rock may have come from the Bampton area. *En échelon* tension gashes in the side of the rock indicate that the sediments have been subjected to shearing stresses caused by earth movements. Descend the track to the Nature Trail and dam. A rock face close to the path on the right, before the dam is reached, shows shiny, weak, finely-laminated slates dipping 63° to the south. The slates represent mud which has been converted into slate as a result of compression rearranging the minerals during the Variscan Orogeny. The slates have been further deformed: close examination will reveal angular folds (kink-bands) a few centimetres apart. These tend to run obliquely up and down the surface of the slate. These indicate that the slates were rucked by sideways, high shear stress after they were formed. This in turn, represents a later phase in the Variscan Orogeny. Superb examples of kink bands can be seen in the old quarry face, behind the barn, near the end of the Nature Trail.

There are also N-S vertical joints in the rock face by the path. Almost every quarry face on Exmoor shows either N-S, or NNW-SSE, joint faces. These represent the effects of yet another stress regime, either during the Variscan Orogeny, or during the Tertiary Period when many NNW-SSE wrench faults were reactivated. The rocks on top of the wall at the lower end of the path are sandy limestones with chert lenses similar to those in the Upper Westleigh Limestones.

Note how the slates weather readily to form friable brown soils. Sunken lanes readily develop and badgers and foxes can easily burrow into the dry weathered material.

Pickwell Down Sandstone

Clatworthy Reservoir is set in Devonian Morte Slates country characterised by subdued, rounded, open hilltops but steep-sided valley bottoms.

To the south of Clatworthy the country has a more hefty look. Here lies the Pickwell Down Sandstone Formation which is composed of massive sandstones reminiscent of the Hangman Sandstone Group which underlie north Exmoor. Indeed, the beds represent a return to large inputs of sands from the Old Red Sandstone continent which lay to the north. These sandstones form a steep north-facing escarpment overlooking Huish Moor; there are roadside exposures and an old quarry at ST 034 284. There is abundant vein-quartz, and the partially-fused grains of sand in the sandstone give the impression of having been affected by heat during the emplacement of the vein-quartz. There is another roadside quarry 400 m south-east of Chipstable (ST 045 268).

The deeply cut valleys are narrower and the slopes steeper than on the Morte Slates. The outcrop runs via Heydon Hill and Haddon Hill to Dulverton and beyond. The soils tend to be sandier, more acidic and less fertile than those on the slates. Pickwell Down Sandstone has been widely used for building.

Chapter 16
Broomfield

(ST 2232) Somerset Wildlife Trust - Countryside - Mining - Mineralisation

Somerset Wildlife Trust

The Taunton geological map shows that the headquarters of the Somerset Wildlife Trust at Fyne Court is on the outcrop of the Devonian Morte Slates rock formation which is exposed in several small quarries along their Nature Trail. A printed guide to the rocks and building stones at Fyne Court and Broomfield church is available from the Trust shop at Fyne Court (Prudden, 2000). The Somerset Wildlife Trust has an important role in supporting the conservation of geological sites in Somerset.

Countryside

The local soils are much more amenable to cultivation than those on the sandstones in the northern Quantocks. The Soil Survey described them as well drained, fine, loamy, reddish soils over rock (see Findlay, 1984 for details). The slates were once mud on the sea floor and they revert to much the same when they weather to become part of the soil profile. Soil rubbed between between the fingers should feel silky indicating of a high silt content. TDBC's Set 1 No. 4 Fyne Court in TDBC's Country Walks around Taunton makes a nice walk passing several old quarries in the Morte Slates.

Collinson, in 1791, was enthusiastic about the landscape:

> .... high ground, beautifully varied, with swelling hills and deep romantic vales, and commanding a great variety of pleasing landscapes, and very extensive prospects.....The lands which are moderately fruitful, are nearly divided between pasture and arable. The soil in general is shallow, and abounds in that kind of rag slate stone, divisible into thin laminae, which is found almost everywhere in the neighbourhood of Quantock.

Mining

Local people today might not react too kindly to news that local landowners hope to start mining operations at Broomfield. A report from the Taunton Courier for April 1853 makes interesting reading:

> Mining operations are about to be commenced on a portion of the Quantock Hills, Somersetshire, which is likely to become an important mining district. It has long been known that these hills contained an abundance of copper; a recent discovery of some valuable lodes at Broomfield on the estates of Colonel Tynte and R. J. Mayo Esq., has given fresh impetus to mining speculation. The matter has been taken up by men of capital and energy and we understand that sanguine expectations are entertained that the mines at Broomfield will form a source of perpetual and increasing wealth. What happened and the story of Quantock mining is told in *Men and mining in the Quantocks by* Hamilton and Lawrence (1970).

Mineralisation

There has been debate concerning the origin of the metal ores found in the Quantocks. It is thought that rising volcanic fluids may have leached base metals and then redistributed them within the Devonian shales and sandstones. Volcanic activity not far away is indicated by the presence of the Devonian Cockercombe Tuff (see Plainsfield chapter). The metals may have been subsequently mobilised and concentrated during the Variscan Orogeny. Fractures and fissures would have provided channels for the mineralising fluids which deposited the metals in ore-bearing lodes.

Chapter 17

Burlescombe and Westleigh

Devon (ST 0716) - Church and landscape - Variscan structures in the Upper Westleigh Limestone - Economic products

Church and landscape

Most of the exterior walls of Saint Mary the Virgin are built of sombre grey Upper Westleigh Limestone from the local Westleigh quarries. These comprise tiny fragments of shells and limestone cemented by calcite. Note the thin layers of secondary chert which have developed after deposition in sediments rich in silica, much as patches of flint developed in the Chalk.

(Courtesy: D. G. Weatherley)

FIG 17.1 The Parish Church of St.Mary the Virgin Burlescombe

There are also purple, pitted blocks on the southeast corner buttresses to the right of the main door. The same rock appears sporadically elsewhere on the building. It is a fine-grained basalt belonging to the Exeter Volcanic Rocks; the holes represent gas bubbles once trapped in the molten lava. Some of the holes have been filled with calcite.

The buttresses on the southwest corner are a Permo-Triassic breccia, possibly from Sampford Peverell. The doorway and window dressings on the north side, together with the arcade pillars, are Beer Stone. This is the furthest north that this stone was used for medieval construction according to the church leaflet.

The altar slab is Purbeck Marble, a freshwater limestone full of the univalve shell Viviparus. These beds take a good polish and have been used extensively in churches and cathedrals for decorative work and tombs as at Burlescombe. The clay content makes it prone to weathering and it is best used indoors.

One can compare Somerset and Nottingham alabaster in the north aisle of the church: the corner memorial of Reginald Ayshford (1610) is Somerset alabaster whilst that of Elizabeth Ayshford (1635) is Nottingham alabaster. The church also allows a comparison between the Devon and Somerset types of capitals.

The British Geological Survey's Tiverton map (Sheet 310) shows that the church stands on a spur underlain by the Budleigh Salterton Pebble Beds (BSPB) formation. The BSPB are more resistant to erosion than the red sandy beds to the south-west which underlie the valley followed by the defunct Grand Western Canal, railway and M5. These pebble beds are well-exposed in the cliffs at Budleigh Salterton and they can be traced northward for some 60 km via Milverton to Williton.

There is a good exposure of the limestones at Fenacre Bridge close to the Grand Western Canal (ST 0711 1770); thick shales and limestone beds have been turned into a vertical position. Permo-Triassic beds appear to be faulted against the tilted Carboniferous strata. Please view from the footpath; visitors are requested not to enter the yard without permission or to interfere with the rock face. The working quarries at Westleigh are not normally open to visitors but there is a good display of rocks from the local quarries on top of the wall on the south side of the churchyard at Holcombe Rogus. The rocks are of Carboniferous age-the same as the Mendip limestones.

Variscan structures in the Upper Westleigh Limestone

Figure 17.2 is a sketch of the 20 m high face in Upper Westleigh Limestone at Greenham Quarry near Gamlins, 3 km north of Burlescombe; note the impressive folding of what were once horizontal sediments on the sea floor. Today the rock face is very obscured and is on private land where access is restricted

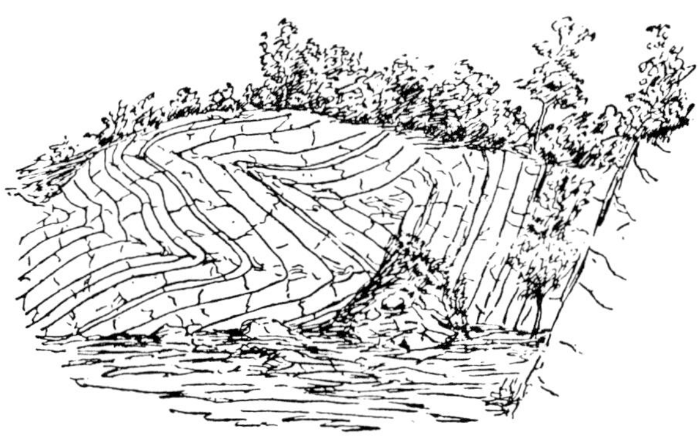

(Ussher, 1906).

FIG 17.2 Contorted beds in Upper Westleigh Limestone, Gamlins Quarry

These structures have fascinated geologists for many years. Note the attitudes of the strata and how steeply dipping beds on the right make contact with the folded beds on the left.

In 1839 Henry De la Beche wrote:

> ...the beds have subsequently suffered from the action of some powerful force which has twisted and contorted them so that probably not a single bed occupies exactly the same position in which it was first formed

Arthur Clayden referred to the structures in this area in his History of Devonshire Scenery (1908):

> They are a necessary consequence of the very great lateral compression acting on a mixture of hard and soft strata which are not at the same time exposed to great vertical pressure. The Culm* beds had only their own weight acting down upon them.

William Ussher (1906) wrote of the structures shown in Figure 17.2

> The structure of Greenham Quarry is no doubt complicated by faults and slides, as it is difficult to connect the partially concealed beds in the west of the section with the sharply zig-zagged structure in the eastern part........The quarry face consists of more or less massive brown and grey limestone, partly crinoidal and irregularly jointed; with bands and lenticles of dark chert, and with veins of calcite.

There has been a lot of controversy and research about the structures seen here, and along the Devon and Cornish coasts to the west, so it is worth taking a closer look at the Gamlins' rock face shown in Figure 17.2. The structures are chevron folds which have long, straight fold-limbs, separated from each other by angular fold-hinges. The axial planes* are near horizontal (recumbent). These recumbent folds may be contrasted with the upright folds at Cockington Head illustrated in Figure 17.3.

(De la Beche, 1839).

FIG 17.3. Upright fold with vertical axial plane Cockington Head Bideford Bay.

We might expect compressive, horizontal north-south forces to result in upright folds with vertical axial planes as shown in Figure 17.3. But the folds at Gamlins have near-horizontal axial planes.

There are a number of mechanisms for generating recumbent folds:

1. Recent geological mapping in Devon and Cornwall has revealed instances of where slices of rock have been thrust over one another. Horizontal compression of strata may result in slices of the crust becoming detached along weak beds (bedding-parallel glide zones or flats) as in Figure 17.4. Ramps may develop below a thrust sheet where the thrust-plane cuts up across more resistant beds. Note how flexures develop where the beds slide over the ramps.

Frequently a thrust sheet becomes stuck and another thrust sheet is propagated ahead of the old one along a new thrust plane. Consequently the first thrust sheet will be tilted to a steeper angle and the pile of beds collapses

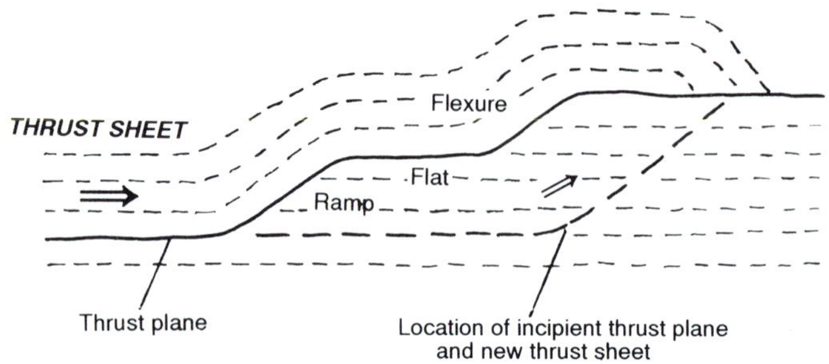

FIG 17.4 Thrust sheet riding up and over ramps and flats.

(footwall collapse) into flat-lying folds. It is pertinent to recall Clayden's observations above that these folds have developed in a 'mixture of hard and soft strata which are not at the same time exposed to great vertical pressure'.

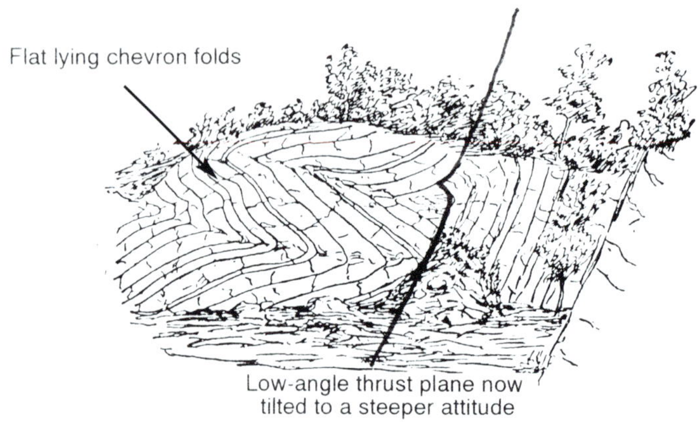

FIG 17.5 An interpretation of the face at Gamlins.

2. An alternative mechanism involves a low angle shear zone where folds, which were initially overturned, tend to rotate to a more flat-lying attitude as in Figure 17.6

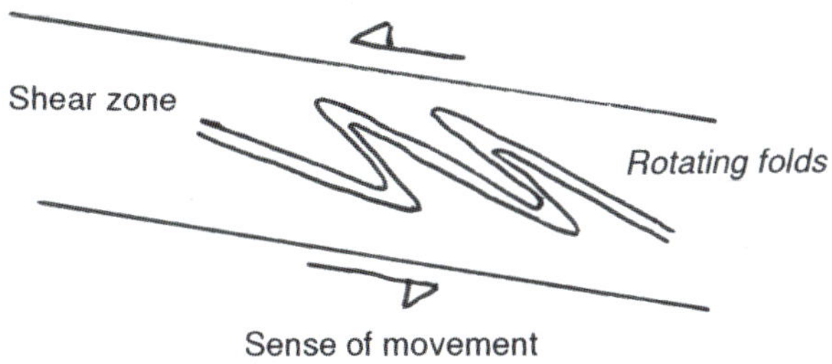

FIG 17.6
Alternative mechanism for generating recumbent folds.

De la Beche (1839) provides an interesting example from a new road cutting in 1837 shown in Figure 17.7.

> From the contorted manner in which the upper rocks rest upon the lower beds, it would appear as if the former were to a certain extent forced over the latter, and contorted at the same time.

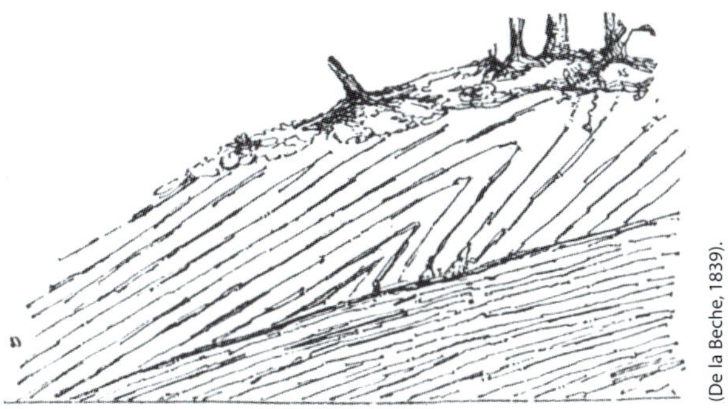

FIG 17.7 Folded rocks above the lower in an unconformable position near Launceston

Since access is difficult at Greenham, we recommend a visit to cliffs at Millook, 7 km south of Bude, which display a spectacular cascade of similar recumbent chevron folds in Carboniferous shales and thick sandstones. There is now a lot of evidence that the chevron folds in the Culm* Basin are thrust related (Andrews et al, 1998, Ch. 6).

Elsewhere, in south Devon, Cornwall and the Mendips, it appears that detached slices of the earth's crust (thrust sheets) have been thrust northwards and upwards at low angles along thrust planes (Bristow, 1996 and Green, 1992). The stacking of the thrust sheets was accompanied by crustal shortening. Previously, the crust had sagged as the thick pile of Devonian and Carboniferous sediments were deposited.

Geologists are busy interpreting these events with the help of concepts associated with plate tectonics theory. Plates are rigid slabs of the Earth's crust and mantle that move relative to other plates. Thrust sheets occur where plates converge; the overlying plate is propelled over the one below. There are similar structures where the plate carrying the Himalayan mountain region is being underthrust by peninsular India.

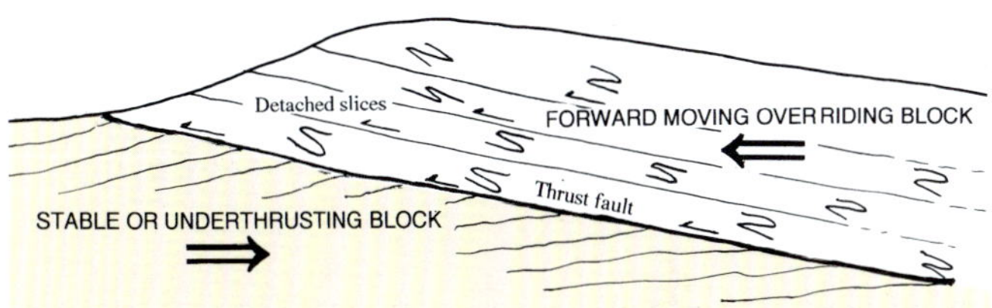

FIG 17.8 The propagation of thrust faults as crustal plates converge.

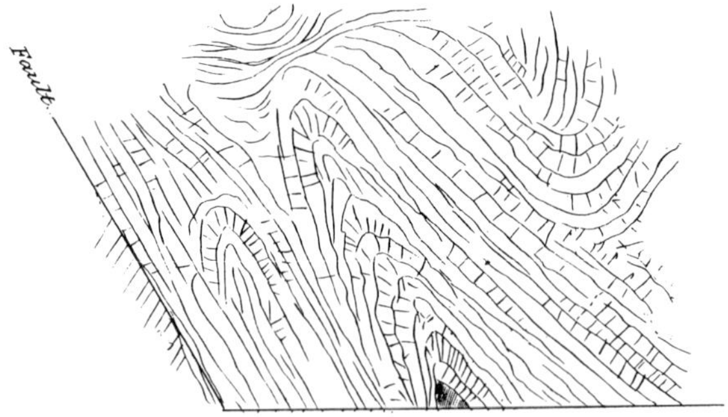

FIG 17.9 A diagram representing the extraordinary contortions in the Culm limestone at Venn. (Lee, 1881.)

Figure 17.9 is taken from Notebook of an amateur geologist by Edward Lee in 1881. The limestone is in beds a few inches thick, separated from each other by thin beds of a rather dark shale. Presumably the axial planes run approximately east-west. Compare the structures with those in the preceding illustrations. It is interesting to note that Venn is near Barnstaple which is on a line to the west-northwest of the structures to be seen in the Westleigh area and in rather similar beds.

Geological structures are a profitable line of enquiry for the amateur and have been sadly neglected in the past in the pursuit of fossils and minerals. They tell a dynamic story of what has happened to the rocks during, and following, their formation. *The Macmillan guide to geological structures* by John Roberts (1989) is an excellent introduction if a copy can be found.

Economic products

Members of the Somerset Archaeological and Natural History Society visited the Westleigh Quarries in 1912. Their visit to the remains of Augustinian Abbey at Canonleigh reminded them that building stone was being extracted locally in the 13th century (Winwood, 1913).

It is interesting to read about the quarry manager's problems in 1912 in view of the problems faced by the quarry industry in the Mendips today. The manager, a Mr G. P. Chamberlain, explained:

> that the stone was not a pure limestone, and a great deal of it could not be burnt into lime. They did a certain amount of limeburning. The lime they produced was not such a good building lime as that made from the Blue Lias, and it was used principally for agricultural purposes. The men who worked in the quarries knew the beds which were suitable for limeburning and picked them out. There were running through a great many of the beds what he regarded as veins of black silex (chert); it was quite black and extremely hard, no steel they used would touch it. Until five or six years ago the stone from the quarry was considered to be the best stone for making roads. Now granite was imported from a long distance, with results disastrous to them from a commercial point of view. There was less sale for their stone and they had to pay rates to meet the cost of stone purchased from their competitors! They hoped that before long the question of the maintenance of the roads would be taken up by a great central body. Then perhaps, as they had gone in for tarring the stone they produced (and with marked success), they might be given a chance. (Winwood, 1913).

The bank of limekilns are no longer working but can be seen near the road junction at ST 065174. Today's manager has problems: the siliceous chert beds rapidly wear the machinery, unlike the limestones; the site is cramped and expansion limited to north and south by both geology and settlements; planning conditions are rigorous. On the other hand the quarry provides a local supply of stone which reduces lorry-miles, provides jobs and, at the end of the day, will hopefully provide a conservation area where geologists can study and debate the many fascinating aspects of the local geology which we have barely touched upon. Readers are referred to the following for further reading: Downes (1878, 1879, 1883), and Durrance and Laming, (1982).

Chapter 18
Cothelstone

(ST 1831) - Gateway and church - Cothelstone Fault.

Gateway and Church

Sitting at the foot of the steep western side of the Quantocks, Cothelstone is both attractive and interesting. The gateway entrance from the lane to Cothelstone Farm incorporates Jurassic Ham Hill Stone, Bath Stone, red Triassic sandstone and North Curry Sandstone. The long wall on the right appears to be a local Devonian limestone which was probably quarried nearby. Access to the church is to the left of the farm where there is a small car park.

The church is mainly constructed of Devonian siltstones and sandstones plus red Permo-Triassic sandstones and breccias. North Curry Sandstone is seen in the tower and doorway on the north side. The effigies to Sir John Stawel and wife are made from Watchet alabaster (1603), one of the earliest examples in which Watchet alabaster was used.

DEVONIAN FAULT OTTER SANDSTONE

FIG 18.1 Section near Bagborough Church showing Otter Sandstone faulted against Devonian slates

The church stands amid fields of red soil with gentle slopes leading up to the very steep sides of the Quantocks. These red sandy soils are much given to erosion when cultivated.

The Cothelstone Fault

FIG 18.1 shows, that near Bagborough, steeply dipping Devonian slates on the left were once to be seen in faulted contact against red Permo-Triassic sandstones. The exposure is no longer visible. The Permo-Triassic rocks are separated from the older Devonian rocks of the Quantocks by a series of faults. The Cothelstone Fault marks a major displacement. Figure 13.5 shows how these faults define the eastern side of a half-graben, i.e. a tilted block forming a basin with a major fault(s) at one side. Permo-Triassic sediments have been preserved in this basin as shown in Figure 13.5 .

The Cothelstone Fault is one of what appears to be a number of faults on the southwest side of the Quantocks and appears to have both vertical and horizontal (dextral*) displacement; it is a major NNW-SSE wrench fault*. Similar faults have been mapped from Cornwall to near Sherborne in Dorset. The most recent movement of the Cothelstone Fault moved the rock strata on each side by 2 to 4 km. Previous episodes of fault activity may have caused greater lateral movement, The evidence comes from comparing the displacement of various large-scale geological features in the Quantocks with their continuation in the Brendon Hills. Some effects of the Cothelstone Fault are featured in the geological trail described in the Cothelstone Hill to Kingston St Mary section below. More details about the evolution of this, and associated, fault systems are in Ruffell (1991 and Miliorizos and Ruffell, (1998).

Chapter 19
Cothelstone Hill to Kingston St. Mary

(ST 1932) A geological ramble in the Southern Quantocks

The walk from Cothelstone Hill (Beacon) to Kingston St Mary church provides a good opportunity to make your own geological survey, much as would a field geologist. There are superb views both in the near and far distance. The energetic can do a circular walk starting at Kingston, lunch at the cafe (ST 2072 3295) or the pub (ST 2100 3340) and then walk downhill taking in the geological localities. Footpaths can be muddy. Parties with two cars can leave one at Kingston St Mary. There are car parks at Cothelstone Hill and next to Kingston St Mary church. Take note of the police warnings not to leave anything on view in the car! Allow 2-3 hours from Cothelstone Beacon.

Walk from the Cothelstone Hill car park (ST 1982 3290) to the viewpoint (Location 1 in Figure 19.1).

Location 1
Cothelstone Hill is one of the outstanding viewpoints in the West Country. Collinson, in 1791, wrote:

> On ascending this eminence, the first object that strikes the sight is the fine succession of hills and valleys round the lodge, cut into rich enclosures; the beautiful vale of Taunton to the south and to the west a series of hills rising in picturesque gradation, bounded by the forest of Exmoor. A great part of Dorsetshire, and part of Wiltshire, are in view. But to the north, northeast, and northwest, the prospect is very extensive, commanding all the middle parts of the county, like a map, from the highlands near Sherborne to the Channel; Mendip bounding the view to the east, at about 30 miles distance. To the north and northwest appear the Channel about 50 miles in length, the mountains about Brecknock, and the greater part of South-Wales. From this delightful spot the eye commands fourteen counties, and with a glass on a clear day, one hundred and fifty churches.

This was in the days before poor air quality in the countryside.

The view point is located on the brow of the Quantock 'escarpment' which presents its face to the south-west. The Taunton sheet shows the outcrop to be the Leighland Slates rock formation which includes the siltstones and sandstone seen here. The vegetation reflects the acidic, infertile nature of the soil: Tormentil, Wood Sage, Heath Bedstraw, Heath Milkwort, Climbing Corydalis, Sheep's Sorrel. But note how the depth of soil and amount of organic matter increases downslope and under woodland.

Take the footpath from the summit to the southeast leading to Ball Lane.

Location 2
Sunken lanes are common in the 'slate' country as the slates are readily pulverised by wheeled traffic and animals; rainstorms wash the debris downslope. The edges of steeply dipping Morte Slates can be seen in the wheel ruts for much of the length of Ball Lane unless obscured by winter mud. The descent down the track gives some idea of the thickness of the beds although it is possible that the original thickness may have been increased or decreased by faults or folds.

Location 3 (ST 1980 3158)
Note the rock face to the left which shows the slates turning over in a downhill direction (terminal curvature*).

Fig 19.1
Geological trail from Cothelstone Hill to Kingston St Mary

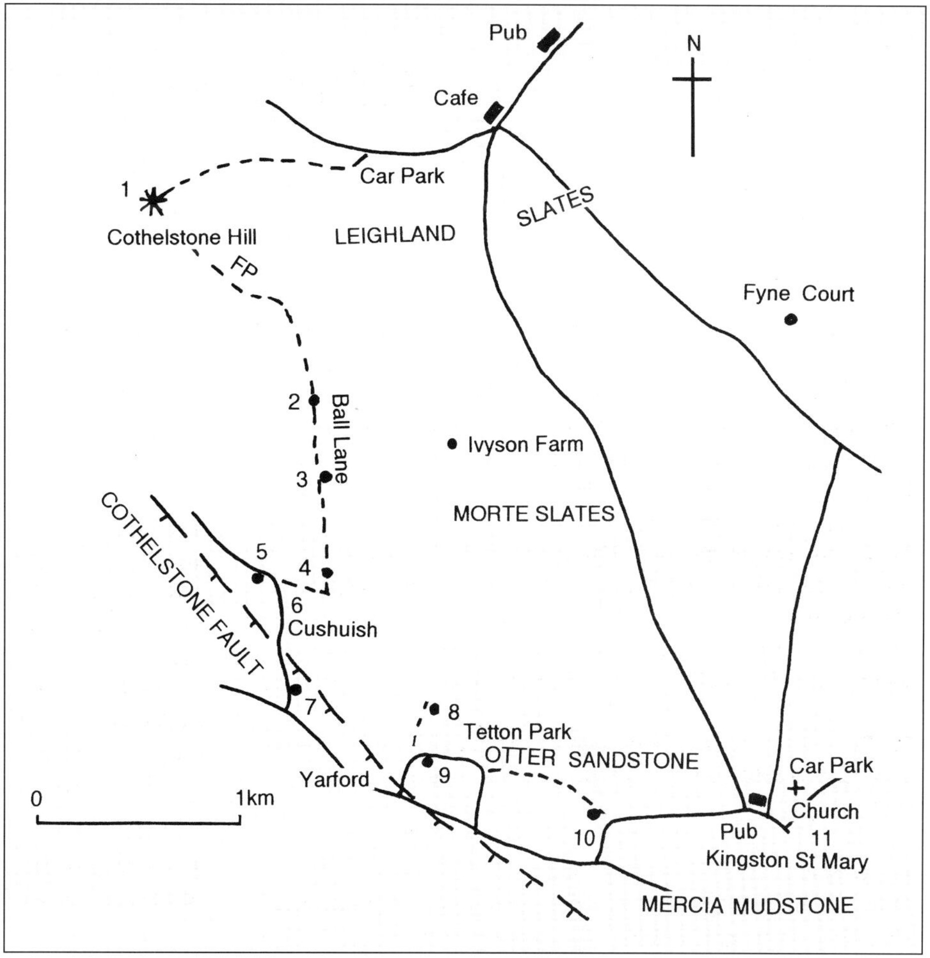

Beware that sandstones seem to have been dumped in the track in order to limit the erosion of the slates and may not indicate the underlying bedrock There are some places where the slates underfoot are reddened; these may mark iron mineralisation, or staining from formerly overlying Permo-Triassic strata penetrating down small faults.

There are attractive views to the left of the southern Quantocks. This southern end of the Quantocks has a number of enigmatic 'benches'. There may have three explanations: (a) there may be an outcrop of stronger rock which has resisted erosion; (b) denudation has removed weaker overlying Permo-Triassic rocks to reveal the ancient landsurface on which they rested; (c) the surface of the eroded stumps of the Devonian rocks has been let down by earth movements.

Location 4 (ST 1992 3085)
Slates, which dip steeply to the south, are bent into gentle curves. This would not seem to be the kind of brittle deformation associated with terminal curvature* which is the result of surface creep and normally shows angular breaks? Instead, these curved slates suggest ductile deformation at depth with greater temperatures and pressures, and possibly associated with movements on the nearby Cothelstone Fault.

Continue down the lane and turn right along the metalled road for 200 m (ST 1952 3089).

Location 5
(A Regionally Important Geological Site). The slates in the road cutting exhibit a distinct type of crumpling and angular folding with axial planes dipping 25° south-east, and a gentle east-northeast plunge (Webby, 1966b). Refer to Figure 19.2 which illustrates these terms. Webby has suggested that sideways movement on the nearby Cothelstone Fault to the south may have rucked the slates into these angular folds. We refer to the movements on the Cothelstone Fault in the Cothelstone chapter above.

The rocks of the southern Quantocks consist of slates sandwiched between massive limestones and sandstones. The angular folds seen in the cutting reflect the susceptibility of the slates to deformation compared with the limestones and sandstones.

The muds deposited in Devonian times were compressed into slates during the Variscan Orogeny*. It follows that the deformation of the slates occurred after the cleavage was imposed since it is the cleaved slates which are folded. Thus we can distinguish various events that occurred during the Variscan Orogeny.

Figure 19.2
Fold architecture showing fold axis and axial plane. 'Plunge' is the inclination of the fold axis if the latter is not horizontal.

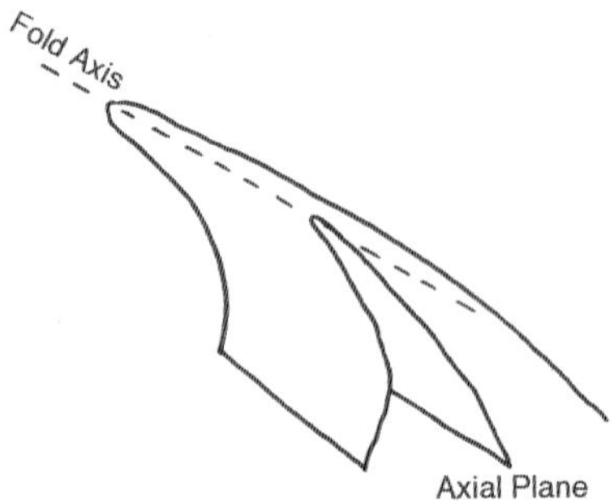

Return back along the road and proceed round the corner to the right down the hill.

Location 6

Notice the deep cutting beyond Yea's Cottage where the road is steepest. Silty-slates can be seen at road level and dip at 35° to just east of north which is unusual as there is usually a southerly component to the dip in the southern Quantocks. The Cothelstone Fault must cross the road somewhere near the entrance to Cushuish Farm but unhappily it is not visible.

Location 7

The rather featureless, thickly-bedded, red and cream, Permo-Triassic Otter Sandstone is met further down the road. These beds do not show the cleavage or crumpling seen in the Devonian slates since they were deposited on top of the slates and after the Variscan Orogeny. They have clearly been let down on the southern side of the Cothelstone Fault.

Continue down the road and turn left. After 700 m turn left again to Yarford.

There are three types of building stone to look out for:
(a) Reddish-brown, smooth-faced but angular Devonian sandstone.
(b) Poorer quality, greenish-grey, rough-faced Devonian silty-slates used for walling.
(c) Red, mottled Permo-Triassic sandstone with a knobbly appearance where lime has concentrated in random patches. This feature is a result of evaporation exceeding precipitation when the sands were deposited in a semi-arid climate to form calcretes*. The latter can be seen in the roadside walls of Wiscombe Cottage in Yarcombe just before the road turns to the right and may come from the old pit around the corner (Location 9).

If there is time, do not turn the corner but continue straight on by the stream on your left for 300 m up an attractive valley to an old quarry (ST 2035 3014).

Location 8

The old quarry shows Devonian purple and grey slates with cleavage dipping at 60° to the south-south-east (Edmonds and Williams, 1985). Some of these beds have been dislocated and intruded by quartz veins (Morte Slates Formation). The sediments on the righthand side of the quarry are smoothed and sheared possibly as a result of movement on the nearby Cothelstone Fault. Note the nearby reddened soil with slate fragments which suggests nearness to the contact with overlying Permo-Triassic sediments. View the quarry face from below.

Return to the road, turn left past the houses at Yarford and observe an old pit on the right but do not enter; the can be seen in the adjacent roadside at ST 2038 2990 beneath the ivy.

Location 9

The memoir for the Taunton sheet mentions a '4 m face of buff and white sandrock overlain by massive red calcareous sandstone'. These beds are at the same height as the Devonian rocks in the quarry at Location 8; in fact, looking north one can see that Devonian slates and sandstones in the Quantock Hills stand over 200 m higher to the north of Yarford. The problem is that the Permo-Triassic beds were deposited on top of the Devonian rocks so how can the latter be higher? Either the Permo-Triassic beds were originally deposited against steep hillsides, or the Otter Sandstone been let down by faults so that Devonian and Permo-Triassic formations are now alongside each other? There may be truth in both explanations.

Continue along the road noting the red sandy soil on the right.

The field shows a typical deep red loamy soil developed on the Otter Sandstone and classified as Hodnet Association by the Soil Survey. These, and similar soils, occur extensively between here and Wellington and are widely used for growing cereals. They are prone to soil erosion on steeper slopes and where subsoils are slowly permeable (Findlay et al., 1984).

Cross the road at the T-junction and take the footpath that passes alongside the south side of the Wessex Water reservoir fence; bear right across Tetton Park and take the road to Kingston.

Location 10

Look out for red sandstones with calcretes where the footpath meets the road to Tetton House.

Tetton Park has one of the many fine houses and parklands that sun themselves on the footslopes of the south and west sides of the Quantocks. The combination of varied slopes, southerly aspect and fertile soils have contributed to a landscape of historic importance which we enjoy today. There are good views southwards to the Blackdown Hills.

Location 11

Kingston St Mary Church and village is mostly built of local Devonian siltstones and sandstones. The outside walls of the church also include blocks of vein quartz and a green stone showing what may be copper mineralisation at the east end of the chancel. The fine tower (1590) has large quoins of North Curry Sandstone with Devonian sandstones, red Permo-Triassic sandstones and North Curry Sandstone in the walls. Ham Hill Stone is used in the dressings and the striking ashlar porch (c1520) on the south side. Inside the church, Doulting Stone, Ham Hill Stone and red sandstone have been used for the pillars. The Warre tomb behind the choir stalls is covered with a slab of Purbeck Marble. This stone consists of the freshwater snail Viviparus set in a clay matrix and used since Roman times for interior decoration. The sides of the tomb are Ham Hill Stone. All this and much more where you can commune with the memorials to the great landowners whose houses and parklands still embellish the Quantocks.

FIG 19.3 Tomb of the Warres of Hestercombe (Carter, 1854)

Chapter 20
Hestercombe Gardens

(ST 2428) - The Edwardian Garden - The Landscape Garden

The Edwardian Garden

Hestercombe is one of the many geological jewels in Taunton Deane. The Edwardian Garden has Devonian siltstones and sandstones which show a variety of ripple marks similar to those seen on modern beaches except that these are some 370 million years old. The use of stone by Lutyens in the design of the formal garden is especially interesting. The garden also includes Ham Hill Stone used to great advantage, especially in the Orangery and balustrade in front of the House. The view to the south is one of the best places to comprehend the geological structure of Taunton Deane using Figure 2.2 .

FIG 20.1 An attractive corner at Hestercombe combining Devonian slates and Ham Hill Stone (courtesy Tony Haskell).

The Landscape Garden

The Morte Slates formation is to be seen in numerous quarries and outcrops. The beds, which were dug for walling, are mainly fine-grained sandstones rather than slates. There are large lumps of vein quartz at the foot of the waterfall. These exposures of Devonian strata are of special interest as they are buried under younger, overlying rocks to the south and east and only revealed in borehole cores..

The charcoal burner's quarry is quite different. It is a reddish igneous rock which has intruded into the Morte Slates. It has been classified in a number of ways but recent research suggests that the term 'diorite' is the most appropriate. The Hestercombe diorite can be seen in the front of Hestercombe House and the tower of St Mary Magdalene in Taunton.

The decorative arch of the Mausoleum is North Curry Sandstone whilst the Grecian Urn is an oolitic limestone from Monks' Park quarry near Corsham.

Visitors should most definitely include a visit to the overflow car park which is at the end of a track leading north from the main car park. Here there is a good exposure of the sandstones in the Morte Slates and is topped with terminal curvature*. The dark rock at the far end is another exposure of the Hestercombe diorite. In fact, it is the chilled margin of the intrusion as is shown by its very fine grain. Here there has been more rapid cooling compared with the outcrop seen in the charcoal burner's quarry where the crystals are much larger having cooled more slowly.

A geological guide to these and many other features is available in the shop at Hestercombe. The exposures at Hestercombe are among Somerset's most important Regionally Important Geological Sites (RIGS).

Chapter 21
Milverton

(ST 1225) - Church-Otter Sandstone-Budleigh Salterton Pebble Beds

Church

The church of St Michael is mainly built of red sandstones and breccias* containing a great assortment of rock fragments of varying shapes, sizes and rock types. The lithology of many of the angular fragments is reminiscent of Devonian rocks found in the Brendon Hills. It therefore seems probable that the material in the breccias is of local origin. The dressings are Ham Hill Stone.

The north aisle has three greyish North Curry Sandstone pillars showing cross-bedding and rip-up clasts*. The printed church guide (Adams n.d.) tells us that the pillars are of 14th century date, and that the golden Ham Hill Stone used in the dressings is 15th Century. Clearly, the quality of Ham Hill Stone made it worth while conveying it for quite long distances in medieval times for specialised uses.

Adams' comments on the Victorian restoration are interesting:

> In 1849-50 a massive rebuilding programme was undertaken, the whole of the southern arcade was taken down and replaced in Bath Stone, also parts of the walls and the south porch, these being rebuilt in the local stone from the old interior (this is weathering rather badly). Inside here and there some of the old stonework was reused, as in the arch over the Lady Chapel......Since the nineteen-sixties a great deal of work has been carried out on this church. The whole roof has been re-slated, the masonry of the tower has been restored...... the window stone has been rebuilt, the lead channels of the roof replaced and the porch re-roofed and fitted with outer doors. It is worthy of note that almost all of this has been paid for by the regular devoted giving of the Parishioners.

This is just one example of the kind of rebuilding that has taken place in so many churches as a result of maintenance problems, the need to enlarge, changing fashions and the availability of materials. Window mullions are particularly vulnerable being thin, exposed on several sides and often laid with the bedding on end. The fact that they have been 'patched' is indicated by the inclusion of more than one type of stone in a single window-a common occurrence.

A great debt is owed to those who have supported renovation of our churches.

Otter Sandstone

There are exposures of the Otter Sandstone in Butts Way leading out of Milverton to Bathealton (ST 119 257). The beds dip at approximately 5° to the east; the cross-beds incline approximately to the east-northeast, thus suggesting a flow of water to the east-northeast when the sediments were deposited. A more interesting exposure of the Otter Sandstone is seen in the road cutting 1 km southwest of Milverton on the B3187 (ST 116 248). There are both sandstone and pebble beds together with a variety of cross-beds indicative of shifting channels as in Figure 21.2. The sketch shows several sets of cross-bedded units; note how the base of an overlying unit cuts across and into the unit below to form an eroded surface. Take care as there is a lot of traffic on the narrow road. There is a splendid view of the Vale of Taunton Deane looking to the east from the top of the hill and the view should be compared with the geological section in Figure 2.2.

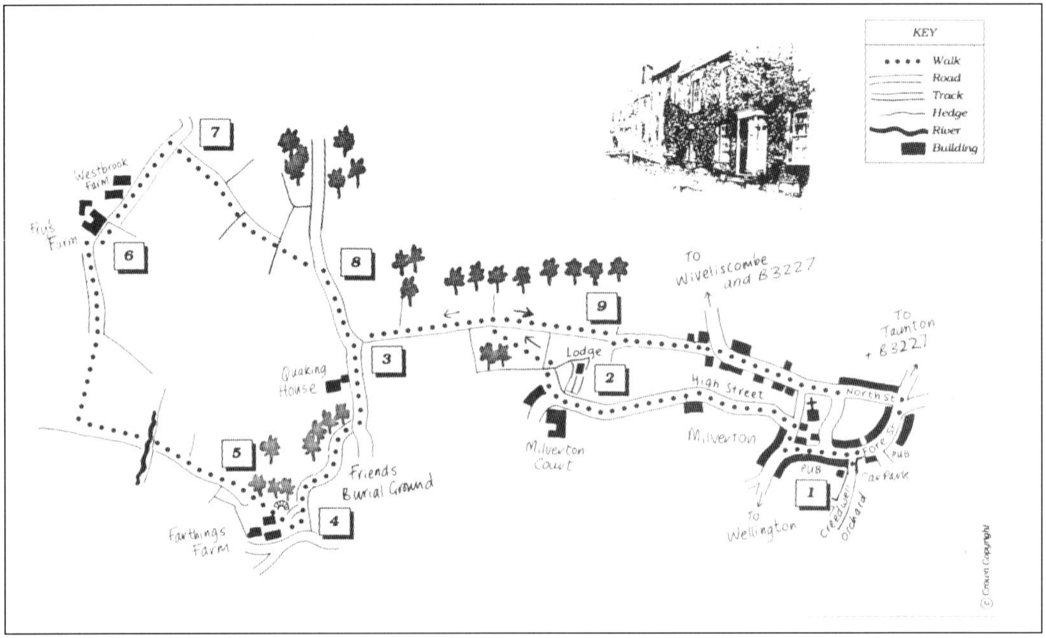

FIG 21.1 The route of No 16 set 2 Milverton (country walks around Taunton, TDBC).

Budleigh Salterton Pebble Beds

TDBC's Country Walks in and around Taunton Set 2 No. 16 (Milverton) is a delightful walk through the hilly, varied landscape provided by the Budleigh Salterton Pebble Beds (BSPB) which form a resistant capping to the hills; in effect they form an escarpment and dip slope (Figure 13.5). The footpath passes close to old quarries in these conglomerates between Locations 4 and 5 near Farthings Farm (ST 104 257). Pause to admire the view to the southeast towards Wellington and the Blackdown escarpment, and the view to the northwest towards Wiveliscombe and the Brendon Hills which are underlain by the much older Devonian slates and sandstones. The BSPB continue to the south towards Langford Budville where they can be seen in the walls of the church and nearby buildings. Note the cut and polished chancel and altar steps which show both angular rock fragments and pebbles set in a finer grained matrix. Ham Hill Stone is used extensively for dressings whilst North Curry Sandstone has been used for coping stones to the left of the entrance gate and in the church porch and tower

There are old quarries in the BSPB which can be seen from the public footpath at the southern end of Langford Heathfield (ST 106 222). Ussher (1906) reports 'a massive, bedded, rubbly conglomerate with pebbles of limestone, grit, and quartz plus an irregular capping of sand.'

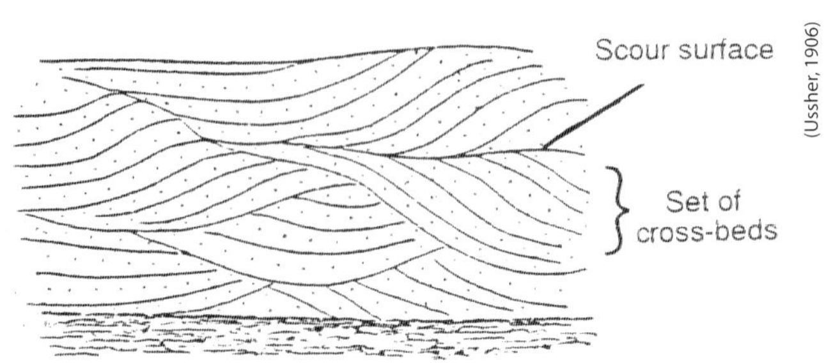

FIG 21.2 Cross bedded sandstone, east of Lower Lovelynch Farm, Milverton.

Chapter 22
North Curry

(ST 3125) - Church - Rocks and landforms

Church

The large church of St Peter and St Paul stands on a broad ridge trending southwest to northeast. The church, especially the tower, is partly built of the local, greenish grey North Curry Sandstone. The best place to examine the stone is the northwest corner of the church where ripple-lamination* indicates deposition by fast flowing water. Its use in church buildings is shown in Figure 4.2.

Ham Hill Stone, which is used for the dressings, has coarser sediments and larger-scale cross-bedding*. There is also a lot of blue-grey Blue Lias limestone showing parallel lamination which suggests that these beds were laid down as mud in more tranquil conditions than the sandstones. Fossils can be observed with the hand lens in some blocks. Fosse Cottage opposite the church is a not unattractive combination of Ham Hill Stone, Blue Lias and Devonian sandstone.

The Somerset Record Office (SRO) holds records for 1443 mentioning sand from 'Corymoursford' and lime and 'limestones' bought at Bathpool; those for 1445-6 include stone from Curry Mallet for a 'wyndore' in the bell tower, and lime bought from both Bathpool and Langport (see reference SRO).

Rocks and Landforms

An exposure of the North Curry Sandstone can be seen near the public footpath that runs northwest from the North Curry-Meare Green road at ST 335 265 to the River Tone via Moredon. TDBC's Country Walks in and around Taunton Set 2 No. 11 North Curry and Knapp could be adapted to take in this path.

Curry Moor and Hay Moor are extensions of the Somerset Levels and are shown as extensive tracts of alluvium on the geological map. Some of these flood plains are used as temporary stores for flood water. The high water table encourages their use as winter feeding grounds for birds. Elsewhere, efforts to raise farm productivity have led to deepening of ditches in order to lower the water table which in turn has mobilised organic acids as shown by the brown water emerging from the peat.

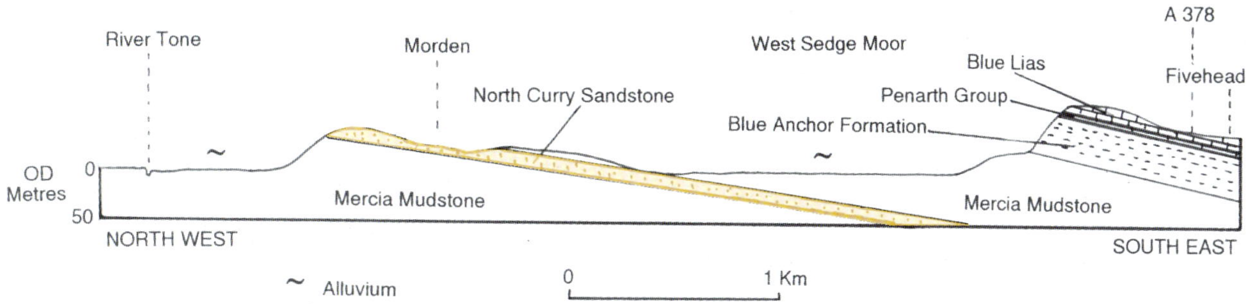

FIG 22.1 Cross section to show the geology and landforms between the River Tone and Fivehead

The North Curry Sandstone forms a steep northwest facing escarpment which is complemented by a dip slope which inclines to the southeast as shown in Figure 22.1. Further to the southeast is yet another escarpment and dip slope-that of the Blue Lias. The Permo-Triassic strata pass below the White and Blue Lias (now known as the Penarth Group-see Appendix C) on the southeast side of West Sedgemoor. The A358 from Taunton to Ilminster crosses these outcrops as one ascends the succession of strata from older to younger rock formations. A journey eastward from Hatch Beauchamp to Shaftesbury crosses eight such escarpments all of which are capped by resistant rock formations.

The North Curry Sandstone Ridges appear on the map showing subdivisions of the physical landscape (Figure A1 in Appendix A). Note how the strikes* of the ridges are N-S to the west of Taunton (strata dipping to the east) and NE-SW to the east of Taunton (strata dipping to the southeast). The alignment of these ridges reflects the geological structure, especially the direction of dip. Clearly, the geological structure has a strong influence on the topography.

The Blue Lias is overlain by the Lower Lias clays. Among the various types of clays are the dark bituminous shales seen in the cliffs at Charmouth. These are very prone to slope failures and have been a problem along the line of the Hatch Beauchamp bypass (ST 2934 1991). There are a number of active shallow slides on slopes close to streams between Hatch Beauchamp and Charmouth as by the River Ding (ST 296 147).

Readers may care to try to trace William Marshall's journey (on horse?) through the area from Taunton to Somerton as recorded in 1794 (see A view of the countryside in 1794 above). Pasture is preferred for the heavy clayland although there has been a considerable increase in arable cultivation in recent years. Today the bicycle would be an ideal means of exploring this area which is much more suited to the cyclist than the 'switchback' topography of the deeply incised valleys of Devon.

Chapter 23
Norton Fitzwarren

(ST 1926) - Church - Terrace Gravels

Church

The church of All Saints is largely built of North Curry Sandstone - indeed it is the best place to examine this particular stone. Note the greenish grey colour of the sandstones plus the many grey pebbles and rock fragments. The latter have been ripped up by strong currents and included in the bedload. Sedimentary structures include ripple-lamination and some splendid cross-bedding. The evidence suggests a high-energy, shallow flow of water. Curiously, these rocks do not exhibit the red coloration seen in the other Permo-Triassic formations.

It is possible that the stone was quarried either at Knowle to the north of the River Tone, or at Hele to the south. Figure 4.2 shows the distribution of churches where this stone has been used; the limited extent reflects the local nature of the outcrops. The dressings are Ham Hill Stone.

Terrace gravels

TDBC's leaflet Norton Hillfort is a useful guide. The hillfort can be approached from the church. The visitor is struck by the masses of rounded sandstone and white quartz pebbles in the red soil. What does the geological map tell us? Sheet 295 (Taunton) shows a 'bird' symbol plus a '2'; this represents a '2nd Terrace River Deposit'. These are gravels which are shown to lie on Permo-Triassic red, silty mudstones (Mercia Mudstone Group). These mudstones do not normally contain gravels, unlike the Budleigh Salterton Pebble Beds. Where have they come from?

They clearly resemble rocks found in the Brendon Hills and Exmoor. The topographic map shows that present-day streams drain from the northwest and it seems likely that these gravels have been derived from the northwest. However, nearby present-day rivers stand at 25m OD whereas Norton Hillfort is higher at 50m OD. Thus the hilltop represents the remains of a gravel-covered valley floor before denudation excavated the adjacent river valleys down to their present-day levels. These terrace gravels are associated with Palaeolithic flint implements and woolly mammoth, woolly rhinoceros and reindeer. In other words they date from the Pleistocene Ice Age.

Note that similar pebbles, derived from yet older rock formations, are found in the Permo-Triassic formations between the Quantocks and the Brendon Hills. It is possible that the pebbles have been recycled several times over geological time.

Please keep to the paths and be careful not to damage the site or the plants growing on it. This is a protected Scheduled Ancient Monument. It is illegal to damage it in any way, or to use a metal detector on it without written permission from the Secretary of state for the National Heritage.

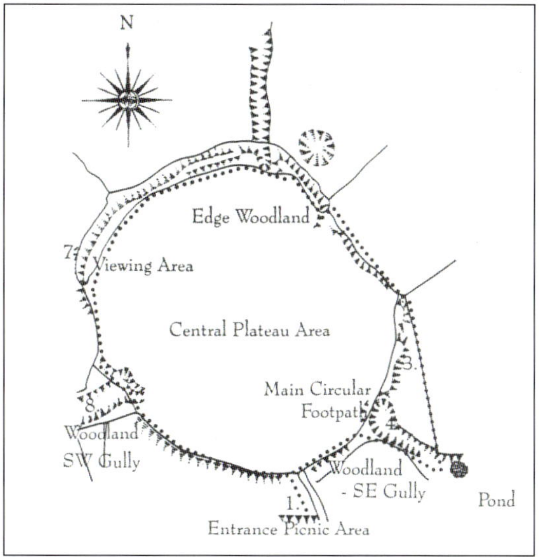

FIG 23.1 TBDC Plan of the Norton Hillfort Nature Trail

Chapter 24
Nynehead

(ST 1322) - Church - Quartz boulders - Otter Sandstone in Nynehead holloway

Church

The church of All Saints has a good display of the local red Permo-Triassic rocks as well as many other interesting architectural features.

Quartz boulders

There is an unusual wall, at the road junction below the holloway, built of white quartz blocks which are thought to have come from the Morte Slates Formation in the Brendon Hills. Heat and pressure during the Variscan Orogeny resulted in silica being mobilised at depth. The silica was later redeposited in the crumpled slates and now occurs as veins and irregular masses. They frequently come to the surface and are struck by ploughs when the surrounding slates break down through weathering processes. They are virtually indestructible. They are often dumped at the edge of fields or now sit on walls as here.

Otter Sandstone in Nynehead holloway

The red sandstones can be examined in the deep holloway east of Nynehead Church. The visitor can use a handlens and fingers to assess the grain size. Are the grains well-worn and rounded, or angular?

Weathering has etched out the outlines of quite steep, thin, concave upwards cross-beds, the slopes of which suggest variable current directions (cf with the sedimentary structures in Figure 21.2). Note the thickness of the sandstone units which can be picked out where finer grained, less well-cemented beds have suffered weathering. Note how the bases of the sandstone units cut down, and across, underlying sandstone beds.

The sedimentary features can be translated into a picture of shallow, swirling currents depositing and eroding unconsolidated sediment in shifting channels. Multi-channelled, braided rivers were moving much of the sandy sediment by traction as bedload across an alluvial plain or fan. Mineralogical comparisons suggest that some of the sediment may have been derived from rocks to the west. The sandstones seen in the Nynehead holloway represent a net accretion of 27m of sediment. It is probable that a lot more sand and gravel was deposited only to be subsequently removed by erosion. The geological record is very fragmentary; the rocks that we study today are those which happened to survive.

These sandstones are mapped as the 'Upper Sandstones' on the Wellington map but the term is now supplanted by 'Otter Sandstone' on Sheet 295 Taunton. These sandstones are now included in the Sherwood Sandstone Group of rock formations. These extend eastwards at depth under Dorset to Hampshire. These beds underlie the finer-grained Mercia Mudstone Group which crops out to the east around Taunton.

The holloway presents a paradox: the walls are strong enough to maintain vertical sides and yet erosion has created the deep cutting! The sands grains are held together with a cement of calcium carbonate and tend not to get waterlogged; hence the sides are less likely to slump which would happen if they were composed of clay. On the other hand carts and feet of animals would have pounded the sandstone in the days before the tarmac was laid; the loosened sand grains would then have been swept down the steep slope when there was heavy rainful. Soil erosion on the Otter Sandstone continues to cause problems in this part of Taunton Deane: fields lose their topsoil, roads are covered with the red sands, and the Environment Agency regard the increased sediment load in rivers as a serious pollutant. The increased use of headlands for nature conservation may serve to trap sediment before it reaches the rivers.

Chapter 25
Otterford and the Blackdown Plateau

(ST 2214) - Otterford Church and Otterhead Nature Trail - The Upper Greensand at Chard - Soils and Vegetation Tertiary deposits on the East Devon Plateau - Churchstanton church and the iron pits.

Otterford Church and Otterhead Nature Trail

The church of St Leonard stands alone by a farm, where sheep graze in the churchyard. Ham Hill Stone table tombs stand in disarray. The walls of the church are mainly coarse chert rubble. There are the usual Ham Hill Stone dressings and Blue Lias flooring. In addition there are blocks of a pale whitish, fine-grained, calcareous sandstone with cross-bedding as in the doorway at the base of the tower. This is the Calcareous Grit from quarries in the top part of the Upper Greensand in the Chard area.

There is a popular walk along the Somerset Wildlife Trust's Otterhead Nature Trail. Park at ST 225 141 and follow the trail for 150 m to the old pit in the Upper Greensand, on the left of the track, shown in Figure 25.1. Examine the soft yellow-brown and green, glauconitic Foxmould Sands. These are overlain by Head: a mixture of chert and sands derived from the higher beds of the Greensand which sludged downslope over Ice Age permafrost during summer thaws. This mixture covers many valley slopes in the Blackdowns. The cherts, being composed of silica, are almost indestructible.

TDBC's Otterford Parish Circular Walk Set 2 No. 17 Otterford traverses both the plateau and the steep sided valleys. Note the incised goyle made by the upper reaches of the River Yarty.

Otterford and Otterhead are set in one of Britain's most significant landforms, namely the plateau feature which extends from the Blackdown escarpment south of Taunton to the English Channel. And not for nothing is the area classed as an Area of Outstanding Natural Beauty with its quiet hidden valleys cut deep into the plateau. Motorists experience either long straight roads along the ridges or circuitous, steep narrow lanes when crossing the valleys. The Countryside Commission has produced a useful landscape assessment of the Blackdown Hills landscape (Cobham Resource Consultants, 1989). Analysis of regional character is now an important part of the planning process and marks a return to the regional studies favoured by geographers in the 1930s.

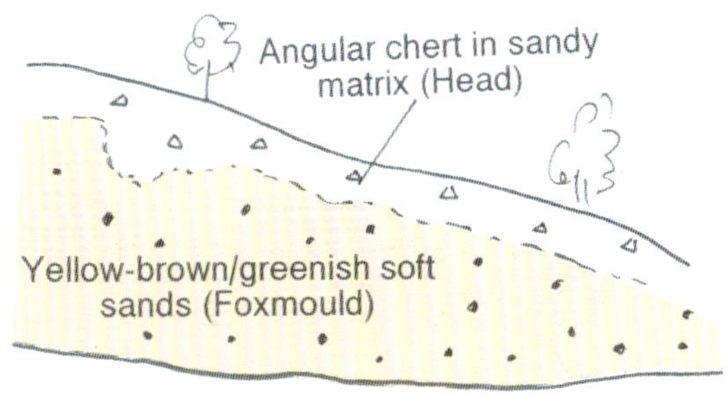

FIG 25.1 Exposure of cherty head over Upper Greensand Foxmould

The Upper Greensand at Chard

The engraving of Snowdon Hill quarry in Figure 25.2, just to the west of Chard, will help the reader to visualise the arrangement of beds in the Upper Greensand. Dark lines of chert nodules can be seen in the lower part of the quarry face (1). They are imbedded in a sand partly composed of very small grains of shell debris (a shell sand). This was a source of building stone with rather poor weathering qualities.

FIG 25.2 Snowdon Hill quarry, Chard. (Woodward 1887)

1. Chert Beds 13' seen.
2. Calcareous Sandstone 7-8'.
3 & 4. Lower Chalk 14' seen.

The lightly shaded beds (2) above the chert are the main source of the building stone used for buttresses and window dressings in many local churches. It is also variously referred to as the Calcareous or Eggardon Grit- a well-cemented calcareous sandstone. Bishop Jocelyn's Charter of 1235 fixed the boundary of the west (Snowdon Hill) side of the Borough of Chard at the 'Staunsmiths' or 'stone-masons. Estate documents of 1424 referring to Chard Parsonage mention that 'freestone' was bought for the the quoins and two masons were paid 5d a day for two days for making the quoins. The Lower Chalk (4) at the top was dug for lime burning.

Readers who are interested in the geology of the Chard area are recommended to seek a copy of *Chard: three aspects of its history* (Chard History Group publication) from which the historical information is taken. It is available at Chard Museum. There is also a delightful book written by John Jones, a local school master in 1860: *Rambles round Chard with a hammer*. There is a copy in the Somerset Studies Library in Taunton.

The quarry face shows vertical cracks which open downwards. These are gulls formed as a result of the foundering of the Upper Greensand and Chalk. This may be the result of the latter sliding over the underlying Liassic clays as in Figure 28.6. However, recent studies of similar features on the Isle of Portland have indicated that flow, or extrusion, of the underlying clays may also be partly responsible (Brunsden, 1996). The Foxmould Sands occur below the Chert Beds and commonly give rise to springs and see pages where they overlie impermeable strata. Waterlogging is yet another reason for the Greensand hills to be ringed with landslips.

Snowdon Hill quarry is a geological Site of Special Scientific Importance. Today, it is heavily overgrown and illustrates the problem of maintaining such sites both for research and to illustrate the all-important rocks below our feet.

Soils and vegetation

Collinson, in 1791, wrote:

> The country here is rough and hilly, but has some good land, which is mostly arable. A great deal is common land, covered with furze and heath, and full of coarse yellow and reddish flints. In some parts which are boggy are found curious mosses.

But we must turn to De la Beche (1839) for a fuller account:

> The chalk and green sand are, indeed, generally so completely covered by the gravels...that those parts, represented in the maps as composed of these rocks, afford a very common agricultural character, and cannot on the whole be considered fertile. Downs of heath and furze are very common upon these gravels; and those portions cultivated as arable land abound in flints and fragments of chert. The gravels also frequently contain much clayey matter intermingled with them, so that water does not readily percolate through them, and black

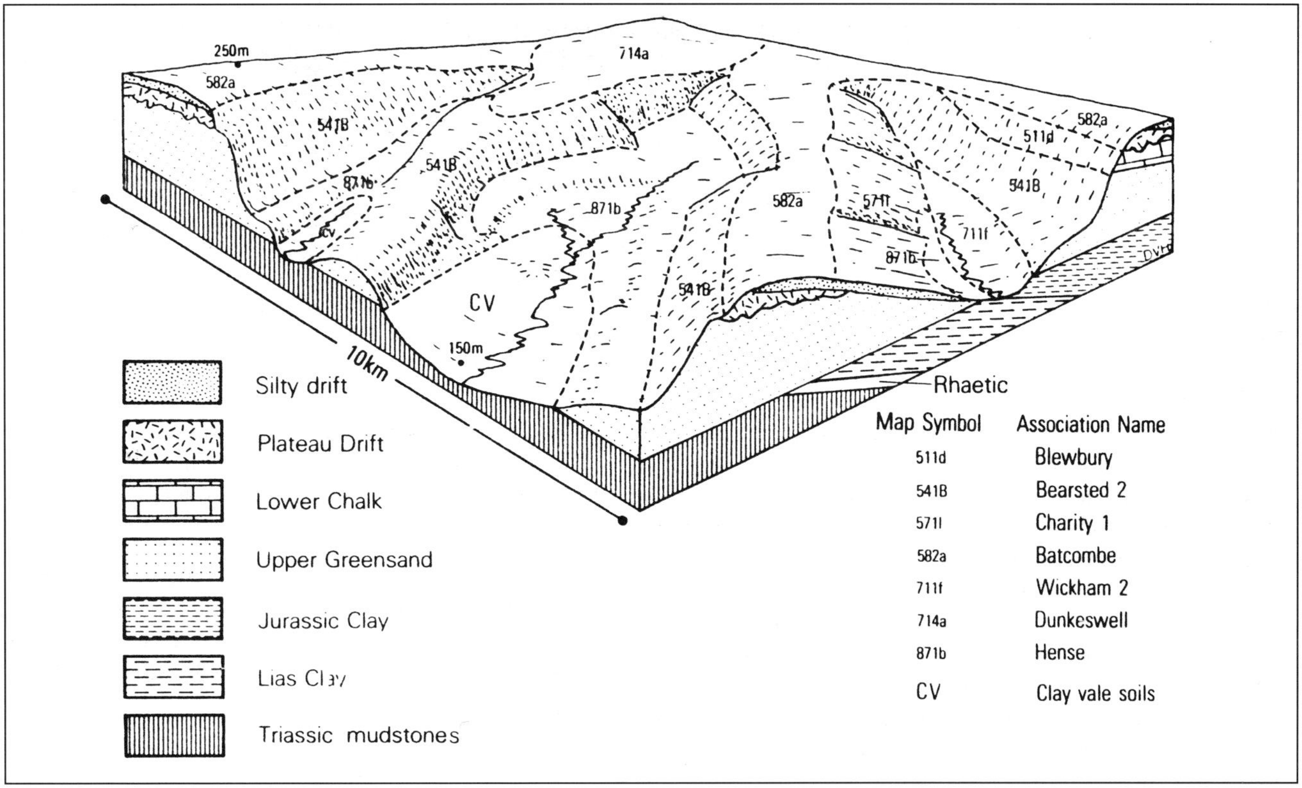

(Findlay et al., 1984 by kind permission of Soil Survey and Land Research Centre, Cranfield University).

FIG 25.3 Soil associations on the East Devon Plateau

peaty soils are often observed. In places where marls, probably the remains of the plastic clay beds, are found near the surface, the agricultural character of the land above the chalk and green sand is much improved, and the country more fertile. In those situations in the Black Downs, where the gravels have not descended thickly spread over the sides of the hills upon the red marls, or lias, beneath the green sand, the contrast offered between the agricultural condition of the country, upon the one and the other, is remarkably striking; indeed a well-marked line of heath and common nearly coincides with the division between the two rocks.

Much of the land has been reclaimed for agriculture but the steep slopes, often with the 'rough and tumble' landslip features together with see pages at the base of the Greensand limit opportunities for farming. *Nature's place: a nature conservation strategy for Devon*, (Chorlton, 1994) published by Devon County Council includes the following summary:

> A number of humid heathland sites survive on the flat plateau of the Blackdown Ridges, particularly where these are associated with areas of common land, while significant number of species-rich grasslands and springline mires are found on the slopes beneath. Small areas of ancient woodland are widely distributed on the steep slopes and at the heads of valleys which, together with long-established hedgerow pattern, serves to highlight the contrast between the 'ancient countryside' of the valley slopes and bottoms and the planned countryside of the Parliamentary enclosures on the high land.

The various soils found in the Blackdown Hills are shown in the idealised block diagram in Figure 25.3 reproduced from *Soils and their use in South West England* to which reference should be made for more detailed information. Brief references are made to the soils in the explanatory notes to Figure A1 (Appendix A). Readers can work out the topographical and geological settings of the various soils. For example, 714a Dunkeswell Association is found on the Greensand hilltops; 871b is on the lower slopes of valley sides and escarpments where the Greensand overlies less permeable rocks which results in see pages (see the chapter entitled *Wellington and the Blackdowns).*

Tertiary deposits on the East Devon Plateau

The Wellington geological map shows that the ridge tops are coloured brown and marked with the sign for Clay-with-Flints. The latter contains the residue of chert and flint weathered out of the underlying Upper Greensand and the Chalk. De la Beche (1839) explains:

> Judging from the accumulation of flints in several places, the quantity of chalk once existing over parts of this district.....must have been considerable. From the unrolled condition of a large proportion of the flints in the neighbourhood of Lyme Regis, Sidmouth, Chard, and many parts of the Black Downs, we are led to suppose that the chalk in which they were once embedded may have been quietly removed from among them, and that these flints have been let down nearly in places above which they occurred in the chalk.

In addition, there are masses of tough, rounded, water-worn flint and chert cobbles together with brown sandstone and white quartz pebbles. Some 3 m of cobbles were visible some years ago in the backscar of a landslip to the north east of the Holman Clavel pub (ST 227 164). The rock face almost resembled a beach deposit; some cobbles were 30 cm long.

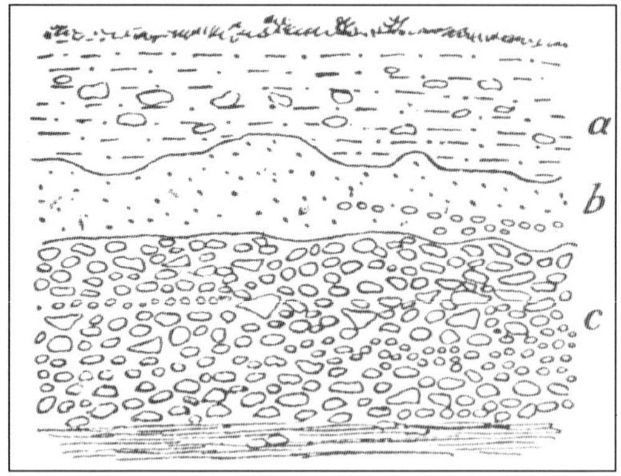

(Ussher, 1906).

FIG 25.4 Pit in Tertiary gravel, north of Burnworthy Farm, north-east of Churchstanton.

a. Reddish-brown loam with quartz pebbles 3-4'.
b. Reddish-brown sand with impersistent seam of water-worn quartz pebbles 2-3'.
c. Gravel of irregular quartz pebbles in clayey matrix plus angular chert 5'.

The rocks represented by these gravels are similar to those found in Devon and Cornwall. Today they lie isolated on the plateau hilltops. They must have been introduced into the area before the present river system and valleys came into being; otherwise the pebbles could not have got across the deep valleys that exist today. Look out for these pebbles especially on North Down (ST 2215), Combe Beacon (ST 2912), Windwhistle Hill (ST 3909). These deposits are quite substantial as is shown by Ussher's sketch reproduced in Figure 25.4.

The gravels and sands would seem to date from the early part of the Tertiary Period when there was low relief and large quantities of abrasion-resistant gravel and sands were on the move. Whilst they may have been moved by rivers at some stage, the consensus seems to be that they mark a marine transgression (Waters, 1960). Where Chalk is present they rest on typical reddish Clay-with-Flints which in turn occupies 'egg box' type depressions, or pipes, in the underlying Chalk. The deep pitting of the Chalk is thought to be the result of chemical decomposition

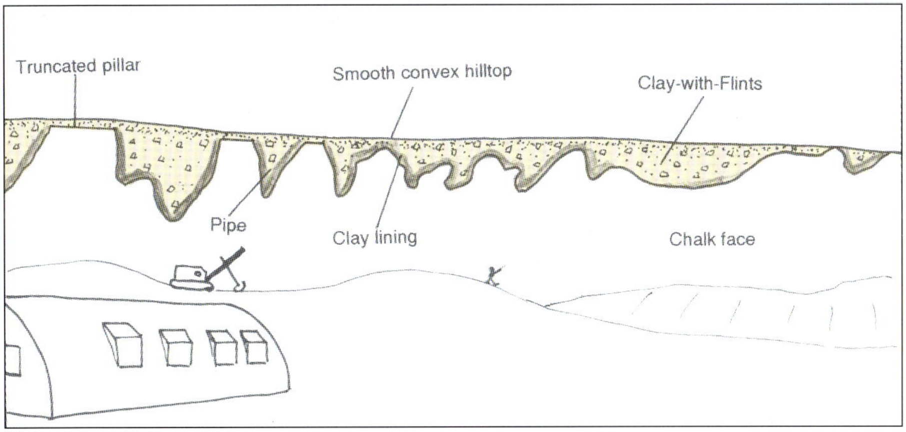

FIG 25.5 Truncated 'pipes' displayed in the Chalk quarry at Beer, Devon.

of the Chalk in a sub-tropical climate and was well-displayed in the old Chalk quarry at Beer in Devon, a sketch of which is shown in Figure 25.5.

The outlines of the pipes are determined both by their shape and how they are cut by the quarry face. The pipes are lined with chocolate-coloured stiff clays; the remainder is a mass of angular flint debris and sand. The surface few metres have been rearranged and partly removed by periglacial processes. The absence of collapse features on the smooth skyline indicates that the pipes are mainly an inactive 'fossil' feature.

The sands and gravels are also found overlying the Upper Greensand outcrops. Ussher (1906) also mentions 'a dark drab-coloured clay without stones' and suggests that these clays may be Tertiary material in situ. Early writers such as De la Beche refer to the 'plastic clay series'.

It was common for students of landforms, some 40-50 years ago, to see staircases of marine planation surfaces, i.e. bevelled hilltops, throughout the West Country. These concepts are now largely discredited. However, the view westward from Golden Cap on the Dorset coast is impressive; the hilltops merge into a level skyline which cuts across Greensand, Chalk and older rocks further west in Devon. The Blackdown Plateau can lay strong claims to be an eroded planation surface; that is, the product of long-lasting denudational processes.

Marine Tertiary sediments lie at over 300 m OD on the Blackdowns and, at the same time, occur below sea level in the adjacent English Channel. These variations in altitude are too great to be explained by the rise and fall of sea levels. There must have been differential vertical movements of the earth's crust. The present height of the Blackdown Plateau is the result of uplift.

The Blackdown Plateau owes its preservation to the resistant capping of Upper Greensand and Chalk. The surrounding clay lowlands provide an indication of the enormous amount of rock that has since been removed; views across the Vale of Taunton Deane from Cothelstone Hill, or from Eggardon Hill in Dorset across the Vale of Marshwood, speak volumes. Periglacial mass wasting has undoubtedly shifted enormous amounts of rock waste during the Pleistocene Ice Age.

Churchstanton Church and the iron pits

Churchstanton Church stands isolated but served by a number of lanes and footpaths which reflect the dispersed settlement pattern of hamlets and farms so typical of the neighbouring county of Devon. Do not be put off by the drab rendering of the tower; there is much of interest both inside and outside the church (Pevsner, 1958; Bush, 1994).

Buttresses, window dressings and arcade are constructed of Calcareous Grit from the Upper Greensand. There is a Ham Hill Stone doorway and the flooring is Blue Lias slabs. The walls are chert, again from the Upper Greensand. Chert is easily dismissed as hard and unfriendly, especially when it is grey throughout but look again: as at Otterhead Church the chert displays a range of warm yellows, browns and reddish tinges, colours associated with staining by iron compounds. The staining is probably caused by the presence of iron compounds in the Upper Greensand. There is also a block of dark reddish-brown fine, subangular sandstone set into the southwest corner of the porch and another in a nearby buttress; they are heavily impregnated with iron.

The transactions and proceedings of the Victorian archaeological and natural history societies are mines of information and accessible in the Somerset Studies Library in Taunton. Hutchinson, in the *Transactions of the Devonshire Association,* records 'iron pits' on the Blackdown Plateau and evidence of smelting. Admittedly it is possible that some of the these pits may have been dug for chert, or sandstones for making scythstones.

Hutchinson records that a Mr James Blackmore of Clivehays, Churchstanton, wrote to a Mr Heineken, August 5th, 1865, that all the extent of Blackdown in his neighbourhood was once worked for surface iron. "My father a few years since dug out several tons of the ore from a space about ten feet square, and it is now besides the wall" (Hutchinson, 1872).

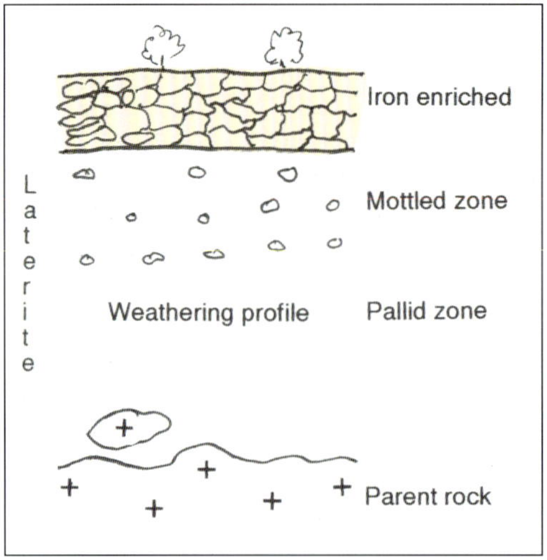

FIG 25.6 Typical tropical weathering profile with ferruginous crust

These iron-enriched deposits may be associated with tropical weathering and lateritic deep-weathering profiles. Figure 25.6 is based on recent research and shows a typical tropical weathering profile (Ollier, 1991). Laterite is a reddish-coloured weathered material of the mottled zone in a deep weathering profile which is sufficiently hard to be used for building purposes. Ferruginously-cemented (iron-rich) deposits may be formed in a wide range of situations and climates.

Iron-rich deposits can occur as vesicular, concretionary or massive forms. The preferred areas for iron deposition in tropical landscapes are the lower slopes of valleys at the upper surface of the water table where oxidation of reduced ferrous iron in solution readily occurs. Iron is brought in by lateral groundwater movement. Crusts often form in material lying unconformably above varied rock types or weathering profiles (Ollier, 1991).

It has to be appreciated that the Tertiary sediments, preserved on the present-day hilltops, were originally deposited in valleys at the time of deposition. Isaac has described and analysed the effects of Tertiary weathering, including a lateritic profile, in the old railway cutting at Combpyne near Lyme Regis (ST 300 923 to 306 923) (Isaac 1981, 1983).

The iron ores, and associated evidence for smelting activity, are the subject of current research among historians and archaeologists. There is a need to record all occurrences of the iron, and especially any exposures of iron in situ.

In 1882 the Rev W. Downes questioned, perhaps unfairly, some of Hutchinson's ideas about iron smelting. However, he did provide more information about the iron deposits on the hilltop above Ponchydown:

> The side of the pit was about two and a half feet in height. The first foot from the surface was of peaty soil, containing a few small pieces of ore. Downward the ore was more plentiful and in larger pieces, mixed with both chert and chalk-flints, the whole being enclosed in a matrix of highly ferruginous earth. The ore seemed to extend downwards below the base of the pit, but we had not with us the means of working for it deeper....I do not hesitate therefore to call it 'vesicular limonite.' It is found filling up interstices in the gravel, and principally in the chert gravel. It is found in pieces varying from the size of a nut to boulders weighing from 1 to 2 cwt. All alike have the same delusive resemblance to slag.

Thus the interests of the geologist, geomorphologist, local historian and industrial archaeologist all come together in the study of the Blackdown iron ores.

Chapter 26
Pitminster

(ST 2219) - Church - Chert and flint head - Blue Lias Escarpment.

Church

Chert rubble walling is widespread in the older buildings in the village as well as in the church of St Mary and St Andrew; a reflection of the location amid large quantities of chert head spread over adjacent hillsides. Chert was also dug from the Upper Greensand on the Blackdowns. Note the greenish-grey, cross-bedded North Curry Sandstone in the porch dressings. Inside the church one can compare the two alabaster memorials: John Colles and wife, on the north side, is East Midlands alabaster whilst John Colles the grandson, on the south side, is Somerset alabaster from Watchet. The latter shows both the blotchy and black varieties of Somerset alabaster. The font is Beer Stone. Look out for the sarsen stone near the Queen's Arms.

Chert and flint head

In 1839 De la Beche commented upon the mass of chert and flint that is spread over the Blackdown footslopes:

> On the north and north-east of the Black Downs there is much gravel composed of chalk-flint and green-sand chert distributed over the red sand stone series and lias...The greater part so occurs that we can scarcely explain its transport from the adjoining high lands by means of river drainage such as we now see.

The processes by which the flint and chert have been spread far and wide would still be a mystery were it not for the widening of intellectual horizons since 1839 to include the climate and landforming processes found in places such as Spitsbergen today. The following descriptions taken from *The first crossing of Spitsbergen* by W. M. Conway may help the reader to visualise the conditions:

> When the thaw sets in and lasts all 24 hours of one day after another it reduces the snow for a considerable depth to mere slush...a stream which by the end of August will be dry, digs into a slope a gully of astonishingly great depth or forms on the flat a fan of wide extent, rendered by countless channels......As the ground beneath is released from its water bondage, the whole becomes softer and less stable. Thus it flows rather than falls, to the valleys below, where it comes to relative repose......Farther up the hillsides one can watch the process whereby the mud is formed out of the soft horizontally bedded rocks of which the hills are built. Melting snow and splitting frost loosen and crack the slabs into a mere slope of debris, all rotten and ready again to split and resplit.

Similar processes would have prevailed in Somerset during periglacial* conditions some 20,000 years ago especially during the great thaw which ended the last cold period. This was the time when the extensive landslides of the Blackdowns were in active mode similar to those at Charmouth today. Recent newspaper reports associate a recent rise in the temperature of the ground ice in Alaska with extensive slumping and ground movement with catastrophic effects on roads and buildings.

We hear a lot about global warming but there may be an alternative scenario waiting in the wings: melting ice in the Arctic might upset the circulation pattern in the North Atlantic with the result that the warm waters from the tropics might be replaced by cold Arctic water. This could reinvigorate hillslope mass wastage processes e.g. solifluction and slides. The effects of these processes can also be seen at Thurloxton (Chapter 32)

The headwaters of many streams have dug deeply into the unconsolidated head and lower beds of the Upper Greensand on the Blackdown slopes to produced deep V-shaped goyles*. Some are over 30' deep.

The Blue Lias Escarpment

The section below the Wellington geological map (Sheet 311) shows that the Upper Greensand cuts across the underlying Lower Lias, White Lias and Permo-Triassic rocks; an indication that the latter were tilted and eroded before the advent of the Greensand sediments. The White and Blue Lias dip to the southeast and therefore the outcrop runs from northeast to southwest. The fine escarpment meets the east-west escarpment capped by the Upper Greensand at an oblique angle south of Corfe. Blue Lias underlies the golf course at Pickeridge Hill and continues southward to the coast at Lyme Regis.

TDBC's Pitminster No 2 Parish Circular Walk traverses the Liassic escarpment at Woodram Copse. Look for fragments of White Lias along the tracks. TDBC's Pitminster No 3 Parish Circular Walk leads to the Upper Greensand.

Chapter 27
Plainsfield

(ST 1936) - Pepperhill Farm-Devonian Limestones-Cockercombe Tuff

(Courtesy: M Fry).

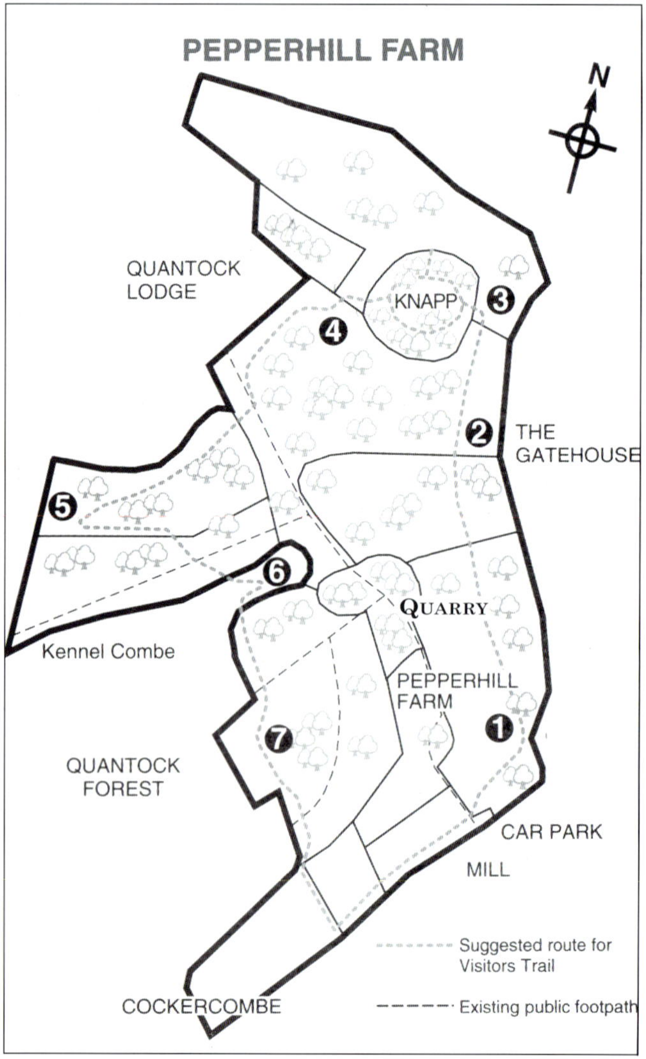

Pepperhill Farm

There is an attractive ramble at Plainsfield through the former parkland of Lord Taunton. It is on the north-east side of the Quantocks where the deep valleys of the latter meet the lowland underlain by Permo-Triassic rocks. Access is supported by the co-operative farmer and MAFF under a Countryside Stewardship Scheme. The map in the Visitors' Guide is reproduced in Figure 27.1 and should be available at the car park (ST 1929 3690).

The quarry at Pepperhill (Stop 1 ST 1933 3698) in the Visitor's Guide is in Devonian Roadwater Limestone and shows massive grey limestone with calcareous sandstone and variegated red and green slates (Edmonds and Williams, 1985). The geological map shows that the hill is surrounded by Permo-Triassic Otter Sandstone. The problem for the geologist mapping the area is to decide whether the hill is a relict of the original Triassic topography that was buried by sandy sediment (Otter Sandstone), or is the sandstone let down by faulting against the Devonian limestone? There is no access to this quarry.

The impressive Gatehouse at Stop 2 (ST 1938 3738) is built of grey-green Cockercombe Tuff*, Bath Stone* (showing calcareous, grain-supported ooliths and skeletal debris), and blotchy red/buff Otter Sandstone. Note that the latter can have poor weathering qualities and is used under the archway.

Fig 27.1
Pepperhill Farm: Visitors Trail and existing footpaths.

FIG 27.2 Overturned syncline in the Rodhuish Limestone at Pepperhill.

Devonian Limestones

Proceed from the Gatehouse via Stops 3 and 4 and turn left onto the footpath, marked in black, that leads to Pepperhill Farm. There is an old quarry shortly to the right in a copse. It is illustrated in Figure 27.2 (ST 1898 3721).

The sketch, taken from the memoir for the Taunton Sheet (Edmonds et al., 1985), shows the Rodhuish Limestone in an overturned syncline; the axial plane of the fold is inclined at 20° to the southeast. It is difficult to visualise the massive bed of limestone being bent as we see it today. Surface rocks tend to be brittle and would shatter if bent. It is much easier to imagine the rocks being deformed if they were deeply buried at depths where temperature and pressure were much higher than at the surface. The fold is the result of broadly N-S compressive forces active during the Variscan Orogeny. Notice how the thin, slaty calcareous rocks underlying and overlying the massive limestone are depicted in Figure 27.2. The hatching represents cleavage parallel to the axial plane* of the fold. The cleavage could easily be mistaken for bedding.

There are a number of abandoned limestone quarries on the eastern side of the Quantocks, most of which are on private land. The significance of the beds of limestone is that they mark a change from periods of large inputs of sediment (mud, silt and sand) to periods of shallow, lime-rich seas with corals. They were worked in the past to make lime and for building stone.

There are some small karstic features in the area such as the cave whose entrance is shown in Figure 27.3 (Crosse, 1852). The entrance to the cave lies in an old quarry 'cut in massive grey sandy crinoidal limestone with some argillaceous limestone and calcareous slates' (Edmonds and Williams, 1985). The relative thinness of these Devonian limestones tends to restrict the size of the caves compared to those in the Carboniferous Limestone of the Mendips.

Crosse describes the crystalline deposits of aragonite and 'common carbonate of lime' on the walls of the fissures in the cave. The processes, by which these minerals are deposited, fascinated Crosse and he describes various experiments using electric currents. He also tells us that 'the aragonite would be slowly increasing were it not for the depredations committed on it for some time past by collectors of specimens, who, not contented with fracturing it in all directions, have partially blackened the roof by the smoke of candles'. Unhappily, vandalism has continued. The cave is on private land; it is essential that permission to visit sites is sought from the landowners. Bryant (1959) provides further information and references.

(Crosse, 1852).

FIG 27.3 Cave entrance and old quarry at Holwell

Cockercombe Tuff

There is an interesting outcrop of volcanic rock in Keeper's Combe-the Cockercombe Tuff. Climb back over the stile and proceed up the valley past the cottages and take the second forestry road which bends back sharply on the right-hand side. Samples of the green volcanic rock can be collected from the roadside; the green colour is due to the presence of the mineral chlorite*.

The old quarry is not readily accessible; it is overgrown and entry is not recommended (ST 1825 3710). However, the memoir for the Taunton Sheet provides useful details of what could be seen and the following quotation will serve as an example of the technical style of writing found in the geological memoirs which are invaluable sources of information:

> An old quarry (ST 1825 3719), now fairly overgrown, shows 18 m of massive greyish green oxide-spotted lithic tuff* cut by cleavage planes dipping at 28° to east or east-south-east; some slates are present.
>
> (Edmonds and Williams, 1985, p15).

Translated into simpler terms, this says that there are 18 m of volcanic ash that have suffered compression that resulted in the rock splitting along planes of cleavage. The presence of cleavage means that the volcano erupted before the Variscan Orogeny unlike the Hestercombe diorite which shows no cleavage.

Webby (1966b), who studied the geology of the Brendon Hills and the Quantocks for his doctorate, recovered fossils from the Cockercombe Tuff which indicated that the volcanic ash had accumulated under the sea and refers to the rock as a spilite. A spilite is a volcanic rock of basaltic composition deposited under water. The minerals pyroxene and olivine are replaced by the green mineral chlorite at temperatures of 250°C-300°C which suggests that the sediments were dragged down to depths at which such temperatures are found. The site of the volcano is unknown but it may have had something to do with the presence of minerals in the Quantocks (see Broomfield chapter). The chlorite contributes to the green colour of the rock and can be seen in walls at Plainsfield and those of the Wyndham Gallery at Taunton Museum.

Jeboult (1893) recounts the following concerning interest in the Cockercombe Tuff:

> When Lord Taunton was about to build his mansion, search was made on the estate for a suitable building stone. In a quarry close by was found this hard, greyish green rock, capable of being worked by the chisel. Since then Mr Davis, builder, of Taunton, has discovered that it will take a high polish. Pillars from this stone have been introduced into the new church at Buckland St Mary.......Before its precise nature was known, some of the stone was forwarded to the Government Museum of Practical Geology, and on being examined by Sir Roderick Murchison, it was pronounced to be a volcanic ash.

Jeboult also considers the possibility of whether or not

> ...the same horrifying eruptions which now terrify those who dwell on the slopes of Etna and Vesuvius would ever pour destruction and death over the fertile plains of Taunton Deane....if an estate standing over the very crater of the extinct volcanoes on Quantock should be offered, we would advise them to accept the offer without hesitation, and to occupy and enjoy it in peace.

As pointed out above, the crater(s) from which the ash was ejected have yet to be located.

The return via Stops 6 and 7 (ST 189 369) makes a very pleasant walk.

Chapter 28
Staple Fitzpaine

(ST 2618) - Blue Lias - Church - Sarsens - Castle Neroche and landslides.

Blue Lias

Staple Fitzpaine is on the dip slope of the Blue Lias. Limestones from the latter can be seen in the walls of The Greyhound. Some walls in the area include the small brachiopod* *Calcirhynchia calcaria* (Figure 28.1). Notice how they are scattered haphazardly through the rock which, of course, would have been mud at the time. They do not appear to be in their 'life' positions and this rather suggests that they were incorporated into the mud chaotically; perhaps a storm, influx of mud or earthquake occurred? Please respect the walls. Most of the old quarries have been filled in long ago. However, Figure 2.1 shows a sketch of an old quarry face in Blue and White Lias at Bishopswood a few miles to the south where the limestones were quarried for making lime.

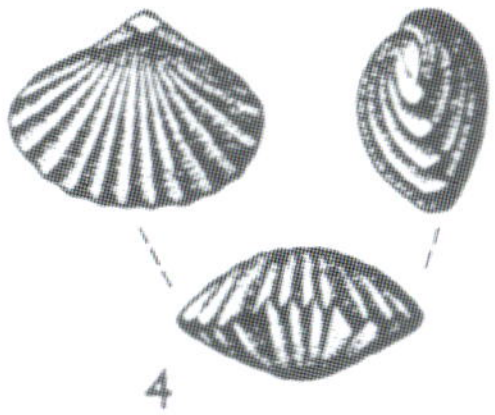

Courtesy Natural History Museum

FIG 28.1. Brachiopod *Calcirynchia calcaria* . S.S. Buckman.

Church

Blue Lias and Ham Hill Stone are seen in the parish church of St Peter. Graham Hutton has written, in *English Parish Churches,* that Somerset stone towers call for special mention including St Mary Magdalene in Taunton (see below) and St Peter at Staple Fitzpaine:

> They all display tall pinnacles, an elaborately worked open parapet, pairs of buttresses clasping the corners, a large west window dwarfing the west door and, in the belfry stage, pairs of windows with perforated tracery instead of common place louvres. (Hutton et al., 1976).

Vivian-Neale has written an account of the heads, carved in stone, which decorate the corbels on the church tower. He suggests that the sculptors were inspired by the livery and personal badges of some of the great families associated with Somerset (Vivian-Neale,1961).

Sarsens

There are superb examples of sarsens*, or silcretes, by the cross-roads in Staple Fitzpaine, at the back of the Greyhound and in nearby fields and stream channels. These are stones up to a metre thick and either tabular or whale-backed. A member of H.M. Geological Survey recounted that one was locally known as the Devil's Stone and adds that 'I was told on the spot by an intelligent native of the neighbouring parish of Curland, that Owd Nick himself put his hands in the holes when he gripped the stone and flung it there, intending no doubt to damage the church, which stands near' (Cameron, 1908). A sarsen from Staple Fitzpaine can be seen in the grounds of the County Museum in Taunton.

The hedges around Curland Common are full of sarsens cleared from the adjoining arable fields (ST 279 168). Many are found by the roadside and where roads and tracks meet. They were possibly used to mark boundaries since they are not easily destroyed. They were widely used in the distant past in buildings and prehistoric monuments such as those at Stonehenge and Avebury especially in places where good stone was not available. There is little evidence for similar uses in southwest Somerset as alternative rocks were available.

In November 1945 Liberator KH126 took off from Merryfield airfield and shortly afterwards crashed into the side of the Blackdown Hills at Hare Lane with the loss of

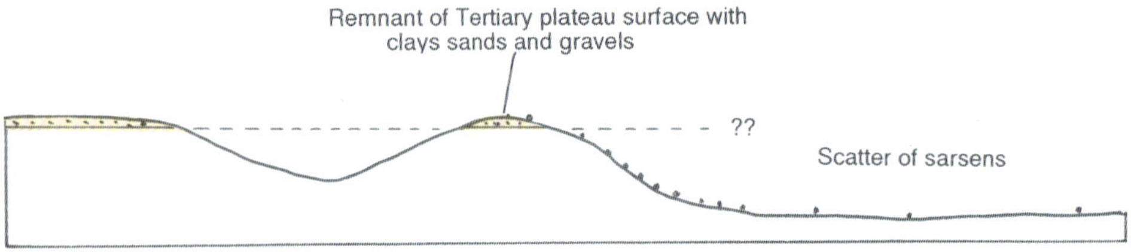

FIG 28.2
Relationship between the present-day location of sarsens and the Tertiary plateau surface.

22 men. A sarsen on the south side of Hare Lane now marks the incident and shows what appears to be an engraving of the American eagle (ST 2772 1550).

Sarsens consist mainly of sand cemented with silica although some show scatters of small, rounded pebbles. Sarsens are relatively resistant to chemical decomposition and physical disintegration in our climate.

Some sarsens are associated with the unsorted mix of clay, sand and chert known as Head which covers many of the hillslopes around Staple Fitzpaine and which flowed downslope (soliflucted) during summer thaws in cold phases of the Ice Age. From this we may infer that the sarsens originated upslope on what are now the Blackdown hilltops. There have been important

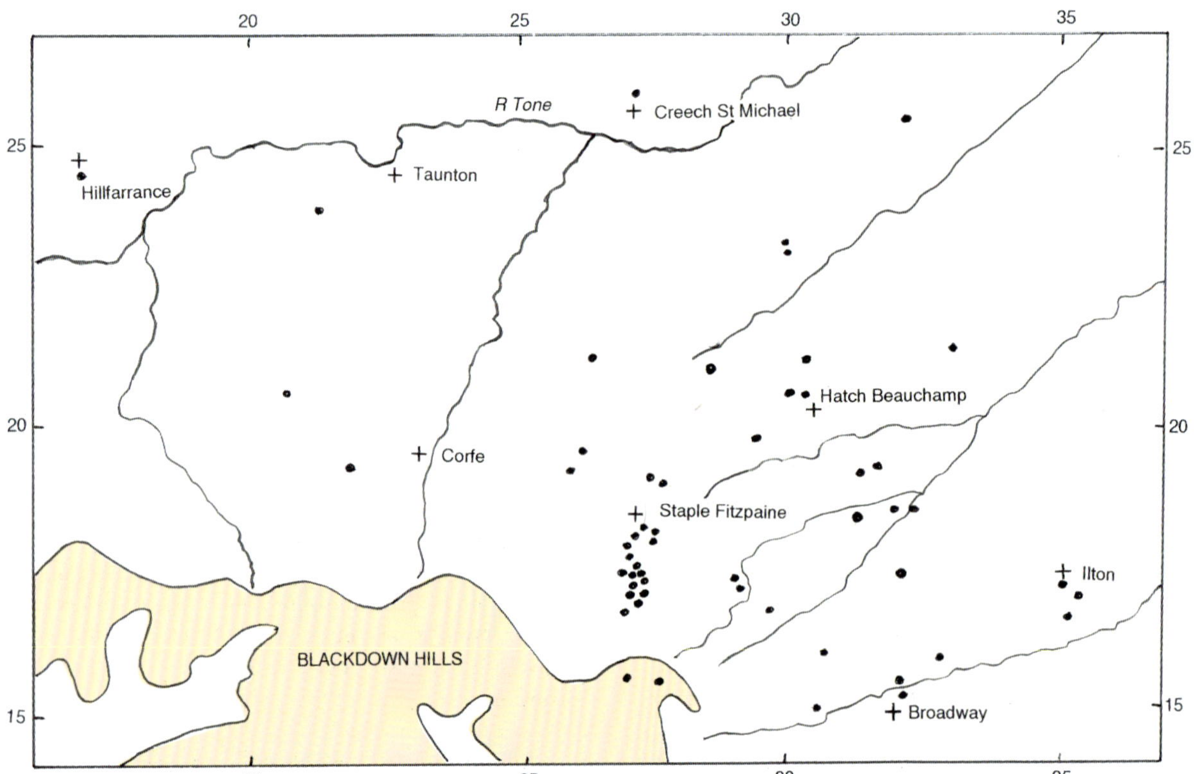

FIG 28.3. Distribution of sarsens in southwest Somerset.

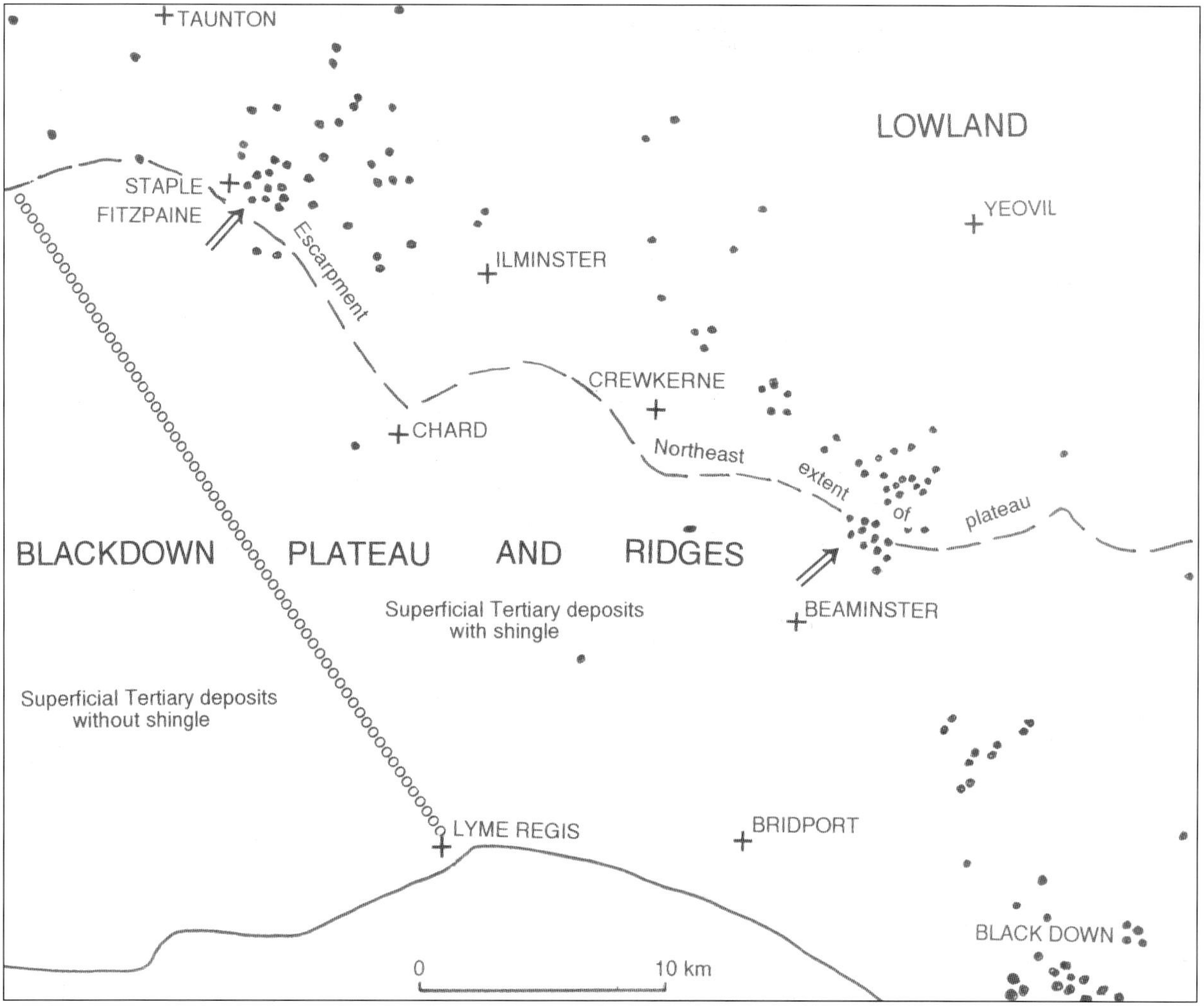

FIG 28.4. Distribution of sarsens in southwest Somerset and West Dorset.

downslope transfers of sarsens both at Staple Fitzpaine and near Beaminster, as shown in Figure 28.4, where the extensive outcrops of clays have facilitated the movement of rock waste away from the plateau. The Black Down sarsens, however, are situated on Chalk and would probably not have been rafted so far as those on the clay outcrops. It would seem that most silcretes have been moved by hillslope processes from the positions where they originated.

Studies of African and Australian silcretes (or duricrusts), very similar in appearance to the Somerset and Dorset sarsens, have provided clues as to how and where they formed (see Nash et al., 1998; Ullyott et al., 1998; Hepworth, 1998). They appear to develop in two situations:

a. As part of distinctive weathering profiles produced by wet and dry phases in a tropical climate where silica was both mobilised and precipitated near the landsurface.

b In valleys where silica was precipitated by evaporating groundwater resulting in linear accumulations of silica-cemented sediments.

The sarsens in Somerset and Dorset seem to have most in common with the latter group which would indicate that sands and pebbles, deposited in low-lying troughs or pans, were cemented as a result of the concentration of silica near the surface. Many sarsens show tubular hollows which are thought to have been occupied by plant stems.

Figure 28.4 shows the distribution of sarsens in south Somerset and west Dorset and raises interesting questions. There appear to be clusters at Staple Fitzpaine, near Beaminster and west of Dorchester at Black Down near the Hardy Monument. There is a broad NW-SE trend. Was this the trace of a river system flowing from the northwest? One has to remember that areas of the Blackdowns which are hilltops today were once lowland basins where sediments collected.

One curiosity is that a continuation of the NW-SE Cothelstone Fault, shown on Figure 28.5, would broadly follow the trace of sarsens although authors vary as to whether it does so continue to the Weymouth area. There has been lateral and vertical movement along this fault at varying times and one might surmise that movement on the fault might have warped the landsurface so as to affect the sedimentation and drainage.

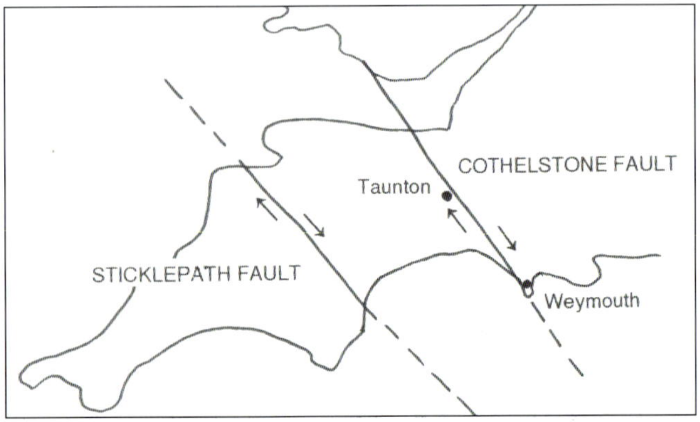

FIG 28.5 Major NW-SE trending faults

A collection of sarsens can be seen at Plantlife's Ryewater Reserve southeast of Crewkerne; a field at the western end of the reserve shows scattered sarsens breaking surface and represents a remnant that has not been cleared for the plough; it is wet, heavy clay country (ST 5085 0645). Sarsens have fallen into the river bed where the streams have undercut the banks.

There is additional information about local sarsens and their occurrence in Prudden (1987).

Castle Neroche and landslides

The active landslides at Charmouth and Lyme Regis have their counterpart in 'fossil' landslides in the Blackdowns. Typical features are shown in Figure 28.6. Instability results from the combination of steep slopes, weak underlying clays and the pressure of water at the base of the Upper Greensand.

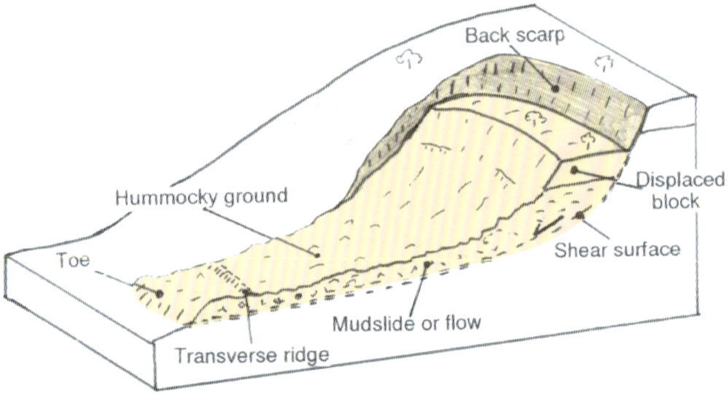

FIG 28.6. Topographic features of landslides

The Blackdown landslides are mostly inactive today, apart from small failures on lower slopes where streams are undercutting the sides of channels as alongside the River Ding (ST 292 146). The large-scale slumping on the Blackdowns may have occurred as ground ice rapidly melted with climatic warming after a cold phase during the Pleistocene Period. Also, the latest thinking suggests that the incompetent clays may have been partially extruded thus leading to the subsidence of the overlying rock.

The coastal landslides are active today because undercutting by the sea steepens the cliff gradients. The account of the west Dorset coast in the Geographical Association's Classic Landform series provides an excellent description and explanation of these features (Brunsden and Goudie, 1997).

The country immediately to the south of Staple Fitzpaine is one of the best areas for exploring the Blackdown escarpment. One can either take to the public footpaths or park on the top at Castle Neroche (ST 2725 1562). TDBC's *Country Walks around Taunton Set 1 No. 5 Castle Neroche* provides a ready made walk. Those who walk will no doubt pass sarsen stones and soils rich in chert debris. The hummocky ground of the lower footslopes indicates fossil mudslides; whilst above these there are indications of rotational slides with wet marshy backslopes. Finally there are the very steep arcuate backscarps where the rotational blocks have pulled away from the ground behind.

There are a number of earthworks at the top including a Norman motte-and-bailey which is perched on the edge of the Greensand backscarp. See Dunning (1995), Adkins (1992) and Davison (1972) for more information. Visitors are recommended to view the landscape from the top of the motte. To the west is Staple Hill and the outline of the Blackdown Escarpment which is joined by the escarpment and dip slope of the Blue Lias. A marked col separates Castle Neroche from Staple Hill where hillslope recession and headwater streams have lowered the drainage divide. To the north the lowland between the Brendon Hills and Quantocks is underlain by Permo-Triassic formations. The southwest side of the Quantocks is a faultline scarp (Watchet-Cothelstone Fault system) where Permo-Triassic beds are let down against rocks of Devonian age as shown in Figure 13.5.

Chapter 29
Stawley

(ST 06 22) - Church and landscape - Pilton Shales - Slate industry

Church and landscape

The fascinating church of St Michael stands remote at the far end of Taunton Deane on a spur overlooking the headwaters of the River Tone and the Devon hill country. Dressings are of Ham Hill Stone and coarse, red sandstone. 'The church is remarkable for possessing an interior practically untouched by the gothic revival or the Oxford Movement' (Eeles, 1935).

Below ground are the grey slates and sandstones of the Pilton Shales. To the east lie the successive outcrops and ridges of the Permo-Triassic formations. To the west are the older rocks of Devonian and Carboniferous age which appear from under the younger Permo-Triassic strata. We are on the transition zone where we pass from 'Lowland Britain' to 'Highland Britain'-that is, from the younger rocks of the east to the generally more resistant rocks of the west. Rock strength is not the only factor that influences the height of the land; the west has tended to rise whilst the east around the North Sea has, and is, tending to sink. But then it gets more complicated-the Bristol and English Channels are areas of downwarping. The general outlines of the British Isles are the result of blocks of crust sinking during and since the Tertiary period.

Jeboult (1873) rhapsodises about the upper reaches of the River Tone:

> The scenery it passes is very beautiful-the hills are full of springs, so green is the grass, so luxuriant is the foliage, and so fine are the numerous ferns and mosses. Many pretty peeps deserve noting, especially at Tracebridge, with its fine slate-quarries and romantic views.

Pilton Shales

The West Deane Way (TDBC, 1999) provides the visitor with a pre-selected route which passes an old exposure in the Pilton Shales in the disused railway cutting near the old viaduct (ST 0550 2458). Planar and cross-laminated fine-grained sandstones occur in beds of variable thickness interpreted as the result of inputs of sediment under low energy conditions. Brown earthy, decalcified limestones show trace fossils (surface tracks) and crinoid columnals. These limestones suggest quiet, sunlit conditions with a lower input of sediment.

The beds dip at 4° to the south-southeast which is a fairly general direction in this area. As a result of the southerly dip the beds appear as east-west belts on the Dulverton geological map. To the north is the outcrop of the Pickwell Down Sandstone which forms the high ground north of Waterrow.

Fallen blocks can be examined but keep clear of the actual quarry face. The beds can also be seen just east of the bridge over the Tone at ST 0545 2475 and by the B3227 south of the Waterrow Inn (ST 0515 2531). The best exposures are to be seen in the cliffs from Morte Point to Croyde Bay in north Devon.

Slate industry

A mile to the south-southeast are the old quarries at Tracebridge which were last worked for slates in 1940 and are now overgrown. The quarries should not be entered. The slates were quarried in the Lower Carboniferous Doddiscombe Beds and can be seen in the old houses of the hamlet and in the car park at the back of the Globe at Appley. Quarrying slate usually involved a lot of waste. Rodwell has researched the industry and describes how the waste material was put to good use for wartime airfields:

> Witnesses report the jagged tops of the rejected stone looked like a range of mountains in misty weather.....Airfields at Dunkeswell and Smeatharpe were planned but the ground at these sites was considered too soft in the winter; the runways might give way under the weight of fully loaded and fuelled four-engined bombers. Large quantities of stone were needed to make a firm foundation to the concrete runways. The piles of waste stone at Tracebridge were deemed suitable and accessible foundation material. (Rodwell, 1984).

Chapter 30
Taunton

(ST 2224) - Rhinoceros in Taunton Deane - St Mary Magdalene - A miscellany of buildings old and new

Rhinoceros in Taunton Deane

In the year 1853, the head and a large number of the bones of the skeleton of a young rhinoceros were found in the alluvial deposit excavated on the site of a portion of the present Taunton Gaol (Wilton). The surrounding debris was evidently washed down from the Blagdon Hills, over the red marl of the Taunton Dean: the fragments of flint and chert mixed up with the marly earth are clear indications of its source...The head of this animal deposited in the Museum, is so perfect with the teeth in their sockets, that there can be no doubt of the species to which it belonged. Professor Quekett has pronounced it to be a young specimen of Rhinoceros tichorinus (Jones, 1856; Ussher, 1906).

(After d'Orbigny)

FIG 30. Skeleton of a Mammoth *(Elephas primigenius)*

Dr Andy Currant, from the British Museum of Natural History in London, has been curating the mammals held in the County Museum and declares that it is now assigned the name *Coelodonta antiquitatis* (Blumenbach) and would be approximately 30,000-40,000 years old (Middle Devensian). Ussher also refers to reindeer and bison under 12 feet of gravel near Taunton Station (Ussher, 1906).

Research suggests that this was a period of 'mammoth steppe' environment with continental conditions: hot summers, very cold winters and low rainfall. Other animals at that time in southern Britain were woolly mammoth, horse, giant deer, very large red deer, spotted hyena, lion, brown bear, wolf and lemmings. These gravels are a clear indication that our river flood plains were choked with rock debris derived from adjacent hillsides which in turn suggests accelerated hillslope processes. The flood plain would have looked different from that of the present; shifting gravel bars would have formed a braided pattern of channels. These gravels form terraces just above and below the present-day flood plain (see the Taunton sheet and the Norton Fitzwarren chapter.

St Mary Magdalene (ST 2290 2457)

The magnificent tower was rebuilt between 1858 and 1862. The new tower has an interesting variety of building stones. One can compare the golden Ham Hill Stone with the red Permo-Triassic sandstone: both show cross-bedding resulting from deposition by fast-running water. However, the Ham Hill Stone is mainly composed of broken sea shells deposited by strong currents in a shallow tropical sea. The red Permo-Triassic sandstone is composed of quartz and other minerals, rock fragments and pebbles transported and deposited by swiftly flowing, overloaded rivers in desert basins. There are also blocks of greenish-grey North Curry Sandstone and pinkish Hestercombe diorite.

There is an account of the debate concerning the old tower and the celebrations which marked the building of the new tower in *The history of Taunton* (Webb, 1874). Webb also provides welcome additional information about the building stones:

> In taking down the old tower, which was generally thought to have been of stone procured either at Norton (Fitzwarren) or Bradford (on-Tone), which forms one variety of the new red sandstone group (sic), large masses of granite (sic), supposed to have been raised from the quarries at Hestercombe, were found in the interior of the old walls, and has been reused, as far as it would go, in facing the present tower. Some difficulty was experienced in obtaining stone for the exterior of a corresponding character, but eventually the remainder was obtained at Williton from the quarries of Sir Alexander Hood, Bart., M.P., by whom the stone was eventually given. The interior of the walls consist of Monkton rag stone.

We should add that the 'granite' is now classed as a diorite.

Walk clockwise around the church to the northeast corner to view the recently constructed Magdalene Centre (1993); a very stylish addition to the church. The dressed stonework is the golden Pont du Gard Limestone from the south of France and which could be mistaken for Ham Hill Stone. The random, coursed, rubble walling is Blue Lias from near Long Sutton. The red squared snecks are St Bees Sandstone from Cumbria. The southeast side of the church has Monkton ragstone alongside cobbles of Devonian sandstone.

(courtesy Somerset Studies Library).

FIG 30.2 St Mary Magdalene before the tower was rebuilt

Stepping inside, there are fine medieval stone carvings of angels throughout the nave. A monument to Robert Grey (1635) on the north wall is made from black and pale brown Watchet alabaster The church guide informs us that the reredos is made of Mansfield Stone (Permo-Triassic dolomitic* sandstone) and Caen Stone. The latter, from France, is a Jurassic fine-grained, pale cream limestone; it will take the most elaborate carving but is unsuited to exteriors in this country.

A miscellany of buildings old and new

Building stones in the town centre have already been mentioned in earlier chapters. In addition, other parts of the town, including former village centres that have been enveloped by the outward growth of the town, are enriched by stone walls and older buildings which give character and a sense of the past.

Shop fronts and public buildings show a variety of rock types, many from outside Somerset and from abroad. The polished limestones on Lloyds Bank in Fore Street are Devonian Limestones from south Devon (Ashburton-Newton Abbot-Torquay). They exhibit crinoidal and coral debris plus sponges set in a dark, calcareous, fine-grained matrix. Devonian limestones can also be seen in the walls of the Magistrates Court. Bath Stone is used at the entrance to County Hall and for the sculptures; Devonian sandstone cobbles are laid around the building.

Various churches are of interest e.g. one can find eight different stones at Staplegrove Church. Jeboult (1873) enthuses about St John Baptist in Park Street designed by Gilbert Scott:

> The interior of the church is richly varied in colour by a skilful mixture of various stone, Hamdon Hill, Bath, and Bishop's Lydeard blending well together.

Walls fronting houses show a great variety of both natural and artificial stone. Bath Stone is to be seen in the dressings in many Victorian villas. There is a lot of drab Upper Westleigh Limestone around the railway station. The former Wilton Gaol is built of Devonian siltstones and sandstones brought from Hestercombe according to Estate papers.

Natural stone has been used for renovation work e.g. Blue Lias on the Riverside Shopping Centre next to the M5. Garden centres have various rock types for sale but hopefully no longer sell weathered Carboniferous Limestone ripped up from Pennine hillsides. Huge boulders have been planted on roundabouts as part of the street furniture.

TDBC's *Taunton Heritage Trail, and Taunton's Historic Chapel's: a visitors guide* provide routes for interesting perambulations around the centre.

Chapter 31
Thurlbear

(ST. 2621) - Thurlbear Church - Thurlbear Wood and Quarrylands Reserves - Blue lias Escarpment and Dip Slope
Fossils in Lower Lias limestones and clays - The Hatch Fault.

Thurlbear Church

St Thomas's handsome 15th century tower stands close to the lane, embellished with dramatic gargoyles...the chancel was rebuilt in the 14th century and its east window is Victorian neo-Norman, while the interior of the nave has two handsome Norman arcades of rare serenity and eloquence, with delicately carved capitals.

The description is from the *Visit churches in Somerset* leaflet produced by The Churches Conservation Trust who look after valued churches which are no longer needed for regular worship.

FIG 31.1 Norman arcade and font in Ham Hill Stone. Illustrated by W W Wheatley.

It is well-worth seeking the key to the church in order to see the Norman font and arcades (Ham Hill Stone) shown in Figure 31.1. Wheatley's sketch has been reproduced by the Somerset Record Society in a valuable collection of church illustrations (McGarvie, 1994). Many show details of churches before Victorian restorers got to work.

The local Blue Lias in the tower does seem to have weathered rather badly and the worst blocks have been replaced by thin slabs of the same. A lot of the local Blue Lias blocks show multiple vertical cracks (joints) which are the result of horizontal shear stresses caused by earth movements in the geological past. Cold brittle rock tends to crack rather than deform like toothpaste. Lines of weakness in a rock open up once a rock is quarried as a result of the removal of the confining pressures. Weathering is also hastened by the decomposition of finely disseminated iron sulphide (pyrites) which causes the rock to crumble.

Note the whitish-grey blocks of stone in the porch. A hand lens reveals small angular translucent quartz grains plus black specks of glauconite* whilst other blocks show larger, rounded sand grains. Look for the same stone in quoins and mouldings. This is the Calcareous Grit* from the Upper Greensand in the Blackdown Hills.

Thurlbear Wood and Quarrylands Reserves

Thurlbear is backed to the southeast by a line of hills with steep northwest facing slopes which we will term, for want of a better word, the Blue Lias Escarpment. The land falls more gently to the southeast (Blue Lias Dip Slope). There are numerous footpaths leading from both Thurlbear and Stoke St Mary. There is open access to the Somerset Wildlife Trust Thurlbear Wood Reserve which is part of the Thurlbear Wood SSS1. This is classed as ancient woodland of oak and ash standards and hazel and field maple coppice. The area is also noted for its butterflies and plants. The entrance is at ST 273 213 as shown in Figure 31.2. The area of the old Blue Lias quarry and limekiln is much overgrown and difficult to access.

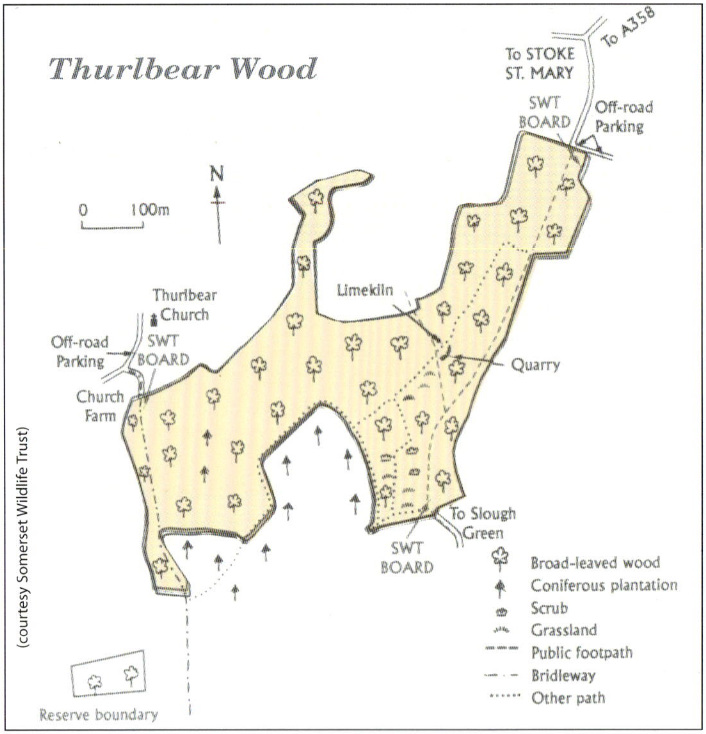

Fig 31.2 Thurlbear Wood

Keep an eye out for indications of the underlying strata when negotiating the deep lanes and tracks on the escarpment, e.g. the lane which ascends the escarpment at ST 2730 3159. A public footpath crosses a point at ST 2685 2051 where a small stream has revealed bedded limestones of variable thickness at the edge of what was once a deep quarry. These beds belong to the Blue Lias. Note the gentle inclination of the beds. Nearby on the edge of the escarpment are some more huge wooded hollows which appear to be old quarry workings.

Visitors in high summer should not omit a visit to the Butterfly Conservation Quarrylands Reserve which lies adjacent to the SWT reserve on its east side. An extensive area of abandoned limestone quarries on the dip slope of the Blue Lias has developed into a nutrient-poor but lime-rich haven for plants and butterflies. Here is a reminder of what is meant by the term 'herb-rich'. Quarrylands sends out a message to planners, conservationists and quarry owners concerning the potential afteruse of old workings for nature conservation. Access is on the south side of the lane some 50 m beyond the entrance to the SWT reserve (ST 2745 2122).

The Blue Lias Escarpment and Dip Slope

The Thurlbear and Quarrylands Reserves are on the Blue Lias escarpment and dip slope which are shown in Figure 31.3; the feature runs from near Corfe in the southwest to Street via Langport and Somerton in the northeast. The escarpment capping is composed of resistant White and Blue Lias limestones which can be seen as brash in ploughed fields and the remains of old quarries. There are clay beds between the limestones. Shales, siltstones and marls appear on the mid and lower slopes of the escarpment below the White Lias and are sometimes exposed in the sides of deeply eroded tracks. The clays show wide cracks during dry weather but are boggy in winter. Top soil has been lost from higher slopes on the dip slope and deposited lower down; as a result many transverse field boundaries show marked changes of level. Steeper slopes on the escarpment may show soil creep, terracettes and slumps.

Soils are mainly alkaline except on the Westbury Beds. The soil series listed on Figure 31.3 belong to a system of soil classification based on the particle-size, parent material, colour and mineralogical characteristics of the various horizons in soil profiles. Readers are referred to the standard text *Soils and their use in South West England* (Findlay et al, 1984) for further details.

The best exposure of these rocks is on the steep slopes near Compton Dundon to the northeast of Somerton where deep gullies score the escarpment. The red, green and grey silty marls readily disintegrate and blocks of turf pull away partly as the result of the weight of grazing animals plus weathering. Loose debris is then washed downslope during storms. It is a remarkable example of accelerated erosion. This area is part of a major downland restoration project and of great interest to naturalists.

There are a large number of Nature Reserves located on this line of hills: Bishopswood Meadows, Thurlbear Wood, Fivehead Arable, Prospect Fields, Aller and Beer Woods, Dundon Beacon, Great Breach Wood, Gilling Down. Information about the reserves, access and membership can be obtained from the Somerset Wildlife Trust at Fyne Court. The transects in Figure 31.3 should help visitors, especially naturalists and ramblers, appreciate the complex nature of the landscape.

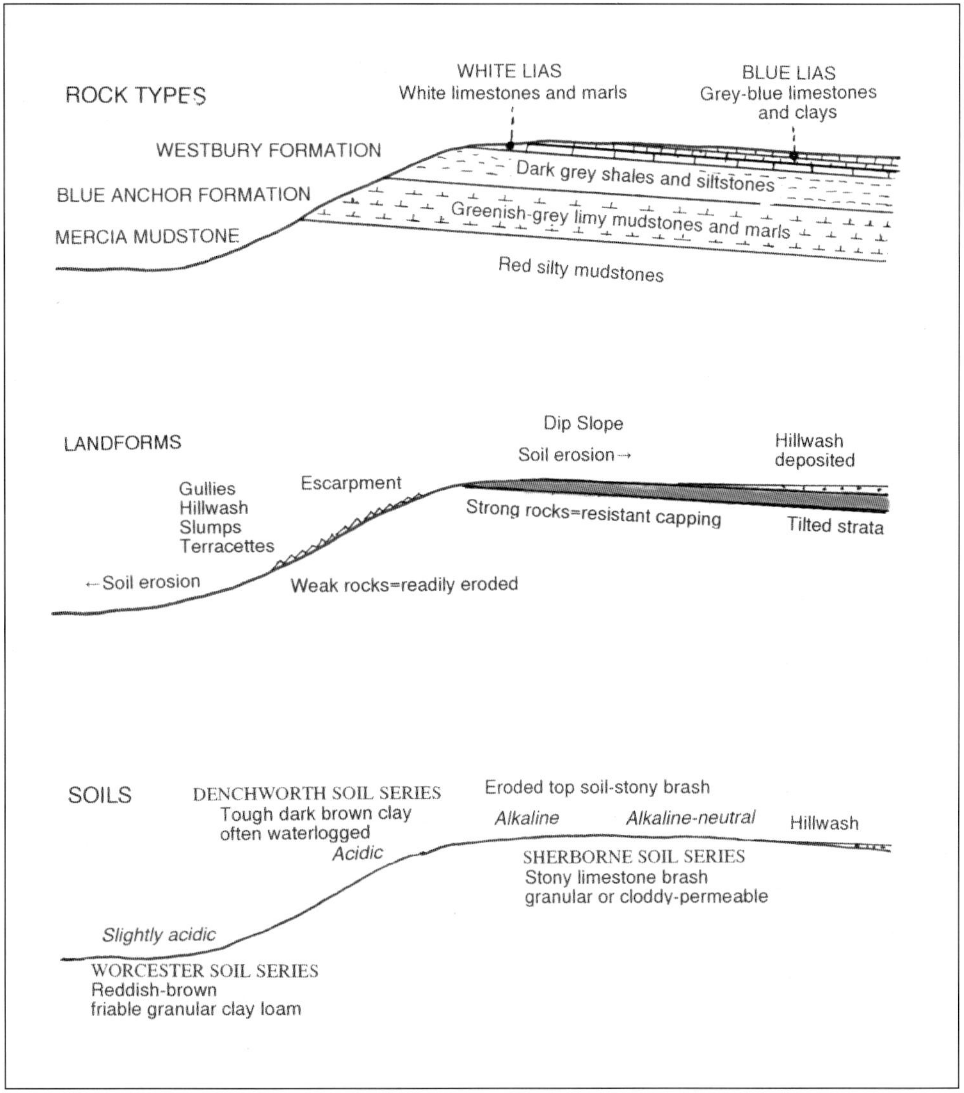

FIG 31.3 Transects illustrating rock types, landforms and soils near Thurlbear

The White Lias is now referred to as the Langport Member in modern terminology. The Langport Member is the upper part of the Lilstock Formation which is, in turn, part of the Penarth Group. However, White Lias is a useful informal term which is still in common use. (See the table in Appendix C).

Fossils in the Lower Lias limestones and clays

The Blue Lias and associated beds continue southwards from Thurlbear underneath the Upper Greensand of the Blackdown Hills and emerge at Bishopswood where they were once dug for lime as illustrated in Figure 2.1.

The same beds continue to the world-famous cliffs at Lyme Regis. There are also extensive exposures of White and Blue Lias of international importance along the Somerset coast between Blue Anchor and Lilstock (King, 1997).

The Blue Lias consists of over 175 m of interbedded limestone, shale or mudstone on the Somerset coast whereas it is only some 29 m thick on the Dorset coast which reminds us that there can be considerable lateral variations within a particular rock formation (Whitaker and Green, 1983). The Blue Lias is overlain by a considerable thickness of Lower Lias clays as seen to the west of Charmouth. These clays underlie the vale traversed by the A358 between Hatch Beauchamp and Ashill.

The Lower Lias is famous for the fossils that draw both professional and amateur collectors. However, there are few opportunities to find these fossils in Taunton Deane although close examination of walls often reveals shell debris, brachiopods* and crinoids*.

Figure 31.4 is an illustration from *The ecology of fossils* (McKerrow ed, 1975). It represents the kinds of animals and animal activity that were typical of the Lower Lias clay communities. The lower half is what we might see today in the cliff face at Charmouth. The upper part is a reconstruction of the original sea floor with its 'life assemblage'.

The creatures now entombed in the rock once swam, floated, crawled, rested or burrowed as a living community until one sad day, a great cloud of dark mud enveloped them to form a 'death assemblage'.

The trace fossils are the remains of burrows and tracks where animals were feeding in the mud or moving over the sea floor. Sediments disturbed by this activity have suffered 'bioturbation'. Some animals lived on the surface of the sea floor (epifauna) whilst others lived in the sediment (infauna).

The key provides names of the animals together with their classification. But perhaps more important for the amateur (and professional?) is the concept that dead fossils were once living creatures dwelling in appropriate habitats and part of a community. They were also

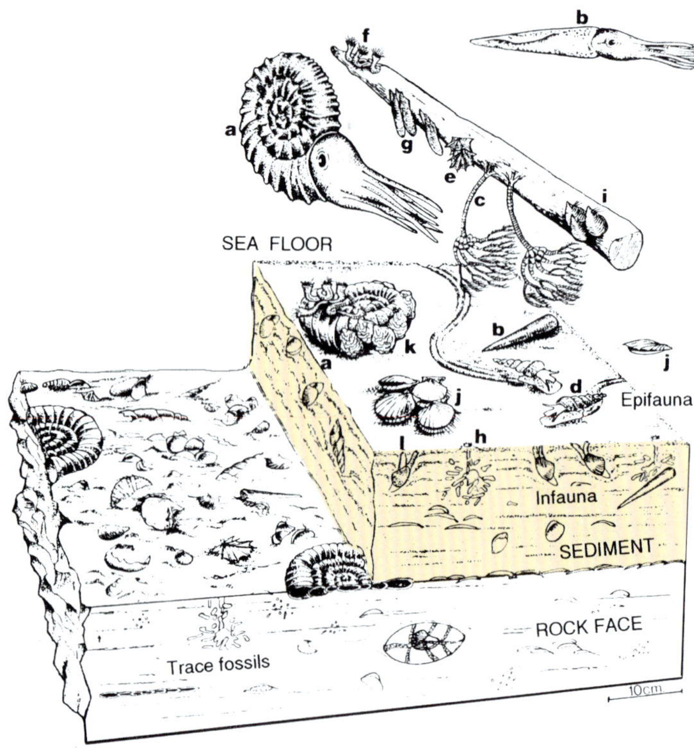

Modified from McKerrow, 1978).

Restricted Clay Communitya

a. Dactylioceras (Mollusca: Cephalopoda: Ammonoidea)
b. belemnite (Mollusca: Cephalopoda: Coleoidea)
c. crinoid (Echinodermat - Crinozoa)
d. Procerithium (Mollusca: Gastropoda: Mesogastropoda)
e. Oxytoma (Mollusca: Bivalvia: Pterioida)
f. serpulids (Annelida - polychaete)
g. Gervillia (Mollusca: Bivalvia: Pterioida)h Chondrites Trace fossil: annelid burrow)
i. Inoceramus (Mollusca: Bivalvia: Pterioida)
j. pectinid (Mollusca: Bivalvia: Pterioida)
k. Liostrea (Mollusca: Bivalvia: Pterioida - oyster)
l. Nuculana (Mollusca: Bivalvia: Palaeotaxodonta - nuculoid)

FIG 31.4 A Jurassic restricted clay community

Fig 31.5
Section of
railway-cutting
Hatch
Beauchamp

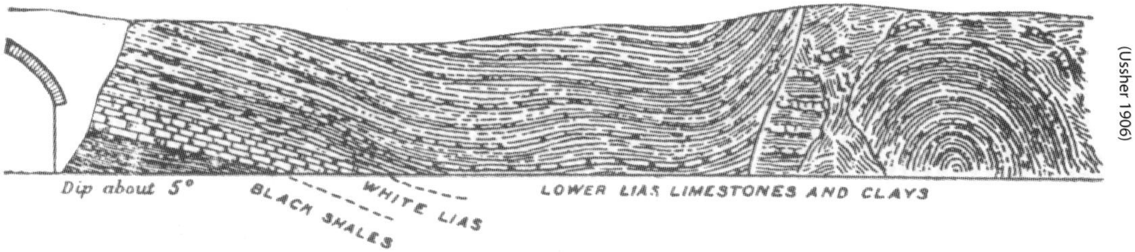

consumers and the consumed within food chains! The fossils in the clay beds at Charmouth were also part of geological history as evolving animals some of which e.g. the ammonites, became extinct. In addition, they became entombed whereupon some were crushed and their soft parts rotted as the soupy sediments turned into the mudstones in which we find them today.

Not only is this evolution in action but the succession of life forms is the basis for one means of dating and ordering the rocks-the science of biostratigraphy. For example, the ammonites found in the Blue Lias enable us to correlate the strata at Kilve on the Somerset coast with those in Swabia in southwest Germany. The Somerset County Museums Service has produced a well-illustrated book on the ammonites in the Lower Lias that are to be found along the Somerset coast (King, 1997).

In passing we may note that Sandford reported in 1859 that the only fossil of importance that the Taunton Museum had received that year was a portion of the skeleton of a large Ichthyosaur from Stoke St Mary.

De la Beche reminds us that many animals falling to the sea floor would normally be recycled, i.e. dissolved or eaten!

> ....these remains are so beautifully preserved, their bones so well connected, with even the contents of their intestines between their ribs, and with traces of skin upon them, that many Ichthyosauri and Plesiosauri must have been suddenly enveloped alive, or immediately after death, by the matter of the rock now enclosing them, so that neither their decomposition took place in the water, nor the predaceous animals existing in the same seas had access to their bodies.

The Hatch Fault

The Hatch Beauchamp bypass on the A358 cuts through the line of Blue Lias escarpment. Figure A1 in Appendix A shows that the line of hills is offset at Hatch Beauchamp. The BGS Wellington geological map (Sheet 311) indicates that a northwest to southeast major fault (the Hatch Fault) passes through Hatch Beauchamp parallel to the old railway cutting. The displacement of the escarpment is due to the strata being let down on the southwest side of the fault.

Disturbed strata were found during the preliminary survey for the M5 motorway on a line between the Hatch Fault and the Cothelstone Fault on the southwest side of the Quantocks (see Chapter 18). The Cothelstone Fault is one of a large group of NNW-SSE dextral faults in southwest England which show displacement to the right when observed from either side. It would thus appear that the Hatch Fault is part of a major fault where there has also been lateral movement.

The Wellington memoir illustrates a northwest to southeast section drawn in the former railway cutting in 1870 which is reproduced in Figure 31.5; some of the cutting is still exposed. The section is parallel to the Hatch Fault. Notice how the beds reflect the regional dip to the southeast near the bridge. Further along, the beds become almost vertical where they are bent against a fault with horizontal beds and a sharp fold to the right. These structures may well be a result of compressive movements associated with the nearby Hatch Fault. The cliffs along the Somerset coast between Blue Anchor and Hinkley Point abound with similar structures and complex arrays of joint patterns which provide evidence for the structural evolution of the region (Dart et al, 1995); Peacock, D C P and Sanderson, D J, 1999; Whittaker, A, 1972).

Chapter 32
Thurloxton

(ST 2730) - Church - Terminal curvature and the Morte Slates Formation - Calcretes - Radial drainage

Church

The walls of the parish church of St Giles are built of local Devonian siltstone and sandstone with sturdy blocks of North Curry Sandstone in the buttresses. Dressings are mainly Ham Hill Stone.

Terminal curvature and the Morte Slates Formation

The sunken lane to the south of the church has been eroded in the relatively weak Devonian slates. The cleavage dips steeply to the south. Note how the slates turn over and disintegrate near the surface. Figure 32.1 is taken from *The Geological Observer* by Sir Henry De la Beche (1853).

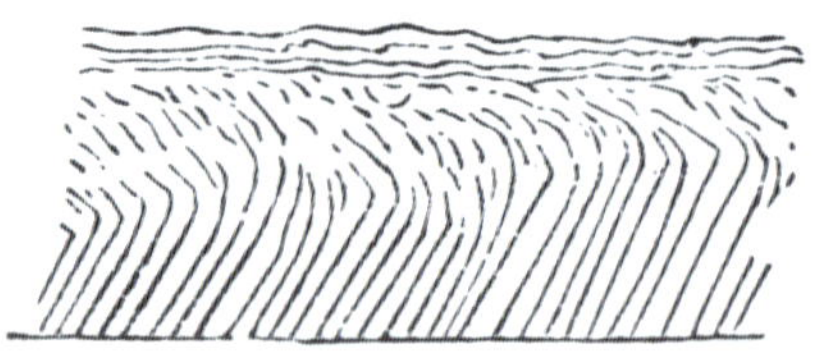
(De La Beche, 1853).

FIG 32.1 Overturned slates showing downhill movement.

De la Beche explains:

> ...The mixed effects of decomposition from atmospheric causes, and of the soaking of the surface on hill sides, are often well shown in slate countries, a certain depth beneath the soil exhibiting the turning over of the edges of the slates towards the valleys; as it were the tendency of the moistened matter of the surface to slide by its gravity to the lower ground.

Note how the slates tend to have sharp angular breaks, sometimes in zigzag fashion. It demonstrates that, at some time in the past, the surface 2-3 m was moving downhill. This turning over must be a relict feature; there is nothing to suggest that the slates are moving downhill at the present day on this scale. This feature is known as 'terminal curvature'.

Mackintosh (1867), in the 19th century, suggested that similar features in the Brendon Hills were the result of the drag of an overriding ice sheet. However, there is no evidence whatever for the presence of any ice sheets this far south in Somerset as Ussher (1878a) pointed out in an acerbic rejoinder.

De la Beche ascribes the phenomena to 'decomposition' and 'soaking' but clearly both must have been more intense than at the present day. The best explanation so far is that freeze-thaw processes, and water logging during the spring melt over permanently frozen ground, were responsible. In other words, this intense denudation occurred at a time when landforming processes in southern Britain were similar to those of Spitsbergen today. Mackintosh also asserted that terminal curvature was mainly to be found on south facing slopes. Is it true? If so, could it be that north facing slopes were frozen solid all of the year?

Very often the slates disintegrate toward the bottom of a slope to form an unsorted mass of angular Head*. This can be seen in the sides of the lane that crosses a narrow valley 0.5 km north of Thurloxton Church (ST 275 308). The slates become progressively fragmented toward the bottom of the lane. The whole mass has a crude horizontal bedding. (See also Webby, 1964.) Additional examples are to be seen in the sides of the lane south of Farringdon Farm at ST 277 312 where the slates have been stained red by the former presence of overlying Permo-Triassic sandstones.

It is fair to assume that periglacial mass-wasting processes, demonstrated in the lane at Thurloxton, were widespread throughout much of southern Britain. In other words, they were a major factor in the development of today's landscape.

The old quarries and woodland, 2.5 km to the north of Thurloxton at King's Cliff, are worth a visit; park at ST 2796 3268 or ST 2709 3205. The extensive quarry faces are in Devonian slates, siltstones and sandstones. Try to distinguish the bedding and cleavage-it is not always easy! The beds dip at roughly 20° to the east-south east and the cleavage a little more steeply to the south-southeast.

Calcretes

If time permits we recommend a visit to a road cutting to the east of the M5 at North Newton (ST 294 310). The red sandstone (Otter Sandstone) shows whitish, blobby calcretes* indicating evaporation of ground water and the concentration of calcium carbonate in soil and subsurface. This suggests that these sediments were part of a land surface and experienced weathering under semi-arid conditions.

Radial drainage

Note that the sandstones in the Morte Slates rock formation are more resistant to erosion than the slates and consequently form steep-sided narrow valleys as at Hestercombe, Thurloxton and west of North Petherton. At Thurloxton the valleys run east to west whilst to the south-west of Thurloxton they are more north-south. Indeed on a wider view, the drainage seems to have a radial pattern with its centre at Broomfield Hill (ST 2132). This could reflect the emergent surface of the older rocks as the Permo-Triassic rocks were stripped off, or it might just reflect a doming at the time that the present stream pattern was established. There is some evidence that earth movements had a similar effect in west Dorset (Chapter 2) and Exmoor (Straw, 1995).

Chapter 33
Wellington and the Blackdowns

(ST 1320) - Church - Brickworks - Wellington Monument -
Culmstock Beacon and Blackdown Common Whetstones and Fossils

Church

Precede a visit to the church by walking away from the town centre past the church to the entrance to Drake Place in order to become familiar with the North Curry Sandstone; note the brownish tints, sandy texture and cross-bedding. The same stone is used in the church of St John the Baptist for parts of the tower, walls, buttresses and some of the dressings. Use Figure 33.1 to identify this and the other building stones.

The square-hewn blocks (ashlar) in the tower contrast with the rubble masonry elsewhere. Note the Beer Stone niches either side of the west door at the base of the tower. The north side of the chancel has some neatly knapped chert.

A red sandstone block on the buttress to the left of the porch, some 1.2m from the ground, includes a grey weathered pebble composed of crinoidal debris probably derived from, what were some 245 million years ago, adjacent outcrops of Upper Westleigh Limestones (use hand lens). The massive blocks forming the gateposts at the entrance to the churchyard show crudely stratified breccias with fragments of Palaeozoic sandstones up to 15 cm in length.

The line of gravestones provides a challenge in identifying the types of stones and the number of different designs. The Blue Lias slabs have weathered badly as usual.

The variety of building stones at St John's reflects the position of Wellington in relation to the availability of building material as is shown in Figure 4.3; it is at the periphery of several 'core areas'. Ham Hill Stone and some Bath Stone from further afield have been used because of their suitability for dressings. However it is a little surprising to see so much Ham Hill Stone used in the tower. An informative booklet about the church is on sale at the bookstall (Isaac, 2000).

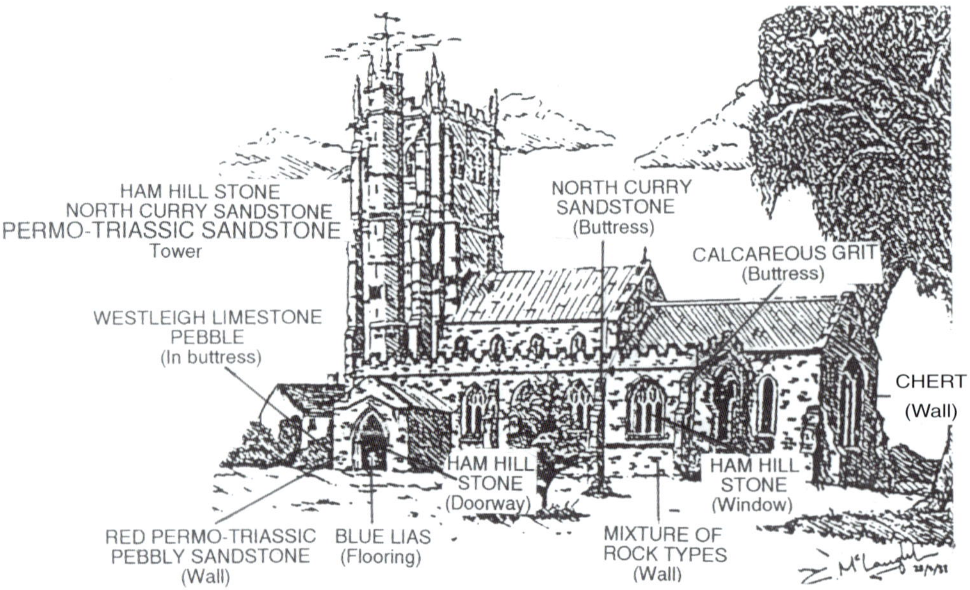

(Courtesy: Craig McLaughlin)

FIG 33.1 Building stones seen on the outside of Wellington parish church.

Brickworks

Much of Wellington is built on the Permo-Triassic sandstones (termed Upper Sandstones on the Wellington sheet) and these can be examined in the deep road cutting at Nynehead (see above). The lower beds, of what were once known as the Keuper Marls (now Mercia Mudstone), have been dug for many years at Poole Brickyard north east of Wellington for the manufacture of a variety of products. Isaac and Parrott (1995) have produced a very readable account of the history of the brickworks.

Wellington Monument

The Wellington Monument is a prominent landmark on the brow of the Upper Greensand escarpment south of Wellington. Park at the NT Monument car park (ST 142 168). The Monument is built of Calcareous Grit- a fine-grained, whitish, quartz sandstone with sporadic black glauconite grains cemented with calcite. It was quarried in the Upper Greensand at Northay some 12 km to the east-southeast of the Monument (Ussher, 1906 p55). The sandstone can be seen in many of the churches in the Blackdowns and in the old quarry at Snowdon Hill near Chard (ST 312 089) shown in Figure 25.2. Further details about the Monument may be found in Girdler (1992).

Culmstock Beacon and Black Down Common

Picnic Sites, Viewpoints and Countryside Car Parks (Somerset Tourism leaflet) recommends the excellent views and walks at Quarts Moor (NT car park at ST 152 168). However, much of the Blackdown escarpment is forested so that views of landslips and distant places are blocked. Nonetheless, the northwest corner of the Blackdowns not only provides panoramic views but much of botanical and geological interest. We suggest that cars are parked at the Wellington Monument and that visitors take the footpath on the southwest side of the Monument, follow the road to Crossways Farm where a bridleway leads to Black Down Common and Culmstock Beacon on the brow of the Upper Greensand escarpment.. There is limited parking on the grass verge in the lane to the farm (ST 152 168).

Use Figure 33.2 to identify three landscape zones:

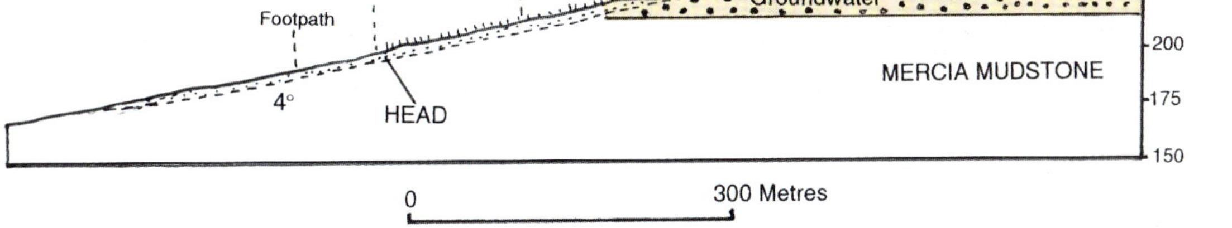

FIG 33.2 A WNW-ESE transect to show features at Blackdown Common.

Zone A The escarpment is formed by resistant beds of Upper Greensand chert which can support a 13° slope. The chert can be seen everywhere. The ridge top has dark peaty silty topsoil over clayey loam (surface-water gley of the Dunkeswell Association 714a). The whiteness of the stones in the eroded paths is due to the infiltrating water from the acidic soils 'bleaching' the underlying rocks. The soils support extensive examples of heathland which were formerly more widespread on the Blackdowns. Chert was dug in many small quarries which were located on the brows of the ridges for ease of access. The old quarries at Sampford Point are good localities for studying soil profiles, and they also show how periglacial freeze-thaw processes have shattered and disturbed the chert beds.

Zone B The middle part of the escarpment displays the lower part of the Upper Greensand (Foxmould Sands) where badgers have been at work.

Zone C The lower part of the escarpment has an apron of sandy cherty head* which mantles the underlying rocks. Part of it is waterlogged marshland and a dark mass of peaty material has formed as a result of the plant remains being waterlogged (humic gley soil of the Hense Association 871b). The block diagram in Figure 25.3 shows how the Dunkeswell and Hense Associations are related to topography and bedrock.

A line of low arcuate seepage steps appear to mark where the surface layers have pulled away from the adjacent beds. From a distance the area looks featureless but there are some low ridges or bulges below the seepage steps where upslope loading pushes forward the saturated debris below. The question has arisen as to whether some of these 'steps' are the result of peat digging. Turbaries were quite common in the Blackdowns. The waterlogging is the result of groundwater emerging where the permeable Upper Greensand overlies the impermeable Mercia Mudstone. The groundwater flows slowly downslope through the mass of sand and chert.

The Head parallels the 4° slope which is, by and large, stable today except for the seepage steps. Jones and Lee (1994) in *Landsliding in Great Britain,* point out that '...under periglacial conditions in the past, seasonal melting would have produced such high pore (water) pressures that movements occurred on very shallow slopes (<4°)'. In fact most of the hillslopes in southern Britain are the product of hillslope recession when ground conditions were very different from those of today.

The marshy grassland has abundant Purple Moor Grass, with Cross-leaved Heath and Bog-mosses co-dominant. In addition, there is Cotton Grass, Sundew, Bog Asphodel, Bog Pimpernel, Devil's-bit Scabious and Bristle Scirpus.

Note the slump at Windwhistle close to the footpath at ST 1136 1660. There are many deep V-shaped goyles (eg ST 1100 1644) cut into the superficial deposits below the springline.

The combination of heathland, carr woodland and marshy grassland, together with the contrasted landforms and soils, earn the site SSSI status. The features are clearly set out for all to enjoy. The area is noted for its butterflies, spiders and heathland birds.

We do not always 'advertise' nature reserves as many are sensitive to visitor pressure. However, we feel that Blackdown and Sampford Commons illustrate the importance of nature conservation and the work of English Nature. Please keep to the tracks and remember that there may be grazing animals present. Avoid the marshy areas as they are very difficult to negotiate

There are panoramic views from Sampford Point and Culmstock Beacon into west Somerset and Devon. Binoculars and a small-scale O S map would help identify landmarks. The practical importance of geomorphology is demonstrated by the siting of the 'Beacon' to convey the warning of invasion to other counties, and the presence of a telecommunications' tower nearby.

The grey outlines of the Haldon Hills and Dartmoor, in the far distance, are views to be savoured. There is an ever-changing skyscape where one can enjoy the glow of winter sunsets to the west or beware the onset of grey rain-bearing clouds coming in from the Atlantic over mid-Devon.

The vast lowland that separates Dartmoor and the Haldon Hills from the Blackdowns is, in itself, a cause for wonder and contemplation. In the 19th century William Ussher crossed swords with a Mr Mackintosh who suggested that a vast mass of solid ice had crossed the region. However, there is no evidence for the latter and Ussher exclaimed:

> How any geologist can calmly contemplate the distant tableland of the Blackdowns from its insulated remnant Haldon, and gazing across the broad valley of the Exe, excavated entirely since the accumulation of the clay with flints, deny the vast contour moulding and surface waste of Pleistocene ages, it is difficult to contemplate (Ussher, 1878b).

The usual concept in Ussher's day was that slow, gradual surface processes could remove vast quantities of rock given enough time. Today we attribute the erosion to accelerated mass wasting resulting in hillslope recession during cold, periglacial phases of the Pleistocene Ice Age. The lowland is the result of the removal of rock since the formation of the East Devon Plateau in the Tertiary Period. Imagine a flat sheet joining the Blackdown and Haldon hilltops with Cothelstone Beacon in the southern Quantocks in order to appreciate the time and space involved. (See also Pitminster and Thurloxton chapters.)

Whetstones and fossils

Some 7 km to the south lies Blackborough which was once the centre of the whetstone mining industry. Whetstones, or scythestones, were made from concretionary sandstones, bound with a silica cement, from the Upper Greensand. They were used for sharpening blades, especially those for use in farming. The topic is fully explored in Stanes (1993).

A by-product of the mining was the recovery of large quantities of beautifully preserved silicified fossils which are on display at Exeter Museum.

(courtesy the Devon Record Office)

FIG 33.3 Drawing by Peter Orlando Hutchinson of a miner using a basing axe. The sketch also shows the entrance to a mine and some partly finished whetstones. The drawing is dated 1854.

Figure 33.4 illustrates the geological structure at Blackborough. Readers should note that the lithology and thickness of the Upper Greensand formation varies laterally. For example, the 'Blackdown facies' is siliceous at Blackborough but calcareous to the east of a line extending from the coast at Seaton north-east to Yarcombe. Edwards (1993) provides an excellent summary of the geological aspects including a bibliography. We also draw attention to two papers by the Rev.W. Downes (Downes, 1880, 1882).

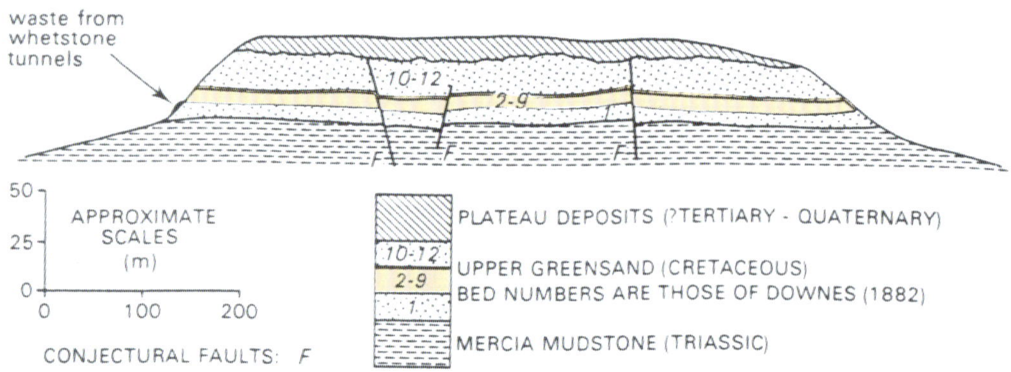

FIG 33.4 Diagrammatic cross section through the upper hill east of Blackborough: all lines shown are conjectual. The beds numbered 2 to 9 are the horizons worked for whetstones.

Edwards, 1993, 110, fig 9 courtesy of the author and the Devonshire Association).

Epilogue

We end by recalling some remarks in a small volume entitled *Outlines of Field-Geology* first published in 1876 by Sir Archibald Geikie who, in his time, was Murchison Professor of Geology and Mineralogy in the University of Edinburgh as well as Director-General of the Geological Survey of Great Britain and Ireland.

"......My aim has been to write primarily for that large and increasing body of readers who have made some general acquaintance with geology but who, though much interested in the subject, find themselves helpless when they try to interpret the facts which they meet with in the field......

....The young geologist, into whose hands this little book may fall, will therefore remember that it is not meant as a systematic text-book on geology....its purpose is to be suggestive to him, rather than didactic; to put him in the way of intelligently observing for himself, rather than to present him with what has already been discovered by others."

Appendix A

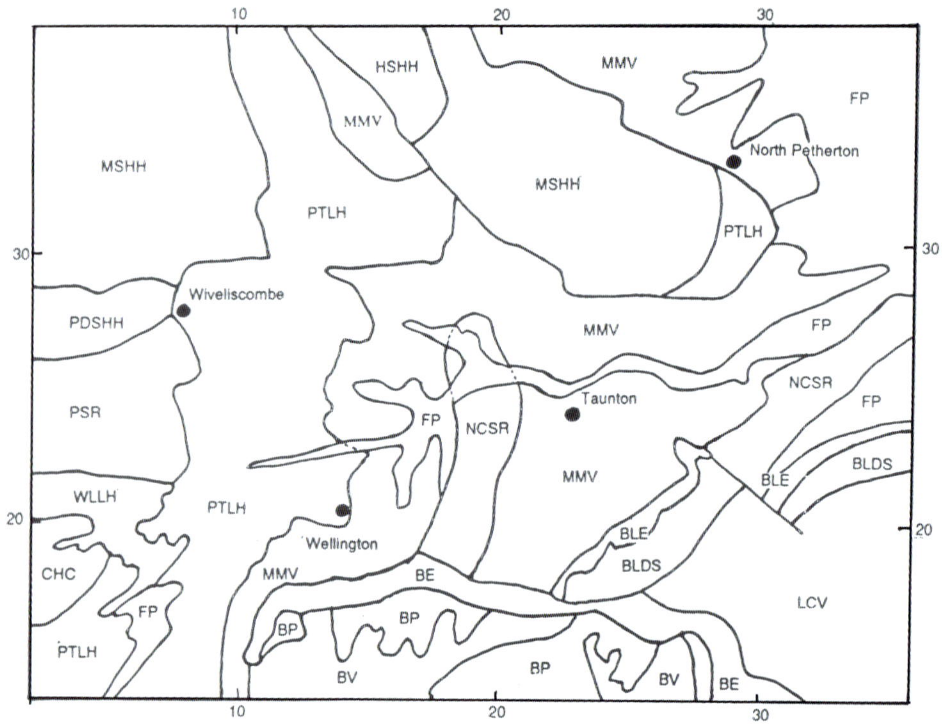

Fig A1 Subdivisions of the physical landscape

Key to classification
(see Figure A1):

BE	Blackdown Escarpment	MMV	Mercia Mudstone Vale
BP	Blackdown Plateau	PSR	Pilton Shales Ridges
BV	Blackdown Valleys	MSH	Morte Slates High Hills
BLDS	Blue Lias Dip Slope	NCSR	North Curry Sandstone Ridges
BLE	Blue Lias Escarpment	PTLH	Permo-Triassic Low Hills
CHC	Culm Hill Country	PDSHH	Pickwell Down Sandstone High Hills
FP	Flood Plains	HSHH	Hangman Sandstone High Hills
LCV	Liassic Clay Vale	WLLH	Westleigh Limestone Low Hills

Subdivisions of the physical landscape of Taunton Deane

Figure A1 is a classification of the physical landscape based upon varying combinations of rocks and landforms which in turn influence the hydrology and the soils. The outlines of the units have been derived by superimposing the 1:50, 000 geological and topographical maps. The selection of criteria and the definition of boundaries is an arbitrary and subjective exercise.

Whilst the information is generalised and simplified, the map does (a) crystallise a mass of information into discrete units, (b) facilitates discussion of regional landscape features, (c) helps build a mental picture of the area and (d) can serve as a basis for planning purposes, conservation studies and reports. Each unit has a degree of internal coherence. Unlike some other landscape assessments, it does not attempt to summarise land use and settlement patterns which deserve separate maps.

Soil information is summarised under soil associations which are groups of soils named after the principal soil type in a soil association and is based on *Soils and their use in South West England* (Findlay, 1984) and the accompanying map, both of which are invaluable sources of information on local soils.

Each unit is summarised as follows:

a. Lithology
b. Landforms
c. Hydrology
d. Soils

BLACKDOWN ESCARPMENT BE

a. Sandy chert beds overlying sands, thick cherty head.
b. North-facing steep slopes with landslip features and deep goyles.
c. Springs and mires at base of Greensand
d. Hense Association: Permeable coarse loamy soils, humose surface horizon.

BLACKDOWN PLATEAU BP

a. Tertiary sands clays and gravels over Upper Greensand.
b. Extensive plateau ridge tops.
c. Permeable; important Greensand aquifer.
d. Batcombe Association: Silty and loamy; slowly permeable subsoil. Dunkeswell Association: Slowly permeable seasonally, waterlogged silty soils some with a humose surface horizon.

BLACKDOWN VALLEYS BV

a. Upper Greensand beds overlying Mercia Mudstone to the west and Liassic limestones and clays to the east; thick chert head; gravel spreads on lower terrace slopes.
b. Deep steep-sided valleys, landslip features, active stream channels with riffles, pools and gravel-filled channels.
c. Upper Greensand an important aquifer with springs at the base; impermeable lower slopes on Mercia Mudstone and Liassic clays.
d. Hense Association: Permeable coarse loamy soils with humose surface horizon on upper slopes. Whimple 3 Association: Reddish fine loamy soils; slowly permeable subsoils on lower slopes.

BLUE LIAS DIP SLOPE BLDS

a. Limestones, mudstones, clays and shales; hillwash on lower slopes.
b. Moderate slopes with the dip of the rocks.
c. Some permeable limestones otherwise impermeable clays.
d. Sherborne Association: Shallow well-drained brashy calcareous soils over limestone associated with calcareous clayey soils. Evesham 1 Association: Slowly permeable calcareous clayey soils associated with well-drained calcareous soils over limestones. See Figure 31.3 for further details

BLUE LIAS ESCARPMENT BLE

a. Sequence of red mudstones, marls, dark clays, shales and limestones.
b. Steep slopes where limestones form resistant capping above weaker beds.
c. Springs where groundwater emerges from limestones.
d. A complex pattern: Calcareous and non-calcareous soils; clayey soils and limestone brash. See Figure 00 for further details.

CULM HILL COUNTRY CHC

a. Sandstones and shaly mudstones (Bude Formation).
b. Broadly convex slopes over sandstones and concave slopes over shales.
c. Extensive poor drainage especially on lower slopes and shales.
d. Neath Association: Better drained fine loamy soils over sandstones. Hallsworth Association: Slowly permeable seasonally waterlogged clayey soils on shales and head.

FLOOD PLAINS FP

a. Alluvial silts and peat.
b. Low-lying, low relief.
c. Liable to flood; variable groundwater table.
d. Midelney Association: Stoneless, clayey-silty soils. (Narrow flood plains on the upper reaches of rivers are not shown)

HANGMAN SANDSTONE HIGH HILLS HSHH

a. Massive well-cemented sandstones with subordinate shales and sandstones; thick sandstone head.
b. Broad ridges; watershed divides the western steep face, with short, deep, narrow valleys from the gentler general slope on the east side, with long, deep narrow valleys.
c. Variable permeability with some ground water.
d. Larkbarrow Association: Reddish, acid, permeable, loamy upland soils.

LIASSIC CLAY VALE LCV

a. Clays, black shales mudstones and occasional thin limestones; stony head on higher slopes.
b. Low-lying vale with rising slopes at the periphery; gravelly terrace remnants alongside flood plains.
c. Impermeable with surface run-off.
d. Denchworth Association: Slowly permeable seasonally waterlogged clayey and fine loamy soils. Evesham Associations: Slowly permeable calcareous and non-calcareous clayey soils.

MERCIA MUDSTONE VALE MMV

a. Red and greenish-grey silty mudstones, thin spreads of river gravel.
b. Low-lying vale with rising slopes at the periphery; gravelly terrace remnants alongside flood plains.
c. Generally impermeable.
d. Hodnet and Whimple 1 Association: Reddish fine and coarse loamy soils; slowly permeable subsoils. Worcester Association: Slowly permeable calcareous and non-calcareous reddish clayey soils over mudstone.

MORTE SLATES HIGH HILLS MSHH

a. Silver and grey slates with some sandstones; thick slaty head.
b. More open valleys and more subdued, convex hilltops than the Devonian sandstones; southern Quantocks has radial pattern of deep, narrow combes.
c. Some groundwater but generally low permeability.
d. Milford Association: Well drained fine loamy reddish soils over rock. Yeolland Park Association: Loamy permeable soils variably affected by ground water; some slowly permeable seasonally waterlogged clayey soils.

NORTH CURRY SANDSTONE RIDGES NCSR

a. Thin greenish grey sandstones and mudstones; red mudstones, siltstones and sandstones.
b. Low escarpment and dip slope.
c. Variable permeability.
d. Hodnet and Whimple 1 Association: Reddish fine and coarse loamy soils; slowly permeable subsoils. Worcester Association: Slowly permeable calcareous and non-calcareous reddish clayey soils over mudstone.

PERMO-TRIASSIC LOW HILLS PTLH

a. Red sandstones, conglomerates, breccias and mudstones.
b. Irregular topography, knolls, narrow vales and escarpments.
c. Permeable, important aquifers for water supply.
d. Hodnet and Whimple 1 Association: Reddish fine and coarse loamy soils; slowly permeable subsoils. Bromsgrove Association: Well-drained reddish coarse loamy sands over sandstones; risk of erosion. Crediton Association: Well-drained gritty reddish loamy sands over breccias, locally stony.

PICKWELL DOWN SANDSTONE HIGH HILLS SHH

a. Purple, reddish-brown and grey well-cemented, often massive, sandstones, siltstones and slates; thick sandstone head.
b. Very steep slopes in deep, narrow valleys; broad convex upper hilltops.
c. Permeable with some ground water.
d. Larkbarrow Association: Reddish acid permeable loamy upland soils; Milford Association: Well-drained fine loamy reddish soils over rock.

PILTON SHALES RIDGES PSR

a. Brown and lilac shales with thin sandstones.
b. Ridges and steep-sided narrow valleys with an E-W tendency.
c. Some groundwater but generally low permeability.
d. Milford Association: Well-drained fine loamy reddish soils over rock.

WESTLEIGH LIMESTONE LOW HILLS WLLH

a. Dense grey limestones and shales.
b. Ridges, knolls, escarpments and valleys.
c. Variable permeability.
d. Neath Association: Well drained fine loamy soils over rock. Nordrach Association: Thin soils over limestone.

Appendix B

Summary of some important rock types and formations

Please see the index for further details.

BATH STONE

An informal term for oolitic limestones containing a mix of ooliths* and other shell debris bound in a calcareous cement matrix which accumulated on the floor of shallow, turbulent, lime-rich seas. It has been, and is, quarried in the southern Cotswolds and was widely used in 19th century buildings.

Jurassic Period

BEER STONE

A white, crystalline, granular limestone, composed of minute, irregular, corroded fragments of shells, foraminifera, echinoderm plates and cemented by a lime-rich crystalline mud. It was deposited in a restricted area of the shallow, warm Chalk seas in what is now south east Devon. (A visit to the caves at Beer is recommended.)

Cretaceous

BLUE ANCHOR FORMATION

Grey and greenish mudstones and siltstones with nodular gypsum horizons exposed at St Audries Bay. Includes what were termed the Tea Green Marls.

Triassic Period

BLUE LIAS

The Blue Lias formation includes alternating beds of black shales, grey mudstones and limestones (see Thurlbear). The limestones began as lime-rich muds deposited in generally quiet, shallow seas. Forms an escarpment and dip slope from Corfe to Langport and Somerton. Well-displayed between Watchet and Hinkley Point on the Somerset coast. Widely used for building work especially to the east of Taunton. (See Thurlbear)

Jurassic Period

CALCAREOUS GRIT

A whitish-grey quartz sandstone cemented with calcite in the Upper Greensand lying above the Chert Beds and below the Chalk as seen at Snowdon Hill in Figure 25.2 There are small black specks of glauconite and increasing amounts of polished yellow-green quartz grains toward the top. It becomes increasingly harder toward the top and forms a marked ledge on the hillsides west of Crewkerne and on Eggardon Hill (Eggardon Grit). It can be seen in the tracery and mouldings in many Blackdown churches.

Cretaceous Period

CLAY-WITH-FLINTS

An unsorted accumulation of angular flints with varying amounts of reddish brown clay overlying the Chalk hilltops and often filling deep pockets in the Chalk. Derived partly from Tertiary sediments and the decomposition of the Chalk.

Tertiary-Quaternary Periods.

COCKERCOMBE TUFF

Volcanic ash deposited on the sea floor, in the area that is now the northern Quantocks, followed by deep burial, compression, folding and faulting during the Variscan mountain building episode (see Plainsfield).

Devonian Period

DOULTING STONE

Brown or grey oolitic and crinoidal* debris deposited in warm, shallow seas on the southern side of the Mendips. Widely used as a building stone e.g. Wells Cathedral.

Jurassic Period

EXETER VOLCANIC SERIES

These include a massive, vesicular purple or reddish rock derived from basalts which flowed from volcanoes in the Exeter area. Rapid cooling resulted in a fine-grained texture whilst gas bubbles in the molten magma are seen today as cavities, some of which are filled with calcite.
Late-Carboniferous-early Permian Periods

FOXMOULD

A dark green, loamy, glauconitic sand forming the lower beds in the Upper Greensand which can often be seen in deep, laneside exposures. The base is often marked by see pages and swampy ground. Readily washed out at see pages causing beds above to founder. May contain large calcareous, concretions. The sands tend to weather to a yellow colour.
Cretaceous Period

GREENSAND CHERT

A hard brownish stone almost entirely composed of silica which is thought to have been derived from the dissolution of sponge spicules and later reprecipitated as beds of nodular chert. Flint found in the Chalk is similar in composition. Widespread in the Blackdown Hills. Occurs between the Foxmould and the Calcareous Grit.
Cretaceous Period

GUITING STONE

A shelly oolite with an orange-yellow tint and prominent current bedding from the Cotswolds deposited under conditions similar to Bath Stone.
Jurassic Period

HAM HILL STONE

Masses of shell debris deposited and moved about on the seafloor by strong currents. Was, and still is, quarried at Ham Hill near Yeovil. An attractive building stone (see Prudden, 1995).
Jurassic Period

HESTERCOMBE INTRUSION

An igneous rock resulting from the intrusion of magma* into Devonian-age rocks. The magma subsequently cooled and solidified. The constitution of the rock suggests that it came from deep down and has been likened to a lamprophyre but has lately been again classified as a diorite. It can be studied in an old quarry in the combe at Hestercombe Gardens.
Permian Period

KEUPER MARL

Part of the higher beds in the Permo-Triassic succession: a mainly red, silty, slightly calcareous mudstone. The term is now subsumed within the Mercia Mudstone Group. Its origin is controversial but it would seem that wind, and possibly waterborne, sediments were deposited in arid inland basins. Includes beds of salt and gypsum. It is well-exposed in St Audries Bay.
Triassic Period

LOWER LIAS CLAY

The thick sequence of clays seen at Charmouth on the Dorset coast which continues northwards to Broadway and Ashill to the east of Taunton. They range from the dark, laminated, organic-rich shales deposited in stagnant water to blocky, pale grey, calcareous mudstones deposited in shallower, more aerated seas. Figure 31.4 shows a typical fossil community associated with the silty clays.
Jurassic Period

MORTE SLATES

Mud, silt and sand, with low organic matter content, was deposited in shallow seas; note the splendid bedding plane ripples at Hestercombe Gardens. There followed deep burial, compression, folding, and faulting during the Variscan mountain building episode which transformed the finer-grained sediments into slates. Note that the so-called Morte Slates contain siltstones and sandstones, especially near West Monkton and at Hestercombe. Widely used as a rough walling stone.
Devonian Period

NORTH CURRY SANDSTONE

Greenish-grey silts and fine-to coarse-grained sands, containing rock fragments and pebbles, deposited in either an estuary, or a delta complex, possibly during a wetter phase of what was generally a semi-arid climate (see Ruffell, 1990; Ruffell and Warrington, 1988; Warrington and Williams, 1984). Best seen at Norton Fitzwarren Church.

Triassic Period

PICKWELL DOWN SANDSTONES

Large inputs of sands from a landmass to the north produced thick, massive beds of sandstones (cf the Hangman Sandstone Formation of north Exmoor and the Quantocks). Used for buildings between Wiveliscombe and Dulverton.

Devonian Period

PILTON SHALES

Brown shales with subordinate calcareous sandstones and silty limestones formed in a shallow sea during the transition from Devonian to Carboniferous times (Edmonds and Williams, 1985). Can be seen at Waterrow in the old railway cutting just east of remains of former viaduct (ST 0552 2458) and by main road (ST 0515 2531).

Devonian-Carboniferous Periods

SARSENS

These are silcretes i.e. sand and pebbles cemented by precipitation of silica when a semi-tropical climate with seasonal rainfall prevailed. They formed on what is now the plateau surface of the Blackdown Hills. The silcretes later broke up and were 'rafted' down slope by solifluction* as the valleys were deepened (see Staple Fitzpaine, and Otterford and the Blackdown Plateau).

Tertiary Period

UPPER GREENSAND

An important rock formation which caps much of the east Devon Plateau (Blackdown Hills). Details are given under Foxmould, Greensand Chert and Calcareous Grit and in Otterford and the Blackdown Plateau, and Wellington and the Blackdowns, chapters.

Cretaceous Period

UPPER WESTLEIGH LIMESTONE

Lime-rich and silica-rich muds deposited on the sea floor. The sediments contain the siliceous skeletons of marine planktonic* radiolaria*. The skeletons have been partially dissolved and the silica reprecipitated to form the bands of replacement chert. The Upper Westleigh Limestones are thought to be associated with submarine debris flows (turbidity currents*) which would have incorporated pebbles and rock fragments. The finer-grained sediments would have settled to the sea floor more slowly thus producing a fining upwards sequence (graded bedding*). The limestones are of similar age to the shallower-water ' shelf' deposits of the Mendips (Carboniferous Limestone). It is useful to remember that in the past, as today, land and sea, shallow and deeper waters, coexisted side by side. The sediments were later subjected to deep burial, compression, folding and faulting during the Variscan mountain building episode. The white veins show where the rock has been stressed and torn apart. Partial solution of the limestone was followed by reprecipitation of the mineral calcite in the cracks (see Burlescombe).

Carboniferous Period

VALLEY GRAVEL

During cold phases of the Ice Age much rock debris was sludged down hillsides and a lot of it accumulated in river channels where it became rounded by abrasion. It occurs either below the flood plain alluvium* or on low terraces adjacent to the flood plain (see Norton Fitzwarren). The change from gravels to the silty-clayey deposits that occurs below many floodplains represents the change from periglacial conditions to the temperate climate of today.

Quaternary Period

VEXFORD BRECCIA, BUDLEIGH SALTERTON PEBBLE BEDS, OTTER SANDSTONE

These sands, silty mudstones, breccias* and conglomerates* of Permo-Triassic age are part of the New Red Sandstone Supergroup. The sands include fine, coarse, angular and rounded grains. Some formations* consist mainly of rounded cobbles (conglomerates). The sediments and sedimentary structures are mainly those of overloaded, multiple-channelled rivers involving lateral accretion and erosion in both braidplain and alluvial fan situations. In addition, there are breccias containing angular rock fragments which have suffered relatively little abrasion. Some of the poorly sorted deposits suggest saturated debris flows following violent storms. The redness is caused by the presence of thin films of iron oxide (haematite) on the particles (see Holloway et al. 1989). Many of the sands, pebbles, cobbles and angular rock fragments are similar to the rocks that make up the Quantocks, Brendon Hills and Exmoor; they represent the rock waste resulting from the destruction of what were, at the time, mountainous areas. (See Appendix C stratigraphic divisions.)

Permian and Triassic Periods

WESTBURY FORMATION

Dark grey shaly mudstones with dark muddy limestones. Deposited mainly in semi-stagnant water poor in oxygen. Crops out near the top of the Blue Lias escarpment where it supports non-calcareous soils and thus adds to the complexity of the soils found on these steep slopes. It can be studied in the cliffs at the west end of St Audries Bay (ST 1038 4412).

Triassic Period

WHITE LIAS

Now referred to as the Langport member of Lilstock Formation. Pale fawn and white, calcareous mudstones and limestones which occur below the Blue Lias; sometimes nodular, laminated or lenticular. Best viewed in Lilstock Bay on the Somerset coast.

Triassic Period

Appendix C

Permo-Triassic stratigraphical divisions.

Ussher 1907 (Sheet 295)	This memoir	Smith and others, 1974 Warrington and others, 1980		
	Blue Lias (lowest part only)		Blue Lias (lowest part only)	
Rhaetic Beds	Penarth Group	Penarth Group	Lilstock Formation	Langport Member (including White Lias of Richardson, 1911)
				Cotham Member
			Westbury Formation	
	Blue Anchor Formation (Grey Marl and Tea Green Marl)	Mercia Mudstone Group	Blue Anchor Formation	
Upper Marls	Undifferentiated (red Mercia Mudstone)		[undifferentiated]	North Curry Sandstone Member
			Somerset Halite Formation	
			[undifferentiated]	
Upper Sandstones	Otter Sandstone	Sherwood Sandstone Group	'Nynehead Sandstones'	
Pebble Beds and Conglomerates	Budleigh Salterton Pebble Beds		'Milverton Conglomerates'	
Lower Marl	Littleham Mudstone	Aylesbeare Group	Littleham Mudstone Formation	
Breccio-Conglomerate	Vexford Breccias		Exmouth Sandstone-and-Mudstone Formation	
Lower Sandstones	Wiveliscombe Sandstones		Clyst Sands and equivalent breccias	

Fig C1. Permo-Triassic stratigraphical divisions based upon a table in Edmonds and Williams (1985) by permission of the British Geological Survey 'IPR/2-108 British Geological Survey © NERC All rights reserved'.

Appendix D
Glossary

**Some technical words are explained in the text.
Others are briefly discussed below.**

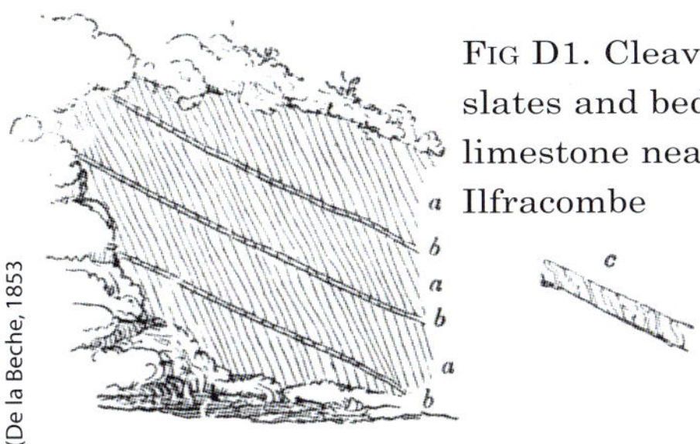

(De la Beche, 1853

FIG D1. Cleaved slates and beds of limestone near Ilfracombe

AXIAL PLANE The surface which separates fold limbs from one another. The dip of the axial plane gives the inclination of the fold (see Figure 19.2).

ALGAL MAT Laminated lime muds resulting from the growth of blue-green algae.

ALLUVIUM Clays, silts and gravels deposited on flood plains.

BIOCLASTIC Broken shell debris.

BRACHIOPOD A marine invertebrate animal with a two-valve shell, each valve being bilaterally symmetrical.

BRECCIA Unsorted angular fragments of rock usually implying transport over a short distance.

CALCAREOUS of, or containing, calcium carbonate.

CALCRETE Calcareous nodules in irregular layers formed by soil processes indicating semi-arid climatic conditions.

CLASTS Rock fragments within a fine-grained matrix.

(De la Beche, 1853

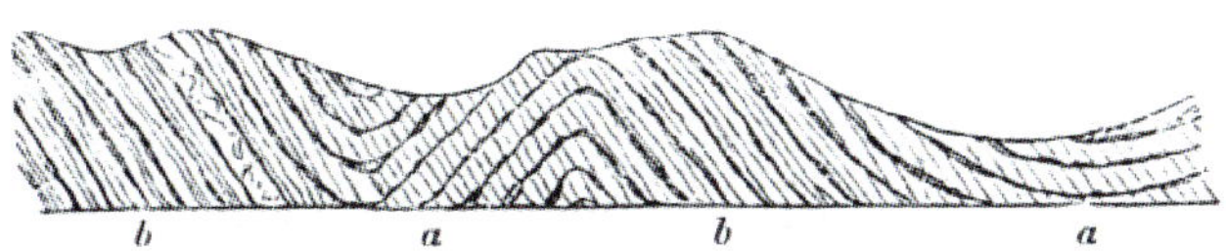

FIG D2. Exposure of Devonian rocks between Morte and Bull Point near Ilfracombe showing folds and cleavage.

CLEAVAGE The tendency of a rock to split along parallel planes along which realignment of platy minerals, such as mica, has occurred as a result of intense deformation (slaty cleavage). The planes are at right angles to the direction of maximum compressive force. Figure D1 shows that the fine-grained sediments (a) have slaty cleavage but not the beds of limestone (b). The latter tend to fracture at a steeper angle (fracture cleavage). Such beds of limestone or sandstones are useful for determining the dip of the beds in areas where slaty cleavage predominates.
Where beds have been folded as in Figure D2 , parallel planes of cleavage may at one place cut the bedding at right angles (a), and at others coincide with it (b).

CHLORITE A green mineral composed of hydrated aluminium, iron, magnesium and silica.

COLLUVIUM Soil and subsoil deposited by hill wash.

CONGLOMERATE Sedimentary rock partly composed of rounded pebbles.

CRINOID Animal related to sea cucumbers and starfish with cup-shaped body and arms attached to the sea floor by a stem.

CROSS-BEDDING Depositional sedimentary structure with inclined sets of short beds (Figure 21.1).

CULM Local name for thin bands of inferior coal in Devon, and thence the name 'Culm Measures' for the shaly and gritty formation containing them.

DEXTRAL MOVEMENT Lateral movement on a fault where the opposite face has moved to the right. 'Sinistral' is movement to the left.

DIP The slope of a rock bed removed from a horizontal plane.

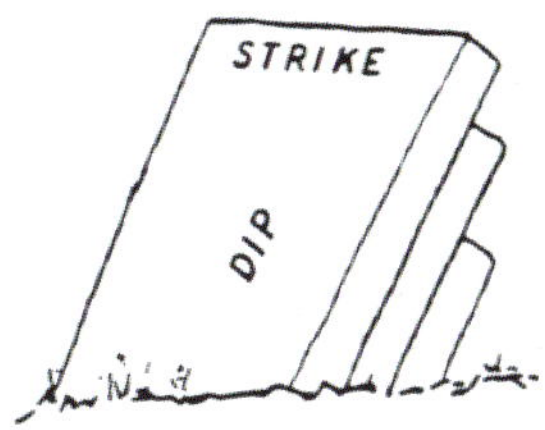

FIG D3. Illustration of dip and strike.

DOLOMITE Limestone with more than 15% magnesium carbonate.

DRESSINGS Carved stone prepared for window and door mouldings, tracery, dripstones and the like.

DIAGENESIS The process whereby a sediment is converted to a rock. These processes include compaction, cementation and recrystallisation.

FACIES A term applied to rocks or fossils to indicate an association of lithological and/or palaeontological characteristics.

FAULT An abrupt dislocation of the rock where the sides have moved past each other.

FERRICRETE Sediment cemented with iron.

FOLD AXIS A line parallel to the hinge of a fold (see Figure 00).

GLAUCONITE A hydrated silicate of iron and potassium.

GRADED BEDDING An upward or downward decrease in particle size.

GREYWACKE As developed in Cornwall, Devon, and west Somerset, the term included chiefly sedimentary deposits, of Lower Palaeozoic age and was used in the early 19th century. (Anglicized form of the German Grauwacke.) Now used for a mixture of muddy and sandy material derived from turbidity currents.

GULL Widened joint formed by the extensional movements of rocks affected by cambering (foundering).

HEAD Surface rock waste formed by periglacial processes.

LIMONITE Hydrated iron oxide.

IGNEOUS Rocks formed by the consolidation of molten magma e.g:
Cockercombe Tuff - ash fallout from a volcano
Exeter volcanics e.g. in Burlescombe Church - solidified lava
Dartmoor granite - intrusive magma which has cooled slowly at depth
Hestercombe diorite - intrusive magma from deep in the crust

Ma Age in million years.

MATRIX A groundmass of clay and silt in which larger fragments are embedded.

MESOZOIC ERA Geological era from 251 to 65 Ma.

MICRITE The matrix to many bioclastic limestones and the main constituent of fine-grained limestones; it consists of particles less than 4mm in diameter. Mostly of biogenic origin.

OOLITH Small spherical carbonate grains formed of concentric layers of calcite or aragonite which have formed around nuclei which may be sand grains, foraminiferal shells or other objects. Figure D4 shows a thin section of an oolitic limestone from near Bath with the grains bound together by crystalline calcite. Note the radial structures. x 80.

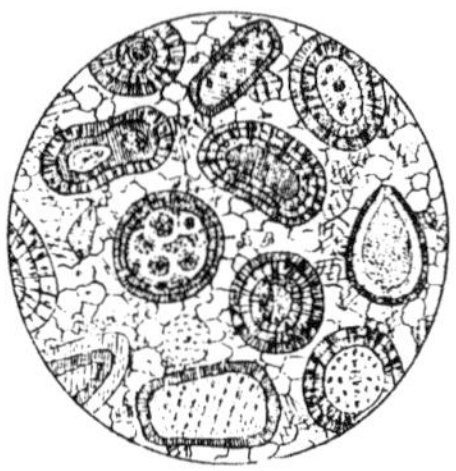

FIG D4 Ooliths

OROGENY The processes that form structures within mountainous areas, including faulting, folding, metamorphism and igneous activity.

PALAEOZOIC ERA The geological era from 570 to 251 Ma.

PERIGLACIAL The area around an ice sheet.

PLANKTON Microscopic organisms that float near the ocean surfaces.

PLATES Discrete units of the earth's crust which converge, separate or slide past one another.

RADIOLARIA Marine planktonic organisms which secrete a symmetrical skeleton with an elaborate lattice-work composed of silica.

RAG Hard, coarse, rough or rubbly stone. Old English raggig, shaggy, ragged, rough.

RIPPLE-LAMINATION Cross-bedding with thin laminae usually composed of sand-sized particles.

RIP-UP CLASTS Fragments of eroded sediments.

ROCK FORMATION A unit of rocks capable of being mapped.

SILCRETE Sediment cemented with silica.

SOLIFLUCTION The process of the flow of a mixture of surface rock.

STRIKE The direction of a horizontal line on a bedding plane (see Figure D3).

TENSION GASHES Openings in a rock as a result of brittle fracture, commonly filled with calcite or silica.

TERMINAL CURVATURE The downslope bending-over of near-surface slaty rocks, especially under periglacial conditions.

TUFF Ash thrown out by volcanic explosions and settled under water.

TURBIDITY CURRENT Bottom-flowing density current of suspended sediment moving rapidly over the sea floor.

UNCONFORMITY The result of non-deposition or erosion followed by renewed deposition. In the engraving Figure D5 the time-gap between the deposition of the Carboniferous Limestone and the Inferior Oolite is some 170 Ma. During that time the Carboniferous Limestone was arched into great folds by lateral compression. The planed-off remnants of the folds that we see today indicate that thousands of feet of rock were removed. The Inferior Oolite was deposited on top of the planed-off beds-a monumental demonstration of the magnitude of geological events.

WRENCH FAULT A dislocation where the movement is dominantly horizontal (= strike-slip, tear fault, transcurrent fault).

a. Inferior Oolite.
b. Arenaceous parting.
c. Carboniferous Limestone.

(Woodward, 1876).

FIG D5 The unconformity in Murder Combe west of Frome

Vernacular geology

It is risky to lay claim to exclusive use of words and phrases for a particular region. However, we draw attention to a few which are of interest. Stone is, and was, a basic need and a lot of these words resonate with the working countryside of the Normans and Saxons.

The *West Somerset Word Book: dialectical and archaic words and phrases used in the west of Somerset and East Devon* by Frederic Thomas Elworthy, is a delightful source for local words and phrases (Elworthy, 1886)).
A more geologically oriented compilation is English rock terms chiefly as used by miners and quarrymen. (Arkell and Tomkeieff, 1953). The selection below have some relevance to the West Country. Some of the names relating to the Blue Lias are still in use in the Somerton area. Certainly 'goyle' and 'shillet' are in everyday use.

CLOG STONE A band of limestone in the Lower Lias (recorded at Beer Crowcombe and Stoke St Mary). Possibly derived from the Celtic clog, clock, a stone. More likely to be derived from the Middle English word clog known since the 14th century and surviving in south-country dialects with various meanings such as block, lump; and cloggy heavy, compact, applied especially to soil or the land.

GRIB Local quarrymen used this term for the Budleigh Salterton Pebble Beds as reported by Ussher (Ussher, 1906). Cf. North Devon dialect gribbly meaning granular, gritty.

FOXMOULD As in the lower beds of the Upper Greensand; broken, or friable earth. Old English molde recorded from the 8th century.

GOYLE [gauy_ul]. A ravine; a deep, sunken, water-worn gully, usually with a running stream down it. A chine in the Isle of Wight; a gill in in Cumberland. 'Let's try the goyle here-uncommon likely place vor a pheasant. A scramble down into the goyal; a clatter up the other side; much crushing in gateways; a heat of sun's rays and anticipation, and we gallop over Wilmotsham Common to the ravine called Nutscale.' Account of Stag Hunt in Wellington Weekly News, Aug.19, 1886. (Elworthy, 1886.)

LIAS Any compact, argillaceous limestone, usually banded with beds of clay or shale, especially those quarried in Somerset but also elsewhere. Also the formation name for the limestones and clays of the Lower Jurassic. Old French liois a compact kind of limestone.

MALMSTONE Hard reddish-grey sandstone in the Trias, Somerset. Old English mealmstan recorded from the 9th century.

MUMBLING BED Two beds in the Blue Lias at Beer Crowcombe. Mumbly is a west Somerset dialect word for building stones which are shapeless, awkward, rounded, likely to fall, having no flat surface. Middle English verb momele, memell?

PAVIOUR Lower Lias blue stone used for indoor flooring. (Middle English pave from French paver.)

POPPLE {paup.l] sb. Pebble. 'That there popple lime idn no good 'bout no buildin' work, but 'tis capical for dressin', idn none better' (limestone pebbles). 'They there white popples be the best vor pitchin' of a path like thick there, but they be skee_us (scarce) to get, now' (quartz pebbles).'

For each pebble (pobbel) set into the pool
Was an emerald, sapphire or some other noble jewel,
So that the whole stream gleamed with light,
So rich was its splendour.

(Elworthy gives the original)
E. Allit. Poems, Pearl, l.117.

'Some limestone and the white popple are also found in the neighbourhood. The latter, when used for the repair of roads, gives them a curious mottled appearance'.
Descr. of Wiveliscombe,
Som. Co. Herald, July 2, 1887.

(Elworthy, 1886.)

POPPLE-STONE-PITCHING [paup.l-stoaun-puch.een].
A pavement made of pebbles. The 'popple lime' presumably refers to mortar made from limestone cobbles dug from the Budleigh Salterton Pebble Beds. The "white popples" must be the white quartz pebbles as seen, for example, in the ploughed soil at Norton Fitzwarren Hillfort. They also appear in the Tertiary gravels on the East Devon Plateau and associated sarsens at Staple Fitzpaine. Visit Angersleigh, Bagborough and Wiveliscombe churchyards to see them used in paths. (Elworthy, 1886.)

POTTLE STONE Local name for the igneous rock at Hestercombe.

SHILLET [shul.ut] Shale.
Used for the disintegrated top layer of the Devonian clay slate so common in West Somerset and North Devon. From shillet-i.e. broken slate. It gradually decomposes into fertile soil.

(Elworthy, 1886.)

Appendix E
Maps

Topographic maps

1:25, 000 Explorer maps

Taunton and Blackdown Hills	128
Quantock Hills and Bridgwater	22

The Ordnance Survey Pathfinder series have now been replaced by the Explorer series in the Taunton area. The latter provides a lot of tourist information. Sheet 128 Taunton and Blackdown Hills is printed back to back and some people may wish to avoid the nuisance of reversing the sheet by buying two copies. It is still good value. These maps really are essential for anyone exploring the countryside especially for information on rights of way.

1:50, 000 Landranger maps

Minehead and Brendon Hills area	181
Taunton and Lyme Regis	193
Weston-Super-Mare	182

Available from local booksellers.

Geological maps

1:50, 000 solid and drift

Taunton	295
Wellington	311

Geology of the country around Taunton and the Quantock Hills by Edmonds, E.A. & Williams B.J. (1985) is a detailed and up-to-date account of the geological features of Sheet 295.

Geology of the country between Wellington and Chard by W.A.E. Ussher (1906) is an account of Sheet 311. It is out of print but nevertheless a mine of information. A copy is available in the Somerset Studies Library.

Maps and memoirs are available from booksellers or the British Geological Survey, Keyworth, Nottingham, NG12 5GG (tel. 0115 936 3100).

Soils

1:250, 000

Sheet 5 South West England. This map is the starting point for any enquiry about soils in the South West. The map is supported by *Soils and their use in South West England* by D. C. Findlay, et al. 1984. It is an essential reference which describes and explains the soils shown on Sheet 5. The text also relates the characteristics of soils to the rocks, landforms and landuse.

The following maps are outside the Taunton Deane area but have much that is applicable to the area:

1: 25, 000

Soils in Devon I Sheet ST 10, Honiton
" " " II Sheet ST 01, Culm Valley
Soils of the Exmoor Forest (Out of print)

1: 50, 000

Soils of the Glastonbury District of Somerset Sheet 296

Available from Soil Survey and Land Research Centre, Cranfield University, Silsoe, Bedford MK45 4DT

Appendix F
References and further reading

Many of the following items are held in the Somerset Studies Library in Taunton.

British Geological Survey

Sheet memoirs

Geology of the Quantock Hills and of Taunton and Bridgwater. W. A. E. Ussher, 1908. Memoir of the Geological Survey of Great Britain. Explanation of Sheet 295. Out of print and superseded by the later Memoir.

Geology of the country between Wellington and Chard. W. A. E. Ussher, 1906. Memoir of the Geological Survey of Great Britain. Explanation of Sheet 311. Out of print.

Geology of the country around Taunton and the Quantock Hills. E. A. Edmonds and B. J. Williams. 1985. British Geological Survey. Explanation of Sheet 295; this is the most detailed and up-to-date account of the Taunton area.

British Regional Geology series

Bristol and Gloucester region (3rd ed.). G. W. Green, 1992.
South-west England (4th ed.). E. A. Edmonds, 1975.

Regional Texts

Exmoor geology: exploring the landscape, rocks and mines of the National Park. R. A. Edwards, 2000. Exmoor Books. At long last we have a popular account of the geology of Exmoor; the area covered is in continuity with that of the present volume.

The geology of Somerset. Peter Hardy, 1999. Ex Libris Press. A very welcome addition to the geological literature of Somerset. The author has lectured on geology and led field trips for Bristol University adult education courses for many years and has written a text designed for the layperson. Essentially, it deals with the character and landscapes of the various distinctive regions of Somerset together with the underlying rocks. It is a book to be read unlike most of the other recommendations which are more technical and useful for reference purposes. The chapters present both a broad view of each region and focus on the highlights. It is well-illustrated with photographs.

Geology and scenery in Britain. J. B. Whittow, 1992. Chapman Hall, London. An updated version of A. E. Trueman's popular classic in print since 1938. Readable.

Geology of England and Wales. P. Mcl. Duff & A. J. Smith, 1992. The Geological Society London. A comprehensive account of the geology of England and Wales, particularly in a stratigraphical context.

Taunton Deane Borough Council publications

Country walks in and around Taunton (2 sets).
A number of these are mentioned in the chapters on various parishes and are highly recommended for exploring the wide variety of landscapes.

Bird watching in Taunton Deane, Somerset.
John Clare, 1998.

Towers and hunkypunks.

Taunton's historic chapels..

Taunton Heritage Trails.

Taunton Deane Church Trail.
A very useful companion to this book.

West Deane Way.

'A circular walk of some 45 miles through the varied countryside of the Vale of Taunton Deane. Surprising vistas, spectacular views, and picturesque villages hidden among gentle hills make it a pleasant introduction to the delights of this unspoilt area'. The route takes in a number of places of geological interest. Please refer to the index. There are many opportunities to make the individual segments into short circular walks.

Listed below are some of the geological highlights section by section. Please refer to Appendix G (Building Stones) for details of stones used in the churches.

1. Ch. 12 County Museum.
2. Ch 23 detour to Norton Fitzwarren Church; Bradford-on Tone Church.
3. Ch 24 detour to Nynehead.
4. Budleigh Salterton Pebble Beds in old quarry face at ST 1205 2170; Runnington Church.
5. Ch 21 Budleigh Salterton Pebble Beds and Langford Budville Church.
6. Ch 29 Tracebridge Quarry-danger keep out!
7. Ashbrittle Church.
8. Ch 29 Pilton Shales exposed in old quarry face in railway cutting and by Waterrow Inn- take care.
10. Wiveliscombe Church.
11. Ch 15 detour via Sandy Lane Hollow and exposures in Grant's Lane.
12. Ch 14 Oakhampton Quarry-danger keep out!
13. Brompton Ralph Church.
14. Ch 14 Tolland Church; quarries (Morte Slates).
15. Lydeard St Lawrence Church.
17. Bagborough Church.
18. Ch 18 Colthelston Church and Fault.

19 & 20. Road cuttings en route at Cushuish.

22 & 23. Staplegrove Church.
Observe variety of stones en route

Other publications

Somerset: the complete guide. Robin Bush,1994, Dovecote Press.

The rural benchends of Somerset: a study in medieval woodcarving. Peter Poyntz Wright, 1983, Avebury. (A large number of the churches cited are in the Taunton Deane area or nearby.)

The Vale of Taunton Deane past. Tom Mayberry, 1998. Phillimore and Co. Ltd. (A book which will appeal to those who wish to know more about the history of Taunton Deane.)

Your handbook and guide to the Blackdown Hills.
Michael Drury-Beck, 1999, MDB Litework.

References in the text

ACKLAND, T. D. and STURGE, W. 1851. *The farming of Somersetshire. John Murray, London.*

ADAMS, H. n. d. *St Michael's Church, Milverton, Somerset.*

ADKINS, R.& J. 1992. *A field guide to Somerset archaeology. Dovecote Press.*

ANDREWS, J. R. 1998. The Culm Basin. In SELWOOD E. B., DURRANCE, E. M. & BRISTOW, C. M. (Eds).1998. *The geology of Cornwall.* University of Exeter Press.

ANON. 1895. Earthquake shocks in Somerset. *Somerset and Dorset Notes and Queries,* **4,** 45-47.

AVERY, B. W. 1955. The soils of the Glastonbury district of Somerset. *Memoir of the Soil Survey of England and Wales.* HMSO, London.

BAKER, W. 1851. Geology of Somersetshire. *Proceedings of the Somerset Archaeological and Natural History Society,* **1,** 127-139.

BARRETT, C. R. B. 1894. *Somersetshire: her highways, byways and waterways.* (Republished Mercer and Bingley 1993)

BARTON, C. M. et al. 1998. Reactivation of relay ramps and structural evolution of the Mere Fault and Wardour Monocline, northern Wessex. *Geological Magazine,* **135,** 383-395.

BAYNHAM, A. W. 1908. *Memorials of Ash Priors. Commin, Exeter.*

BENTON, M . J. 1997. The Triassic reptiles from Devon. *Proceedings of the Ussher Society,* **9,** 141-152.

BETJEMAN, J. 1952. *First and last loves.* Murray.

BILLINGSLEY. J. 1797. *General view of the agriculture of the County of Somerset, with observations on the means of its improvement.* Bath.

BRYANT, A. R. et al. 1959. Holwell Cavern, Quantocks.. *Wessex Cave Club Journal,* **6**, 54-59.

BRISTOW , C. R. et al. 1995. Geology of the country around Shaftesbury. *Memoir for1:50 000 geological sheet 313 (England and Wales).* HMSO

BRUNSDEN, D. 1996. Landslides of the Dorset Coast: some unresolved questions. *Proceedings of the Ussher Society,* **9,** 1-11.

BRUNSDEN, D. and GOUDIE, A. 1997. *Classic landforms of the west Dorset coast.* Geographical Association and British Geomorphological Research Group.

BUCKLAND, W. 1851. Dr Buckland's address to the first annual meeting of the Somerset Archaeological and Natural History Society. *Proceedings of the Somerset Archaeological and Natural History Society,* **1,** 9-21.

BUSH, R. 1988. *Taunton Castle: a pictorial history.* Somerset Archaeological and Natural History Society.

BUSH, R. 1994. *Somerset: the complete guide.* Dovecote Press.

CAMERON, A. G. C. 1908. In reference to the sarsens, or greywether-sandstones, at Staple Fitzpaine, near Taunton. *Proceedings of the Somerset Archaeological and Natural History Society,* **54,** 153-159.

CARTER, E. C. 1854. The church of St Mary the Virgin at Kingston. *Somerset Archaeological and Natural History Society,* **4,** 36.

CENTRAL ELECTRICITY GENERATING BOARD (CEGB). *1987. Proposed Hinkley Point 'C' PWR power station.* Environmental statement.

CHARD HISTORY GROUP, 1970. *Chard: a geological survey.* Publication no. 3. Republished 1988 in Chard: Three aspects of its history.

CHORLTON, E. 1994. *Nature's place: a nature conservation strategy for Devon.* Consultation draft. Devon County Council.

CLAYDEN, A. W. 1906. *The history of Devonshire scenery: an essay in geographical evolution.* Commin, Exeter.

CLIFTON-TAYLOR, A. 1987. *The pattern of English building* (2nd ed.) Faber.

COBHAM RESOURCE CONSULTANTS. n. d. *The Blackdown Hills: a landscape assessment prepared for the Countryside Commission.*

COLLINSON, J. 1791. *The history and antiquities of the County of Somerset.*

CROSSE, A. 1851. Holwell Cavern. *Proceedings of the Somerset Archaeological and Natural History Society,* **2,** 14-32, 123-124,

DANIEL, P. 1988. Limekilns at Castle Hill, Wiveliscombe (ST 096285). *Bulletin of the Somerset Industrial Archaeological Society,* **49,** 10-13.

DANIEL, P. 1990. Limeburning and geology in Somerset. *Bulletin of the Somerset Industrial Archaeological Society,* **55,** 6-14.

DART, C. J. 1995. 3D analysis of inverted extensional fault systems, southern Bristol Channel basin, UK. In (Buchanan, J. G. & Buchanan, P. G eds) *Basin Inversion.* Geological Society, London, Special Publications, **88,** 393-413.

DAVISON, B. K. 1972. Castle Neroche: an abandoned Norman fortress in south Somerset. *Proceedings of the Somerset Archaeological and Natural History Society,* **116**, 16-58.

DAVISON, C. 1896. On the Exmoor Earthquake of January 23, 1894, and on its relation to the Northern Boundary Fault of the Morte Slates. *Geological Magazine,* **3,** 553-556.

DE LA BECHE, H. T. 1839. Report on the geology of Cornwall, Devon and west Somerset. *Memoir of the Geological Survey of Great Britain.*

DE LA BECHE, H. T. 1853. *The geological observer* (2nd ed.) London.

DOLLAR, A.T.J. 1963. The seismicity of the Cornubian Peninsula in relation to its structure. Proceedings of the Ussher Society, **1,** 43-46.

DOWNES, W. 1878. The fossils of the Culm Measure limestones around Holcombe Rogus. Report of the *Transactions of the Devon Association for the Advancement of Science,* **10,** 330-334.

DOWNES, W. 1879. The limestones of Westleigh and Holcombe Rogus. *Report of the Transactions of the Devon Association for the Advancement of Science,* **11,** 433-441.

DOWNES, W. 1880. Blackdown. Report of the *Transactions of the Devon Association for the Advancement of Science,* **12,** 420-446.

DOWNES, W. 1882a. Chert pits. A stray note on Blackdown. *Report of the Transactions of the Devon Association for the Advancement of Science,* **14,** 317-321.

DOWNES, W. 1882b. The zones of the Blackdown Beds, and their correlation with those at Haldon, with a list of the fossils. *Quarterly Journal of the Geological Society of London,* **38,** 75-94.

DOWNES, W. 1883. On the occurrence of barytes in the Culm Measure limestones of Westleigh. *Report of the Transactions of the Devon Association for the Advancement of Science,* 15, 453-454.

DUNNING, R, 1987. *Elworthy St Martin of Tours Somerset.* Redundant Churches Fund (now the Churches Conservation Trust), London.

DUNNING, R. 1995. *Somerset castles.* Somerset Books, Tiverton.

DUNNING, R. 1996. *Fifty Somerset churches.* Somerset Books, Tiverton.

DURRANCE, E. M. and LAMING, D. J. C. (Eds) 1982. *The geology of Devon.* University of Exeter.

EELES, F. C. 1935. Stawley Church. *Proceedings of the Somerset Archaeological and Natural History Society for 1934,* **80,** xxxiii-xxxv.

EDMONDS, E. A. and WILLIAMS, B. J. 1985. Geology of the country around Taunton and the Quantock Hills. *Mem. Br. Geol. Surv..* Explanation of Sheet 295; this is the most detailed and up-to-date account of the Taunton area.

EDWARDS, R. A. 1993. Geology of the Whetstone Industry. *Report of the Transactions of the Devon Association for the Advancement of Science,* **125,** 106-112. An appendix to paper by Stanes, 1993.

EDWARDS, R. A. et al. 1997. The Exeter Group, south Devon, England: a contribution to the early post-Variscan stratigraphy of north-west Europe. *Geological Magazine,* **134,** 177-197.

FINDLAY, D. C. et al. 1984. *Soils and their use in South West England.* An essential reference text for soils at the regional level to accompany the 1:250,000 South West England soil map.

FIRMAN, R. J. 1989. Alabaster update: research in progress. *Mercian Geologist,* **12,** 63-70.

FIRSOFF, V. A. 1958. When earthquakes shook Somerset. *The Somerset Countryman,* **19,** 159-160.

GEIKE, A. 1892. *Outlines of field geology.* Macmillan.

GERRARD, C. M. 1985. Ham Hill Stone: a medieval distribution pattern from Somerset. *Oxford Journal of Archaeology,* **4,** 105-115.

GIRDLER, J. 1992. *The Wellington Monument.* Leaflet available locally eg museum.

GREEN, G. W. 1992. Bristol and Gloucester region. *British Regional Geology series.* British Geological Survey.

HAMILTON, J. R. and LAWRENCE, J. F. 1970. *Men and mining in the Quantocks.* Town and Country Press.

HEATH, M. J. 1991 Radon in the surface waters of southwest England and its bearing on uranium distribution, fault and fracture systems and human health. *Quarterly Journal of Engineering Geology,* **24,** 183-189.

HEPWORTH, J. V. 1998. Aspects of the English silcretes and comparison with some Australian occurrences. *Proceedings of the Geologists' Association,* **109,** 271-288.

HICKS, H. 1897. On the Morte Slates and associated beds in north Devon and west Somerset, Part 2. *Quarterly Journal of the Geological Society,* **52,** 438-462.

HOLLOWAY, S. et al. 1989. The Sherwood Sandstone Group (Triassic) of the Wessex Basin, southern England. *Proceedings of the Geological Association,* **100,** 383-394.

HOSKINS, W. G. 1955. *The making of the English landscape.* Hodder and Stoughton.

HUNT, T. J. 1971. Some 13th Century building accounts for Taunton Castle. *Proceedings of the Somerset Archaeological and Natural History Society,* **114,** 39-44.

HUTCHINSON, P. O. 1872. Iron pits. *Report of the Transactions of the Devon. Association for the Advancement of Science,* **5,** 47-50.

HUTTON, G., COOK, O. and SMITH, E. 1976. *English parish churches. Thames and Hudson.*

ISAAC, K .P. 1979. Tertiary silcretes of the Sidmouth area, east Devon. *Proceedings of the Ussher Society,* **4,** 341-354.

ISAAC, K. P. 1981. Tertiary weathering profiles in the plateau deposits of east Devon. *Proceedings of the Geologists' Association,* **92,** 159-168.

ISAAC, K. P. 1983. Tertiary lateritic weathering in Devon, England and the Palaeogene continental environment of southwest England. *Proceedings of the Geologists' Association,* **94,** 105-114.

ISAAC, L. and PARROTT, I. 1995. *Brickmaking in Wellington.* (2nd ed.) Wellington Museum Society.

JEBOULT, E. 1873. *A general account of west Somerset, description of the valley of the Tone and the history of the town of Taunton.* Taunton.

JONES D. K. C. and LEE, E. M. 1994. *Landsliding in Great Britain.* HMSO.

JONES, M. H. 1985. *Harry Frier: Somerset's unknown painter.* Somerset County Council Library Service.

JUDD, J. W (ed.). 1896. *The student's Lyell.* John Murray, London.

KING, A. et al. 1996. *Earth heritage conservation in England: a natural areas perspective.* English Nature research reports no. 158.

LEE, J. E. 1881. *Note-book of an amateur geologist. London.*

LOMAS P. R. et al. 1996. *Radon Atlas of England.* NRPB-R290. National Radiological Protection Board.

MACKINTOSH, D. 1867. On some striking examples of the terminal curvature of slaty laminae in West Somerset. *Quarterly Journal of the Geological Society,* **23**, 323-327.

MARSHALL, W. 1796. *Marshall's rural economy of the West of England 1796).* (Reprinted David and Charles.)

MAUDE, T. 1997. *Guided by a stone mason: the cathedrals, abbeys, and churches of Britain unveiled.* I. B. Thomas.

MAY, D and BUTCHER, W. 1997. *Taunton Deane Biodiversity Action Plan.* Prepared for Taunton Deane Borough Council at Somerset Environmental Records Centre.

MAYALL, M. J. 1983. An earthquake origin for synsedimentary deformation in a late Triassic (Rhaetian) lagoonal sequence, southwest Britain. *Geological Magazine,* **120,** 613-622.

MCGARVIE, M. (ed) 1994. Sir Stephen Glynne's church notes for Somerset. *Somerset Record Society,* volume 82.

MCKERROW, W. 1978. *The ecology of fossils. Duckworth.*

MILES , J. C. H., GREEN, B. M. R. & LOMAS, P. R. 1992 Radon affected areas: Derbyshire, Northamptonshire and Somerset. *Documents of the NRPB,* **3,** 19-27.

MILIORIZOS, M AND RUFFELL, A. 1998. Kinematics of the Watchet-Cothelstone-Hatch Fault System: implications for the fault history of the Wessex Basin and adjacent areas. In: UNDERHILL, J. R. (Ed) *Development, evolution and petroleum geology of the Wessex Basin.* Geological Society, London, Special Publications, **133,** 311-330.

MONTGOMERY, F. J. 1902. *Halse village notes.*

MUSSON, R. M. W. 1994. A catalogue of British earthquakes, *BGS Global Seismology Report No. WL/94/04.*

NASH, D. J. 1998. Drainage-line silcretes of the Middle Kalahari: an analogue for Cenozoic sarsen trains. *Proceedings of the Geologists' Association,* **109,** 241-254.

NATIONAL RIVERS AUTHORITY SOUTH-WEST REGION. 1995. *River Tone Catchment Management Plan: consultation report.*

OLIVEY, H. P. 1901. *North Curry: ancient manor and hundred.* Barnicott and Pearce.

OLLIER, C. D. 1991. Laterite profiles, ferricrete and landscape evolution. Zeitschrift für Geomorphologie, **35,** 165-173.

PEACOCK, D. C. P. & SANDERSON, D. J 1999 Deformation history and basin-controlling faults in the Mesozoic sedimentary rocks of the Somerset coast. *Proceedings of the Geologists' Association,* **110,** 41-52.

PEVSNER, N. 1958. South and west Somerset. *The buildings of England.* Penguin Books.

PRUDDEN, H. C. 1987. Notes on the distribution of sarsen stones in south Somerset and west Dorset. *Proceedings of the Ussher Society,* **6,** 557.

PRUDDEN, H. C. 2000 *The building stones and geology of Fyne Court and Broomfield.* Leaflet available from the Somerset Wildlife Trust.

PRUDDEN, H. C. 1995. *Ham Hill: the rocks and quarries.* South Somerset District Council.

ROBINSON, E. 1992. *Geology in the churchyard.* Leaflet published as part of the Living Churchyard Project, obtainable, along with others on wildlife, management etc., from the Church and Conservation Project, Arthur Rank Centre, National Agricultural Centre, Stoneleigh Park, Warwickshire CV8 2LZ.

RODWELL, E. G. 1984. Tracebridge, Stawley. *Proceedings of the Somerset Archaeological and Natural History Society,* **128,** 95-108.

ROGERS, P. n. d.. *Quantock geology.* Leaflet available from the Somerset Wildlife Trust, Fyne Court, Broomfield, Bridgwater, TA5 2EQ.

RUFFELL, A. 1990. Stratigraphy and structure of the Mercia Mudstone Group (Triassic) in the western part of the Wessex Basin. *Proceedings of the Ussher Society,* **7,** 263-267.

RUFFELL, A. 1991. Palaeoenvironmental analysis of the late-Triassic succession in the Wessex Basin and correlation with surrounding areas. *Proceedings of the Ussher Society,* **7,** 402-407.

RUFFELL, A. and WARRINGTON, G, 1988. An arenaceous member in the Mercia Mudstone Group (Triassic) west of Taunton, Somerset. *Proceedings of the Ussher Society,* **7,** 102-103.

RUTHVEN, N. 1998. Hammer and tong. *Somerset Magazine,* **8,** 21.

SHERRELL, F. W. 1970. Some aspects of the Triassic aquifer in east and west Somerset. *Quarterly Journal of Engineering Geology,* **2,** 255-286.

SHOEL, T. 1819. *Miscellaneous pieces in verse.* J. T. Boucher, Yeovil.

SMITH, N. J. P., CORNWELL, J. D., HOLLOWAY, S. and EDWARDS, R. A. 1999. High velocity layer beneath seismic 'reflector x' in the Bristol Channel may be Carboniferous Limestone: implications for a possible Exmoor-Cannington Park Thrust *Proceedings of the Ussher Society,* **9,** 358-364.

SMITH, S. A. and EDWARDS R. A. 1991. Regional sedimentological variations in the Lower Triassic fluvial conglomerates (Budleigh Salterton Pebble Beds), South West England: some implications for palaeogeography and basin evolution. *Geological Journal,* **26,** 65-83.

SOMERSET RECORD OFFICE. North Curry item: DD/CC 131908 5/12 and 131914 6/18.

STANES, R. G. F. 1993. Devonshire batts: the Whetstone Mining industry and the community of Blackborough, in the Blackdown Hills. *Report of the Transactions of the Devon Association for the Advancement of Science,* **125,** 71-112. See also Edwards R. A. 1993.

STRAW, A. 1995. Aspects of the geomorphology of Exmoor. In: *The changing face of Exmoor* (Binding, H. (Ed.). Exmoor Books, Tiverton.

TAUNTON DEANE BOROUGH COUNCIL, 1997. *Taunton Deane Nature Conservation Strategy.* (See also May and Butcher, 1997).

TAUNTON DEANE TOURISM UNIT. n. d. *On the trail of towers and hunkypunks.* Churches of Taunton Deane Series.

TILLEY, C. The west Somerset slate industry. *Exmoor Review,* 34, 72-74. Also in *Bulletin of the Somerset Industrial Archaeological Society,* no. **61,** 20-24.

ULF-HANSON, P. F. and BOYCE, D. C. 1998. *Exmoor and the Quantocks Natural Area Profile.* English Nature and Exmoor National Park.

ULLYOTT, J. S. et al. 1998. Recent advances in silcrete research and their implications for the origin and palaeoenvironmental significance of sarsens. *Proceedings of the Geologists' Association,* **109,** 255-270.

USSHER, W. A. E. 1878a. On terminal curvature in the South-Western counties. *Quarterly Journal of the Geological Society,* **34,** 49-55.

USSHER, W. A. E. 1878b. On terminal curvature in the south-western counties. *Geological Magazine,* **Dec 2** (5), 237.

USSHER, W. A. E. 1906. Geology of the country between Wellington and Chard. *Memoir of the Geological Survey of Great Britain.* Explanation of Sheet 311.

USSHER, W. A. E. 1908. Geology of the Quantock Hills and of Taunton and Bridgwater. *Memoir of the Geological Survey of Great Britain.* Explanation of Sheet 295, but now superseded by the later Memoir.

van ROSE, S. and MUSSON, R. M. W. 1997. *Earthquakes: our trembling planet.* British Geological Survey. NERC.

VIVIAN-NEALE, A. W. 1961. Livery badges and personal badges in early Tudor Work at Cheddon Fitzpaine and Staple Fitzpaine. *Proceedings of the Somerset Archaeological and Natural History Society,* **105,** 77-86.

VIVIAN-NEALE, A. W. and GREY, H. St. G. 1941. Materials for the history of Taunton Castle. *Proceedings of the Somerset Archaeological and Natural History Society,* **86** 45-78.

WARRINGTON, G, and WILLIAMS B. J. 1984. The North Curry Sandstone Member (late-Triassic) near Taunton. *Proceedings of the Ussher Society,* **6,** 82-87.

WATERS, R. S. 1960. The bearing of superficial deposits on the age and origin of the upland plain of east Devon. *Transactions of the Institute of British Geographers,* **28,** 89-97.

WEBB, C. G. 1874. *The history of Taunton in the County of Somersetshire* (Supplement p. 28). Webb, Taunton.

WEBBY, B. D. 1964. Sedimentary, tectonic and superficial structures, and iron mineralisation in the Devonian rocks of the Brendon Hills, west Somerset. *Proceedings of the Bristol Naturalists Society,* **31,** 69-81.

WEBBY, B. D. 1966a. Of stones, from the manuscript of John Strachey's proposed Somersetshire Illustrated. *Proceedings of the Bristol Naturalists Society,* **31,** 311-330.

WEBBY, B. D. 1966b. The stratigraphy and structure of the Devonian rocks in the Quantock Hills, west Somerset. *Proceedings of the Geologists' Association,* **76,** 321-343.

WHITAKER, A 1972. The Watchet Fault-a post-Liassic transcurrent reverse fault. *Bulletin of the Geological Survey of Great Britain,* No **41,** 75-80.

WHITTAKER, A. and GREEN, G. W. 1983. Geology of the country around Weston-super-Mare. *Memoir of the Geological Survey of Great Britain.* HMSO

WILSON, R. C. V. (ed). 1994. *Earth Heritage Conservation.* The Geological Society , London in association with The Open University, Milton Keynes.

WILSON, V. et al. 1958. Geology of the country around Bridport and Yeovil. *Memoir of the Geological Survey of Great Britain.* HMSO.

WINWOOD, H. H. 1877. Notes on the Rhaetic and lower Lias section on the Bath and Evercreech line, near Chilcompton. *Proceedings of the Bath Natural History Field Club,* **3,** 300-304.

WINWOOD, H. H. 1913. The Westleigh quarries. *Proceedings of the Somerset Archaeological and Natural History Society,* **58,** 49-54. (Good photographs of structures.)

WOODWARD, H. B. et al. 1876. *Geology of the east Somerset and Bristol coalfields.* Geological Survey of England and Wales. HMSO.

WOODWARD, H. B. 1887. *The geology of England and Wales.* Philip and Son.

Appendix G
Building Stones

Parish churches

The list below refers to the building stones used in walls and buttresses of parish churches. Capital case is used where significant quantities are used; lower case for lesser amounts.

KEY	
BL	Blue Lias
CGRIT	Calcareous Grit
CH	Chert
D	Devonian slates and sandstones
DLST	Devonian limestone
DTG	Doulting
EXV	Exeter Volcanics
HHS	Ham Hill Stone
HIG	Hestercombe intrusive igneous
MRLS	Marlstone
NCS	North Curry Sandstone
PT	Permo-Triassic
WL	Westleigh Limestone
WTLI	White Lias

1 Aisholt D/pt
2 Angersleigh CH/cgrit
3 Ashbrittle WL
4 Ashill CH/bl/hhs
5 Ash Priors PT
6 Bathealton D/wl
7 Beercrocombe BL/hhs
8 Bishops Hull NCS/pt/wl/d/ch
9 Bishops Lydeard PT/hhs
10 Bradford on Tone CH/NCS/hhs
11 Bridgwater PT/hhs/dtg/bl
12 Broadway BL
13 Broomfield D/pt/hig/bl/wtli
14 Brompton Ralph D/pt
15 Burlescombe WL/exv
16 Charlynch PT
17 Cheddon Fitzpaine D/bl/hig/hhs/ncs/pt
18 Chedzoy BL/ncs/hhs/dtg
19 Chipstable D
20 Churchstanton CH/cgrit/hhs
21 Clayhidon CH/cgrit/hhs
22 Combe Florey PT
23 Cothelstone PT/DLST/ncs
24 Creech St Michael D/hhs/bl
25 Crowcombe PT/d
26 Culmstock CH/wl/cgrit/
27 Curry Mallet BL/hhs
28 Donyatt MRLS/hhs/cgrit
29 Durleigh PT/bl
30 Durston D/bl/hhs/ncs
31 East Lyng BL/D
32 Elworthy D/pt
33 Enmore D/PT/bl/hhs
34 Fitzhead PT
35 Fivehead BL
36 Goathurst D/hhs/ncs
37 Halse PT
38 Hatch Beauchamp BL/hhs
39 Heathfield PT/ncs
40 Hemyock CH/hhs/cgrit
41 Hillfarance NCS/PT
42 Hockworthy WL
43 Holcombe Rogus WL/hhs
44 Huish Champflower D/pt
45 Ilton BL/MRLS/cgrit/hhs
46 Kingston St Mary D/pt/ncs/hhs
47 Kittisford WL/D/pt/exv
48 Langford Budville PT/ncs
49 Lydeard St Lawrence PT/ncs/hhs
50 Milverton PT/ncs
51 Monksilver D/PT
52 Nettlecombe D/pt
53 North Curry BL/ncs
54 North Newton PT/bl/d/hhs
55 North Petherton PT/BL/D/ncs/hhs
56 Norton Fitzwarren NCS
57 Nynehead PT
58 Oake PT/ncs
59 Otterford CH/cgrit/hhs
60 Pitminster CH/hhs/cgrit
61 Runnington PT
62 Ruishton BL/d/hhs
63 Sampford Arundel CH/pt/wl
64 Spaxton PT/d
65 Staplegrove NCS/PT/wl
66 Staple Fitzpaine BL/hhs/cgrit
67 Stogumber PT
68 Stoke St Gregory BL/hhs/ncs
69 Stoke St Mary BL/hhs/wl
70 Taunton St Mary PT/D/hhs/ncs
71 Taunton St James D/PT/hhs\ncs
72 Thornfalcon BL
73 Thorne St Margaret WL/pt
74 Thurlbear BL/cgrit
75 Thurloxton D/ncs
76 Tolland PT/d
77 Trull CH/NCS/bl
78 Wellington CH/NCS/pt/hhs
79 Wembdon PT
80 West Bagborough PT/d
81 West Buckland CH/NCS/pt
82 West Hatch BL
83 West Monkton D/hhs
84 Western Zoyland BL/hhs/ncs
85 Wilton D/CH/hhs/ncs
86 Wiveliscombe PT

Further reading on building stones

The building stones of Devon. 1992. The Devonshire Association. A booklet with colour photographs, distribution maps and text relevant to south-west Somerset.

Devon: a new survey. Hoskins, W. G. 1954. Collins, London. Chapters 1 and 16 deal with geology and building stones and are embued with Hoskins' enthusiasm for landscape and buildings.

The pattern of English building. Clifton-Taylor, A. 1987. 4th ed. Faber and Faber, London. A sensitive account of regional variations in building stones.

Guided by a stonemason: the cathedrals, abbeys and churches of Britain unveiled. Maude, T. 1997. I. B. , London. A readable introduction written from the viewpoint of a stonemason with many references to Somerset and nearby counties.

Appendix H
Useful Organisations

There are a large number of organisations involved with geology, landscape and heritage. Details of organisations rapidly become dated. Therefore a file has been deposited with the Somerset Studies Library at Taunton Library, Paul Street, Taunton TA1 3XZ (tel: 01823 340300), and with the Heritage and Landscape Section, Taunton Deane Borough Council, Deane House, Belvedere Road, Taunton TA1 1HE (tel: 01823 356356).

British Geological Survey; Churches Conservation Trust; English Nature; Environment Agency; Geologists' Association; Hanson Environment Fund; Kilve Court Residential Centre; Leonard Wills Field Centre; Quantock Hills AONB Service; Royal Society for Nature Conservation; Soil Survey and Land Research Centre; Somerset Archaeological and Natural History Society; Somerset County Council; Somerset County Museum; Somerset Environmental Records Centre; Somerset Geology Group; Somerset Industrial Archaeological Society; Somerset Studies Library; Somerset Tourist Information (Taunton); Somerset Wildlife Trust; Taunton Deane Borough Council; University of Bristol (Department of Continuing Education); University of Plymouth (Department of Geological Sciences); Ussher Society; Wessex Water.

Index

The index has a thematic structure in order to bring together information on various topics and places. Please refer to the various appendices for further information.

BUILDING STONES

Rock type

Miscellaneous

CAVES

CHARTS AND TABLES

CHURCHES

Parish churches

Miscellaneous

RADON

RIVERS

SOILS

SEDIMENTARY ROCKS

STRATIGRAPHY

STRUCTURAL GEOLOGY

TRAILS AND WALKS

UNCONFORMITIES

VIEWPOINTS

VEGETATION

ACKNOWLEDGEMENTS

Financial support for the publication from the following is gratefully acknowledged: British Geological Survey, English Nature, Environment Agency, Hanson Environment Fund and the Royal Society for Nature Conservation, Quantock AONB JAC, Service, Quantock Geological Services, University of Plymouth, Somerset Wildlife Trust, Wessex Water plc and Wyvern Waste. Harvey Ham Hill Stone, Geologists' Association Curry Fund.

The author wishes to acknowledge and thank the large number of people who have been consulted: Dr Jim Andrews (Southampton University), Dr T. K. Ball (BGS), Derek Briggs, David Bromwich (Somerset Studies Library), Roger Carter, Garry Dawson, Phil Parker, Professor M Benton (Bristol University), Bob Corns (English Nature), Dr Andy Currant (Natural History Museum), Peter Daniel, Dr Robert Dunning (Victoria County History), Dr R. A. Edwards (BGS), Francis Farr-Cox (Environment Agency), Michael Fry, Gilbert Green (ex BGS), David Hughes, Leonard Isaac, Dr Andy King (English Nature), Dr Derek Laming (Herrington Geoscience), Graham McKenna (BGS), Dr Roger Musson (BGS), Dr Kevin Page (English Nature), Dr Alastair Ruffell (Queen's University Belfast), Dr Robin Shail (Camborne School of Mines), Mick Storey (Quantock Geological Services), Bob Thomas, Dr Mike Thomas (Exeter University), Dudley Weatherley, David Westbrook (Somerset Wildlife Trust), Philip White (Hestercombe Gardens), Dr Geof Warrington (BGS), Brian Williams (ex BGS).

Wherever possible, credits are quoted in the text. The following have kindly given permission for use of the following figures: 1.1 Department of Geology, National Museum of Wales; 2.4 Professor M. Benton; 2.3 and 31.2 Somerset Wildlife Trust; 3.3 Cambridge University Press; 25.3 Soil Survey and Land Research Centre, Cranfield University; 7.1 National Radiological Protection Board; 8.3 Sites and Monuments Record, Somerset County Council; 14.2 & 31.1 Somerset Archaeological and Natural History Society; 31.4 Stuart McKerrow Oxford University; 17.1 Dudley Weatherley; 33.1 Craig McLaughlin copyright held by the Wellington Museum Society; 20.1 Tony Haskell; 3.2, 8.1, 13.5, 13.6, 27.2, Appendix C/1 British Geological Survey; 28.1 Natural History Museum; 33.3 Devon Record Office; 33.4 Dr R Edwards and Devonshire Association. Ian Clarke; Taunton Deane Borough Council.

The following figures are by the author: 13.6, 17.4, 17.6, 17.8, 19.2, 22.1, 25.5, 28.2, 28.3, 28.4, 28.5, 28.6, 31.3, 33.2.

Ian Clark, of the Heritage and Landscape Department of Taunton Deane Borough Council is thanked for his support and encouragement as are members of the Graphics Department.

The Author

Hugh Prudden has lived and taught in Somerset for forty years, read geography at Cambridge and was awarded the Halstead Medal by the Geologists' Association.

British Geological Survey Publications

The British Geological Survey (BGS) is the nation's foremost supplier of geoscience solutions and custodian of much of the country's geoscientific information. It also publishes maps, guides, books and reports, covering many geoscience topics and ranging from general to specialist publications. The major publications series include the following:

Earthwise™ Books and Guides

The Earthwise™ range includes books and guidecards covering that present geological topics to a non-specialist audience. The books cover wider themes like earthquakes, groundwater and origin of life. The guidecards, published as Holiday Geology Guides and Fossil Focus Guides, cover specific topics such as the geology of major scenic areas – the south and south-west coasts, Lake District, Peak District, etc – or fossil groups – trilobites, corals, fish, ammonites, etc.

Small Scale Geological Maps

Maps of the British Isles and the adjacent sea areas are published at small scales (between 1:1.5million and 1:625,000) and provide a national view of the United Kingdom' geology, mineral resources and related geoscience themes.

British Regional Geology Guides

Guides to the geology of each of 21 regions of the United Kingdom provide an excellent introduction for students, geologists and specialists. These guides describe the stratigraphy, structure and mineral resources of each region, and are illustrated with photographs and diagrams.

1:50 000 Scale Geological Maps

Geological maps show "the occurrence, nature, extent and stratigraphic age of rock strata in a district". The maps have been published since the 1830's and are regularly revised. Many maps are available in different versions, for example: the bedrock geology only ('solid' version), or the bedrock geology *and* the superficial deposits such as sand, gravel, and alluvium which may overlie the bedrock ('solid and drift' version). Variations on these types are also employed where appropriate.

The 1:50 000 maps provide the best synthesis of the geology of a district and include vertical and horizontal sections illustrating the geological structure and, often, marginal text and diagrams. Over 500 maps are published for England and Wales, Scotland and Northern Ireland each covering an area of approximately 20 x 30km.

Geological Sheet Memoirs

Sheet memoirs, published as books, present a comprehensive account of the geology shown on the 1:50 000 series maps. Memoirs are aimed at geologists and specialists, and contain a wealth of facts, tables and diagrams, illustrating almost every aspect of the local geology. Memoirs are progressively being replaced by shorter brief Sheet Explanations which are complemented by more detailed digitally produced reports.

Large Scale Geological Maps and Explanatory Notes

The primarly geological survey scale is 1:10 000, and "print-on-demand" National Grid maps are available for most parts of the UK this scale. (Some areas may only be covered by earlier County Series 1:10 560 maps). For many areas surveyed since the 1970s accompanying explanatory notes may also be available, providing key interpretations of the local geology.

Information on the full range of BGS publications is available from:

British Geological Survey
NATURAL ENVIRONMENT RESEARCH COUNCIL

British Geological Survey, Keyworth, Nottingham NG12 5GG

Tel. 0115 936 3241 Fax 0115 936 3488

Email: sales@bgs.ac.uk **or** enquiries@bgs.ac.uk

Main internet site: www.bgs.ac.uk

Internet shop: www.thebgs.ac.uk